EXPERIENCES IN
SOCIAL DREAMING

EXPERIENCES IN
SOCIAL DREAMING

Edited by

W. Gordon Lawrence

KARNAC

LONDON   NEW YORK

First published in 2003 by
H. Karnac (Books) Ltd.
6 Pembroke Buildings, London NW10 6RE
A subsidiary of Other Press LLC, New York

British Library Cataloguing in Publication Data

A C.I.P. for this book is available from the British Library

ISBN 1 85575 916 0

10 9 8 7 6 5 4 3 2 1

Edited, designed, and produced by Communication Crafts

Printed in Great Britain

www.karnacbooks.com

For Dr VERA PETTITT
with profound gratitude

CONTENTS

ACKNOWLEDGEMENTS

I am grateful to the contributors who took up the challenge of writing for this book. I owe, as do my writing colleagues, an enormous debt to all the people who have taken part in social dreaming matrices since 1982. Through them has come my education in social dreaming.

To the editors of *Socio-Analysis* (the Journal of the Australian Journal of Socio-Analysis), Professor Susan Long and Dr Allan Shafer, I am grateful for permission to reproduce the article by Hanna Biran (chapter seven).

Thanks are also due to Judith Lawrence for her painstaking work on the bibliography and, also, to Bipin Patel, who shepherded my badly house-trained computer and myself to completion of this text. Finally, I wish to thank my editors, Eric and Klara King, who are such painstaking professionals.

Any mistakes and omissions are mine, for which I apologize.

W. Gordon Lawrence
London

CONTRIBUTORS

Laura Ambrosiano is a full member of the International Psychoanalytic Association (IPA) and the Italian Psychoanalytic Society (SPI). She is Scientific Secretary of the Centro Milanese di Psicoanalisi "Cesare Musatti". She also teaches in psychoanalytic training and in the "Area G" Psychological School in Milan. As an organizational consultant, she specializes in group process and in organizational development and examines the dreaming process in groups. Her publications have focused recently on the relations between clinical experiences and institutional experiences.

Lilia Baglioni is a member of the SPI, the IPA, and the International Group Psychotherapy Association (IGPA). A former researcher at the National Research Council (CNR) physiological and clinical psychology departments, she currently collaborates with the Faculty of Theory and Technique of Group Dynamics at the University of Rome, "La Sapienza". She has been National Scientific Director of ABA (Association for the Study of Anorexia and Bulimia), and is a co-founder of ARGO (Association for the Research on Homogeneous Groups). She has participated in many social dreaming matrices, nationally and internationally, exploring its applicability in professional conferences, academic institutions, and health organizations.

Alastair Bain is a Founder Member, Fellow, and Director of the Australian Institute of Socio-Analysis (AISA). He has had thirty years' experience working as a socioanalyst in the United Kingdom, Europe, the United States, and Australia. He worked at the Tavistock Institute in London from 1968–1983. His interest in social dreaming began with the first Australian conference in 1989. Since then he has been a consultant to a weekly matrix over five years and has incorporated social dreaming within the Lorne conferences, the "Authority for Faith" conferences, the "Authority for Spirituality" conferences, two international conferences in 1993 and 2002, and the Socio-Analytic Fellowship Programme. He is currently a member of a social dreaming matrix that meets as part of the development of consultancy within AISA.

Ron Balamuth, a psychoanalyst and a clinical psychologist in private practice in New York City, is a graduate of the New York University Postdoctoral Program in Psychotherapy and Psychoanalysis. He is an Adjunct Associate Professor of Psychology at Columbia University, Faculty and Supervisor at the William Alanson White Institute Child and Adolescent Programme, and Faculty and Supervisor at the National Institute for the Psychotherapies. Originally from Israel, where he grew up, he moved to the United States twenty years ago. He has a life-long interest in fairy tales, mysticism, spirituality, meditation, and Tai Chi Chuan, all of which inform his psychoanalytic practice with children and adults. He specializes in treating very young children, often those diagnosed as autistic. He has an interest in the body–mind matrix and has written and presented on this topic. He published a chapter in *Relational Perspectives on the Body,* edited by L. Aron and F. Anderson (1998). He is currently involved in setting up child social dreaming matrices in various school settings in New York and elsewhere.

Hanna Biran, a clinical psychologist and organizational consultant, is a lecturer on Group Psychotherapy at the Tel Aviv University School of Medicine and on Group Relations at the School for Social Workers. She is a co-founder and member of the Innovation and Change in Society Foundation, which conducts seminars and conferences based on the Tavistock tradition. She also works with individuals and groups in private practice and as a consultant to organizations, including the Ministries of Health, Education, and Defence and to business companies. Her publications include *The Relationship between the Conductor and the Group According to Object Relations Models* (1983), "To Dream the Impossible Dream" (*Changes,* 1989), "Fear of the Other" (*Palestine Israel,* 1994), and "Myths, Memories and Roles" (*Free Associations,* 1997).

John Clare has a multidisciplinary background in sociology, musicology, art, and psychoanalysis. He now works as a psychoanalytic psychotherapist and is a founding member of the Multilingual Psychotherapy Centre, London. He was formerly a lecturer and researcher at London University in Sociology and the Study of Deviance. For two decades, he ran a specialist music venture comprising shops, a record label, and live-music venues in central London. His specialist areas are jazz and Afro-American music. He is also a painter, with two recent shows in London. Influenced by the writings of Christopher Bollas, his interests lie in the processes of free association in music, painting, and literature. His involvement with social dreaming was developed by working first hand with Gordon Lawrence, and for two years he has been a facilitator of the IMAGO social dreaming matrix and is particular interest in the socio-political contextualization of dreaming and dream-telling. He presented a paper on "Samuel Beckett and Psychoanalysis" at the conference on Exile and the Loss of Mother-tongue, London and Paris (2001). He currently works in private practice as a psychotherapist in London.

Mira Erlich-Ginor, a clinical psychologist and organizational consultant, is Training Analyst and Faculty, Israel Psychoanalytic Society and Institute; Co-Founder and former Chairperson of the Israel Association for the Study of Group and Organizational Processes (OFEK); Faculty and Management, the Programme in Organizational Consultation and Development at the Freud Centre, Hebrew University of Jerusalem, and OFEK; Co-Director of the course in Psychotherapy run by the Israel Psychoanalytic Society; and a Member of the International Association for the Psychoanalytic Study of Organizations (ISPSO). As an organizational consultant she specializes in social organizations in transition as well as designing specific experiential workshops for organizations, with a special interest in the use of social dreaming.

Stephen Fitzpatrick holds a degree in philosophy and is a fellow of Kingston University's International Business Unit. He is Director of Strategic Innovation in the Interactive Division of Saatchi and Saatchi in London. He is originator and director of the "Saatchi Smart Network", a convergent coalition of specialists drawn from the arts, academia, the media, and emergent technology. He was formerly director and co-founder of Knowhaus, an award-winning digital-media company, and has also directed Internet projects for Greenpeace, the National Theatre, and Charter 88. He was a panel member of the Government's 2000 Creative Industries Task Force. He is currently writing a book about the Internet, entitled *The Tao of Insurgent Marketing*.

Franca Fubini, a psychotherapist, group analyst, and organizational consultant, has lived and trained in the United Kingdom, in India, and in Italy, where her practice is based. She has been teaching Management of Human Resources at Perugia University. She is the co-founder of a centre for the integration of the arts in the psychotherapy of psychosis and was recently involved in the creation of "Blossoming in Europe", a programme that links European countries in an exchange of cultural events.

W. Gordon Lawrence, MA, Dr rer oec, is a former member of the Tavistock Institute of Human Relations, where he discovered social dreaming in the late 1970s and early 1980s. Currently, he is a visiting Professor at Cranfield, the University of Northumberland at Newcastle, and the New Bulgarian University, Sofia. He is a Fellow of AISA and is on the editorial boards of *Free Associations, Freie Assoziation*, and *Organization and Social Dynamics*. He has published a number of books as well as writing numerous articles and papers of which the most recent are *Roots in Northern Landscape* (1996), *Social Dreaming @ Work* (1998), and *Tongued With Fire: Groups in Experience* (2000). He is a managing partner of Symbiont Ventures, London, which is directed at advancing the idea of social dreaming and its application.

Suzanne Leigh-Ross, a psychologist and psychotherapist, is a Fellow of AISA. Her present role is Director of Counselling and Training at St. James Ethics Centre, Sydney. There, Suzanne's work ranges from training ethics counsellors to "Organizational Character and Culture Analysis". She also practices privately in transpersonal psychotherapy (dream work, sand play) and shamanic counselling and training, having trained extensively in core shamanism with renowned anthropologist Michael Harmer in the United States. She includes social dreaming matrices as an integral part of her work and co-directed the social dreaming matrix with Gordon Lawrence at the 1993 International Group Relations and Scientific Conference in Australia.

Paul Lippmann is a Training and Supervisory Analyst at the William Alanson White Institute in New York City and an associate Clinical Professor at the New York University Postdoctoral Program in Psychotherapy and Psychoanalysis. He is Director of the Stockbridge Dream Society in Stockbridge, Massachusetts, where he is a psychologist and psychoanalyst in private practice. He has written and lectured for over twenty-five years on dreams and their use and misuse in psychoanalytic therapy.

Marc Maltz is currently the Co-Director and Faculty Member of the William Alanson White Institute of Psychiatry, Psychotherapy and Psychoanalysis Organization Program and Visiting Faculty at Columbia University Teachers College Graduate Program in Organizational Psychology. He is a Registered Organizational Development Professional and a member of the A.K. Rice Institute and the International Society for the Psychoanalytic Study of Organizations. He is a co-founder and Managing Partner for the New York-based TRIAD Consulting Group LLC and has been practising for over fifteen years. He is also a founding member of Symbiont Technologies LLC. Prior to developing his consulting practice, he held executive positions at AT&T, Westinghouse Electric Company, NYNEX Corporation, and Music Mining Co., Inc.

Thomas A. Michael is Professor Emeritus at Rowan University in New Jersey and Principal and Senior Consultant at the Dialogue Centre for Counselling and Consulting. He taught organizational development, organizational behaviour, and business policy in the College of Business at Rowan for over twenty-five years. He was founder and administrator of the Master of Administration Program at Antioch University in Philadelphia. He is an ordained Presbyterian minister, having served two congregations in New York State, and is on the national staff of the Presbyterian Church USA in personnel referral and career counselling. He is a member of the International Society for the Psychoanalytic Study of Organizations, the Colloquium on Violence and Religion, and the A.K. Rice Institute Philadelphia Centre for Organizational Dynamics. He has consulted, conducted workshops, and published in the field of organizational development and social dreaming.

Claudio Neri is a full Professor at "La Sapienza" University of Rome and visiting Professor at the Universite Lumiere-Lyon, France. He is a Fellow of the IPA and has been a Training Analyst with the SPI for many years. Among his current positions, he is editor of the electronic journal *Funzione Gamma*. He has published several books, of which *Group* (1998) has been translated into Italian, French, Spanish, and Portuguese. He is editor with Malcolm Pines and Robi Friedman of a recent book, *Dreams in Group Psychotherapy: Theory and Techniques* (2002). He has worked widely using the group setting in therapy and training, and in the last few years he has conducted social dreaming matrices in various countries: Italy, Australia, Israel, and Switzerland.

Dr Judit Szekacs is a bilingual psychoanalyst and psychotherapist. Born and educated (mostly) in Budapest, Hungary, she has taken the way of thinking and ideas of Ferenczi, the Balints, and Rajka as the integral part of a "professional mother tongue". The experience of living and working in a totalitarian regime and the transforming years leading to the fall of the Berlin Wall sensitized her to the social and individual aspects of trauma, identity formation, and strategies of survival. She moved in 1990 to London, where, with Gordon Lawrence and a small group of colleagues, she founded IMAGO East–West and the Multilingual Psychotherapy Centre to create a space for studying the socio-cultural effects of immigration. During the past fifteen years she has worked with Gordon Lawrence through diverse experiences in social dreaming.

Peter Tatham is a medically qualified doctor who retrained at the C. G. Jung Institute in Zürich. Since returning to England in 1979, he has had an analytic practice outside London. He has lectured in England and abroad on Jungian subjects and also conducted social dreaming in various places and situations. His book *The Makings of Maleness* was published in 1992, and he continues to research and lecture on new attitudes to male archetypes and fathering. He recently published a chapter in *Creative Approaches to Group Work*, edited by A. Chesner and H. Hahn (2001).

E. Martin Walker grew up in Argentina, Brazil, Chile, Denmark, India, Nepal, Switzerland, and the United States. Following undergraduate degrees in Management, Religion, and Psychology at New York University, he received a doctorate in Clinical Psychology from the City University of New York. As a Fulbright Scholar (Mexico), he lectured at the Universidad Iberoamericana and did research on the psychosocial aspects of the North American Free Trade Agreement. He is a managing partner of Symbiont Technologies LLC, New York, and is currently finishing his candidacy at the William Alanson White Institute for Psychiatry, Psychology, and Psychoanalysis, where he has directed an annual social dreaming matrix. He has a psychoanalytic practice for individuals, groups, and organizations, and he consults in hospitals on issues of long-term care and the final stages of life.

INTRODUCTION

I n editing the contributions to this volume, I have been struck by
how the idea of social dreaming has caught the imagination of the
writers and those with whom they worked. I am also struck by the
quality of thinking of the contributors. Although social dreaming has
a short history, it is now well-enough established in a range of countries, like Australia, Denmark, Finland, Italy, France, Israel, Ireland,
the United Kingdom, and the United States. As yet, there is no well-
rehearsed theory, but there are working hypotheses, which are testi-
mony to the fact that social dreaming is always in a process of
becoming

I set out in chapter one some ideas on the phenomenon called
social dreaming. This is a version of a lecture delivered at the William
Alanson White Institute in New York. In it an epistemic theory of
dreams is outlined. I also suggest that in social dreaming the terms
"finite" and "infinite" might better be used than the conventional
conscious–unconscious division.

This is followed by Claudio Neri's (chapter two) account of social
dreaming matrices in Israel. Neri is a psychoanalyst who has made
the transition from the individual perspective to the social one. This

he does in relation to a dream about a warship, referring to what he would have thought of as an analyst but focusing instead on the social, which led to a rich mosaic of associations and thoughts that reflected what the participants in the matrix were thinking about the then current war in Afghanistan.

John Clare (chapter three) has taken a year-long matrix, held in London, and identified the themes and issues that arose from it. In a detailed account of the dreams, associations, and thought processes, he gets at the pain that people are experiencing at the margins of existence, at this point in history. Two of his five hypotheses draw attention to the idea that social dreaming can be a way of delineating the experiences of people at the margins of society and that the freedom of expression experienced in a social dreaming matrix is based on contingency and on the absence of certainty and finality. This clears the way for freedom of thought.

Alastair Bain (chapter four) was one of the first to see the potential of social dreaming, and he writes on the associative poetry that arose from matrices in Australia. These he couples with the free associations. This is followed in chapter five by Suzanne Leigh Ross's thinking about the matrix, introducing the history of social dreaming ideas of complexity and chaos. She, too, was an early devotee of social dreaming and has gone on to do interesting programmes in Australia.

Laura Ambrosiano (chapter six), who came to social dreaming comparatively late, writes with freshness on the discovery of social dreaming and makes some acute observations. She starts by questioning the accepted idea that dreams are personal, referring to Bion, who doubted the accepted spatial definitions of mind that were current at the time. He saw the mind as a process. Ambrosiano details dreams from a programme in Rome and draws attention to the fact that social dreaming encourages "negative capability" in a liberating way.

Hanna Biran has been a pioneer in using social dreaming in organizational consultancy. Here, in chapter seven, she describes a consultation in a school with the teachers, who were experiencing violence in the school. She points to the distinction between consultancy as salvation and consultancy as revelation (Lawrence, 2000a, pp. 165ff). In her view, social dreaming falls into the category of the latter and so is more effective.

On the theme of schools, Ron Balamuth (chapter eight) writes engagingly of work he is doing in a New York school with pupils and staff. This is truly pioneering work as, to the best of my knowledge, no work has been done using social dreaming in schools. In a fascinating account he traces the development of the dreams in what he calls a "childreamatrix". He concludes that social dreaming transcends the individual and that, by listening to children's dreams, we may learn more of our culture and society.

Thomas Michael (chapter nine) is in the world of adults and writes of social dreaming in the context of churches. The dreams are wonderfully human and illustrate something of the dynamics of being a church member at a time when churchgoing is not highly valued. An important element in this rich account is the effect of the September 11 tragedy in America. He asks the question: can we experience the transcendent infinite? He concludes that social dreaming may be one way that we access the infinite depth that calls to the depth of ourselves across the ordinary barriers of our humanity.

Similarly, Mira Erlich-Ginor (chapter ten) describes a matrix in Israel that had strangely predictive powers. She writes of the matrix in the context of the Israel–Palestinian conflict and the *Intifada*. She reaffirms Pedro Calderón de la Barka's view in the seventeenth century that all life is a dream and that even dreams are just a dream.

Turning to the world of the National Health System in the United Kingdom, Peter Tatham (chapter eleven) writes of his attempts to run social dreaming with health managers. He regards social dreaming for people in commercial situations as important, though he is aware of the ordinary person's distrust of dreaming.

Marc Maltz and Martin Walker (chapter twelve) take the idea of dream intelligence much further than anyone has to date. In their discussion they set forth key points that have to be taken into account in this work.

This is followed in chapter thirteen by an interview conducted by Martin Walker with Paul Lippmann, who is a distinguished worker with dreams in the United States. Paul Lippmann disentangles his thoughts on dreaming and social dreaming by separating the thinking of social dreaming from the group relations tradition, where it had its roots.

In chapter fourteen, Martin Walker writes engagingly of the confusion of dreams between selves and others, and he points to the nonlinear continuities present in every matrix.

Stephen Fitzpatrick (chapter fifteen) writes of the numinous and the holy as these are evinced in a social dreaming matrix. He takes quite a new perspective on social dreaming.

Judit Szekacs (chapter sixteen), a psychoanalyst, takes up the issue of transference in a social dreaming matrix and postulates that the transference is to the dream and not to the dreamer or the "takers" of the matrix. This move has been implicit for a number of years but is now made quite explicit, using, as she does, the work of John Byng-Hall in family therapy.

Lilia Baglioni (chapter seventeen) reflects on social dreaming in the experience of the matrix and offers some quite novel insights.

Franca Fubini (chapter eighteen) writes of doing consultancy with a business firm using social dreaming. She goes on to discuss the idea of dreams in search of a dreamer, using Bion's idea of thoughts in search of a thinker.

Finally, in chapter nineteen I offer some thoughts on social dreaming that have been puzzling me for some time. I say something more about matrix and the necessity for having more work done on this subject. I also point to the role of not-knowing in a social dreaming matrix and the value of negative capability in this work of the exploration of dreams. Through negative capability, we allow ourselves to be available for the divergent thinking that social dreaming can produce.

CHAPTER ONE

The social dreaming phenomenon

W. Gordon Lawrence

The purposes of this chapter are (1) to describe the phenomenon of social dreaming and (2) to consider the relevant theories of dreaming in the light of this experience. I shall approach these through presenting working hypotheses. A working hypothesis is a sketch of the emergent reality which illumines it that reality. If the sketch is found wanting, another working hypothesis can be substituted that better fits the reality that is always in the process of becoming.

The chapter is structured in three parts:

- The phenomenon of the social dreaming matrix.

- Towards a new way of understanding dreams: the epistemic theory.

- Social dreaming @ work.

This chapter is a version of the Harry Stack Sullivan Society Program Lecture, given at the William Alanson White Institute in February 2000.

The phenomenon of the social dreaming matrix

1.   The dream is always enlarging the space of the possible. Through the dream we are brought into the tension between the finite (that which we know) and the infinite (that which is beyond our ken). In the context of social dreaming, I am persuaded that the terms "finite" and "infinite" be used instead of the terms "conscious" and "the unconscious". The infinite is a mental space that contains all that has ever been thought and is capable of being thought. This space is not "outside" us but is contained in our inner worlds. All thinking begins from no-thought, from an absence, which we experience in our inner world. We make the thought present from first recognizing that it is not there.

Harry Stack Sullivan wrote about the "unattended" when referring to the unconscious. This seems right to me, because the unconscious does not become a thing, is not reified. It is a process.

The first working hypothesis is that *dreams, dreaming, and dream work is always inducting us to the tension between the finite and the infinite.*

2.   Social dreaming takes place in a matrix. People come together to share their dreams. Someone will give an account of a dream at the beginning of a session. Others follow. There is a flow to the dream in that one dreamer intuitively fits his or her dream into the previous one. The taker will offer a comment on the possible links and connections between the dreams. The term "taker" is used to describe the persons who are convening the matrix. Their role is to further the work of the matrix, which is stated in the primary task: to associate to one's own and other participants' dreams that are made available to the matrix so as to make links and find connections.

The seating of the matrix is designed to facilitate this work. The chairs are arranged in clusters of five to seven, depending on numbers. All the chairs are linked but are ordered in a pattern, and they all face into the centre of the room. Together the clusters of chairs represent a star-like shape, a bit like a snowflake when seen through a microscope. In a matrix of thirty or so participants, there will be about four to six clusters of chairs. The takers sit anywhere in the matrix.

3.   Dreaming is respected as being a representation of the truth of the images and proto-thinking that is the infinite, which is in the minds of the participants. A dream will often be a fragment but, nevertheless,

is seen as a potential synthesis. Social dreaming is a method of arriving at the meaning of the dreams through dream work.

The key tool is "free association". Free association was proposed by Sigmund Freud in *The Interpretation of Dreams* (1900a), though it was not his original idea. The takers' work is basically to associate to the dreams in order to find connections among them. In this, the takers are working at the finite of the dream and the emotional experience of the infinite from which dreams arise. In this way, they, in a sense, model how to work with dreams in a matrix.

4. I have used the term "matrix" to describe the configuration of participants. This term was first proposed when social dreaming existed only in the mind, in imagination. To the best of my knowledge, such a configuration had never been consciously convened before Patricia Daniel and myself did so. It was thought that if it was to be called a "social dreaming group", it would be in the area where what had been learned about groups would obtrude into the work of the matrix, which is to transact dreams and to be working at the multiple dreams-in-association. In short, the fantasy was that dreams would speak with dreams. Although we each dream individually, participants seem to intuit that their dream is not a personal possession but belongs to the larger whole matrix, which is always in a process of discovery, or of meaning becoming a version of the truth.

In the first social dreaming matrix in 1982 (conducted in the Tavistock Institute) the hypothesis that it would be possible to dream socially was quickly established. Not only was dreaming over and above the individual participants, so to speak, but it also evoked new dimensions that had rarely been possible in the classic, dyadic situation. Social dreaming ushered us into a new experience of dreaming. Why was this so?

The term "matrix" had been intuitively chosen. It proved to be correct. A matrix is different from a group. A matrix is derived from the word for a "uterus" or "womb". It is a place from which something is bred, grows, and develops. Matrix describes the space from which everything that exists in our Universe, indeed the cosmos, has its origins. Matrix exists before mankind developed groups. And it may well be that group is a defence against the experience of the formlessness of matrix. The social dreaming matrix, purposely convened in the here-and-now, is a reflection of the primordial matrix of humanity.

What can be said about the matrix in the context of social dreaming can be offered as a second working hypothesis: *a matrix is a
different "container" for receiving dreams, and so the "contained" of the
dream alters. The "content" of the dream becomes different from that delivered in other contexts.*

5. A social dreaming matrix evokes a different array, or suite, of
dreams. Transference and countertransference would be part of the
domain of a "group". It was felt intuitively that such issues would
interfere with the work of a matrix, just as would basic assumption
behaviour and the like. In a social dreaming matrix, transference and
countertransference issues are not addressed directly in the here-and-
now of the matrix. If the participants have faith in the dream and
dreaming, such issues will be voiced in the dream. We have found
that if they are addressed directly they rob the dream of these emotional experiences. Once they are indicated in a dream, the takers will
make some comment. For instance, from our work in companies we
know that such issues will be present. Once feelings on authority
figures are verbalized in the dream, they can be associated to and
developed. The transference is to the dream, not to the dreamer or the
takers.

Participants in a group are concerned, at some level, about being
part of the universe of meaning, and the group spends most of its life
tussling about the meaning and non-meaning of being in the group. In
a social dreaming matrix, because of its work of free association, what
emerges is a multi-verse of meaning. A matrix can tolerate this, and
the members do not think they are going mad (psychotic), because
such a multi-verse makes sense for them. This is consistent with
dream life.

The third working hypothesis is: *the dream arises from the matrix of
emotional experience that exists prior to the formation of group.*

6. Grotstein (1979) makes a useful distinction between the dreamer
who dreams the dream and the dreamer who understands the dream.
In a social dreaming matrix, there are as many dreamers-who-under-
stand-the-dream as there are participants. It tends to be that the taker
is the first to free associate, but it can happen that participants will be
associating before the takers. In the end, it is the dreamer-who-
dreams-the-dream who takes on the function of understanding in the

sense of making meaning. The social dreaming matrix is a socio-democratic endeavour.

7.   When in 1982 in the first social dreaming matrix it became apparent that the act of dreaming was enlarged in the matrix, I could not formulate the experience.

I now see dreaming quite differently. Here, I follow the philosopher Schopenhauer, who posed the question: "May not our whole life be a dream or more exactly is there sure criterion of the distinction between dream and reality?" Miguel de Unamuno gave an answer to the question when he wrote that the poets of all ages always have been dismayed at the passing of life. He goes on to make the point that whereas Calderón de la Barca simply said that "life is a dream", it is to Shakespeare that we owe the insight that "we are such stuff as dreams are made on". Shakespeare "makes ourselves a dream, a dream that dreams" (Unamuno, 1954, p. 39).

8.   The social dreaming matrix has caused me to reflect on the content of the dream, and what it is achieving. I believe that dreaming in a social dreaming matrix inducts us to the world of the socio-centric. Bion makes a very useful distinction between the world of the ego-centric and that of the socio-centric. This distinction is between narcissism and social-ism. In the introduction to *Experiences in Groups* (1961) he says that as a psychoanalyst one can look at groups via two vertices. The first is that of the pair and all the minutiae of transferential detail between the consultant and the participant. This is the oedipal situation. It is also, I think, to do with what takes place within the individual. But, second, Bion writes that one can also look at the group in terms of what he calls sphinx. This is related to problems of knowledge and scientific method—that is, how one arrives at knowledge. Very firmly, a social dreaming matrix takes us into thinking about the other and frees us from being gagged and bound in the world of the "I".

So I have a fourth working hypothesis: *the experience of a social dreaming matrix places participants in the domain of sphinx—that is, in the realm of knowledge, scientific method, and truth searching.*

In this hypothesis I am reflecting something of the social character of dreams. Paul Lippmann, in a brilliant article on the nature of dreams (1998), makes the hypothesis that the nuances and styles of social influence can be found in dreams. He refers to Erich Fromm, Erik Erikson, and Montague Ullman and suggests that dreams contribute to social life and character.

> The varied experiences in dreams may be thought of as continuously exploring, portraying, rehearsing, commenting upon, criticizing, adding to, varying and improvising on aspects of the socially shared characteristics of a people . . . in the deepest privacy of dreaming, the culture's ways are being developed, tested, explored, and reinforced. [Lippmann, 1998, pp. 203–204]

Towards new ways of understanding dreams

1.   I begin with a dream on social dreaming, which occurred during the night of 13 September 1999.

In the dream, two of us are rebuilding an ancient, fortified tower on the top of a low, craggy mountain, which commands a view of a valley. My colleague, who is a co-founder of Symbiont Ventures, is the builder. He is studying a report that has come from the expert on historical monuments. In the report it says that we have to build an extra floor between the first two stories and the final one, which is a battlement. The extra floor looks like a pudding, or a soufflé. It is like the bulbous towers that one finds in a Russian Orthodox church, but not so regular. Then the topmost fortifications will be superimposed.

As happens in many dreams, this building work is done instantaneously. My colleague is querying this opinion of the expert, but I am insisting that we follow his advice. During this we have found the visor of William Wallace. We are not sure if it is empty or not. It is not, we find, and we scoop the head out.

Later in the dream I descend to the valley. There are two perfect Georgian houses, each a mirror of the other from a distance. When one gets closer, I find that one is made of stressed concrete, mimicking in every detail the features of the original house. I find that the concrete house has been built by trade unionists as a conference centre only a few years ago. In the dream I go down the long drive that leads from these two houses. I hear voices. Recognizing that apparently one woman talks in the same way as both my mother and my wife, I go towards them/her across some wild moor, which is reached through a gate. The woman is talking to the others in her group of the opinion of the historical monuments' expert. She says, in effect, that both opinions are right: to have an extra floor and not to have one. I meet with them, and the dream ends abruptly and I do not have the answer I crave.

Associating afterwards to the dream. There is something around about my willingness to listen to experts. William Wallace was a great Scottish leader who challenged the king of England. Do I want to be a leader against the Central Europeans? Why are we in the dream scooping out his head from his visor? To get at his brains! (William, of course, is one of my first names.) I have been digging out the brains of people for years, from books.

The stressed-concrete Georgian house built by trade unionists? Who built which house—Jung or Freud? Assume that the trade unionists are those who follow the rules of their masters but at the same time are often in conflict. Are they psychoanalysts?

The dream illustrates vividly the dilemma I face in pursuing social dreaming. Do I enter into understanding it without memory and desire? Does the matrix interpose itself between dream and reality? In terms of my dream, the restored tower on top of the crag is social dreaming, which has a long past but a short history. The soufflé-like structure—is that the social dreaming matrix?

Can I allow myself to try to understand it with negative capability—that is, being in mysteries and doubts without irritably reaching after reason? Can I experience social dreaming as it is? Like all of us, I have been listening to the voices of the dead and, on occasion, imbuing their words with tongues of fire.

2.   Erich Fromm wrote in *The Forgotten Language* (1951) that there were three approaches to the understanding of dreams. First, the Freudian view postulates that all dreams are expressions of the irrational and asocial nature of human beings. Second, Jung's view is that all dreams are a revelation of unconscious wisdom, a wisdom that transcends the individual. Third, there is the view that dreams express mental activity of whatever kind and are expressions both of our irrational strivings as well as our reason and morality; dreams express both the best and the worst in us as human beings, for they cannot be controlled or managed.

3. To go back to my dream of September 1999, for something like twenty years I have been hewing out the brains of previous writers on dreams and dreaming. Of the three views, I empathize most with that of Jung. At the same time, I do not know which of the smaller eighteenth-century houses, representing Jung and Freud, is the facsimile or not. But one was built by trade unionists. I think that they are those people who know about dreams and, by extrapolation, believe they know about social dreaming. When I took the first social dreaming matrix in Israel I was assured by one psychoanalyst before the matrix began that there was nothing new in this, that she had been doing it for years.

4. I have sympathy with Fromm's third way of interpreting, which says that dreams are an expression of mental activity. It is possible to cut through the various "schools" of interpretation if we ask ourselves from what or where do dreams arise.

5. Trying to understand the conscious mind and disentangling it from what we know of brain is notoriously difficult. The brain is, like the body, objective, exposed, external, and public. Mind, on the other hand, is a subjective entity, is private, internal, and hidden. To identify the nature of consciousness depends on the existence of that same consciousness.

    The brain registers everything that happens to the individual. This can be called the "movie-in-the-brain" (Damasio, 1999b, p. 77). The movie is a metaphor for the integrated and unified composites of diverse sensory images that can be experienced. We generate a sense of self in relation to this movie. The self is nested in the movie. But we are never fully consciously attentive to this movie. Much of it will be unattended to, and this is the content of dream. It is almost as if dream comes from the movie seen from the rear of the screen.

6. I follow an epistemic theory of dreams first propounded by Wilfred Bion. This takes us much further than Freud, Melanie Klein, or Jung. The theory is based on Bion's view that psychoanalysis is about the evolving process that make for mind: "the mind is seen to develop on the basis of the acquisition of knowledge, knowledge about itself and knowledge about its objects, internal and external" (Meltzer, 1984, p. 68).

Bion outlined his theory of thinking/dreaming through three functions: alpha functions, alpha-type elements, and beta-type elements. To be sure, Bion (1967b) makes clear that this is a mythical apparatus, and he invites others to fill out these functions from their experience to make them meaningful and useful (Meltzer, 1984, p. 72).

Bion proposed that the alpha functions operate on the sense impressions and the emotions. If they are successful they are transformed into alpha-type elements that are suitable for dream storage and subsequent thinking. If they are not capable of transformation, they remain as beta-type elements; they remain as undigested facts and not available for thought; they become things in themselves. He describes beta-type elements as being "the matrix from which thoughts can be supposed to arise. It partakes of the quality of inanimate object and psychic object without any form of distinction between the two. Thoughts are things, things are thoughts, and they have personality" (Bion, 1963, p. 22).

7.   Since the times of Freud, Jung, Fromm, and Bion, quantum physics has been developed and this can now help in our understanding of the processes of thinking. Though they each foreshadowed quantum mechanics, particularly Jung with his concept of synchronicity and Bion with his elements, there was no theory of dreaming firmly grounded in the new sciences.

Every atom of our body and mind contains, at the sub-atomic level, both waves and particles simultaneously. Every elemental event in neurophysiology is related to the other elemental events as entities in the cosmos at large through waves and particles. The Heisenberg principle states that you can measure either one or the other, but never both at the same time. This is because only a wave or a particle exists at one time. In a superimposed state, a wave of all the atoms we possess contains all that has ever been known and all that ever will be known of the Cosmos. Waves periodically collapse, or coalesce, or configure, as particles. When it is in this form it becomes a piece of information, a fragment of knowledge, a shard of the infinite. Waves are immortal, invisible, and hidden from our eyes.

Bion foreshadowed this. Beta-elements are waves; when they coalesce into particles, they become alpha-elements. As beta-elements they become part of a universe of strong emotions, though we are unable to use them for thinking. They constitute the infinite that each of us contains, which becomes a formidable obstacle for making experiences finite. The tension between the finite and the infinite arises because the emotional elements sabotage the process. "In effect, there exist things that are too frightening or too difficult to contemplate (Biran, 1997, pp. 31–32).

8.   The quality of the information contained as a particle in our dreaming and thinking will depend to an extent on our ability to comprehend—our intelligence—but, most important of all, on the mental disposition we bring to bear on the act of participation. A dream is a subjective experience that no one else has had in exactly the same form. I use the term "participation" in two senses: the first, to partake of; the second, to engage subjectively with the dream. The dream is not an object to be regarded through the equivalent of a one-way mirror. It has to be made in the inner world of the observer, as natural scientists found out well over fifty years ago.

I can illustrate what is in mind here by referring to Harold Bloom's anti-reductionist point about poetry. He says that the meaning of a poem can only be another poem:

> The sad truth is that poems don't have presence, unity or meaning. . . . What then does a poem, possess or create? Alas, a poem has nothing, and creates nothing. Its presence is a promise, part of the substance of things hoped for, the evidence of things not seen. Its unity is in the goodwill of the reader . . . its meaning is just that there is or rather was, another poem. [quoted in Rorty, 1989, p. 41]

I submit that this could equally well apply to dreaming and dreams. A dream is a particle. To arrive at the meaning of a dream requires free association, through which a fresh meaning for the dream is minted. The poem is replaced with another poem of the reader. We participate in the dream work of a matrix through free association, which is to give our subjective feelings and experiences the highest value and acclaim. Free association is the most subversive of activities in the twentieth century. Christopher Bollas writes in *The Mystery of Things* (1999) that in our linear and goal-directed world, where consciousness is highly focused and is directed at redemption through the scientific and technological endeavour, to free associate—where one says whatever crosses one's mind—is "to undermine the structure of Western epistemology" (Bollas, 1999, p. 63).

9.   To engage in free association in the matrix—to be taking the dream as a particle and thinking around it in a free way in order to find/make meaning—is to be approximating, to a greater or lesser degree, what is contained in infinity. Infinity will never be known. As Wilfred Bion pointed out, the *noumenon* can never be known. Infinity is the O, the god-head. The dream, which is a state of thinking, can be termed the phenomena. ("All dreamers are thinkers", as Bion reminds us.)

10.   The evidence for the infinite being made present in dreaming comes from Bollas, who has written on the "unthought known". The unthought known has proved to be a useful concept in organizational analysis. The unthought known is not a collection of abstract representations but is the outcome of countless meetings, often in tranquillity, between the infant as a subject and his or her object world (Bollas, 1987, p. 52). I think that embedded in these encounters is an inkling of the infinite as we make our relationships in the finite world. The infinite is not only something out there as objective fact but is also in here in our inner worlds. To engage with the infinity that is publicly construed, we have first to construe it in ourselves. The ecology of forgotten dreams is the infinite.

What comes to be known when it is thought depends on the opportunities and the impediments presented by the eco-niche that each of us inhabits. By "eco" I am referring to the whole natural world in which we are located. Loosely, I am using it in the sense of ecological. By "niche" I mean the slice of the environment that we occupy. I have the idea that even a single-cell organism dreams, or participates in proto-dreaming. Thus, evolution comes about in the context of the eco-niche the organism inhabits.

The eco-niche occupied by an Indian peasant's child is different from that of someone born in Scotland, or born in Kosovo in the last ten years, or born in Manhattan or the Bronx. This is further complicated for the child by the wealth of the parents, their psychopathology, the educational opportunities he or she has, and so on. The figures in, and the context of, the eco-niche are always presenting opportunities or thwarting the child. It is the child's ability to construe these events as providing a chance for his or her development that introduces him or her to fate and a sense of destiny (Bollas, 1989).

Dreams reflect life in the eco-niche and are always encouraging us to expand the space of the possible. The dream will be a mirroring of actual experiences lived in the day-to-day world. So, from the residues of dreams, forgotten or otherwise, we make a life from their shadows.

11. Ullman (1975) writes that dreams come from the "black hole of the psyche" (p. 9). This is a wonderful image. The dream has an "explicate" meaning or interpretation. Through the process of "revealing the unknown implicit in the known" (Sharpe, 1937, p. 18), one can experience the growth of language. In particular, there is a growth of "poetic diction" which has its roots in the infinite as well as the poetic. The poet and the dreamer have the same task, which is to convey experience through language that is "simple, sensuous and passionate" (Milton). Simile, metaphor, metonymy, synecdoche, or onomatopoeia, for instance, all have their place in how communication is framed as the dreamer struggles in the immanent world of the day-to-day to give a sense of having been in the transcendent world of the night. These figures of speech are ways whereby in common discourse we convey our sense of the infinite. In short, in a matrix participants are discovering the difference between thoughts of the forgotten past and thinking that is of the present. Within the explicate meaning is another set of meanings embedded in the "implicate". So working out the meaning of dreams is a continual movement between the two—between the explicate and the implicate.

The fifth working hypothesis can be stated. *Social dreaming ushers into the infinite the implicate—the distinction between alpha-type and beta-type elements—which signals the world of quantum reality that leads us away from the intrapsychic, narcissistic mode of understanding dreaming.*

Social dreaming @ work

1. We work in organizations as social systems. This conceptualization was introduced about sixty years ago. There are two social systems in operation at one and the same time. There is the overt one of consciousness. This is where people share a primary task and cooperate about what work is to be done. Alongside this is the other—the system of parallel processes. This is the one of free association, the stream of consciousness, the musings in the mind, possessed by every human being. All the people in a company share this stream of con-

sciousness, composed of waves and particles. There is a communication at a primordial, intuitive level, which we would want to deny.

The world is composed of an infinite number of social systems, in each of which there is the unattended parallel social system of free thoughts and dreams, unencumbered by logic. Every person who participates in these has dreams. They may be forgotten or regarded as so much junk mail, to be discarded. But we know that people dream. The dream is a particle version of the dreaming that goes on all the time as a wave. The means by which the particle becomes apparent to us is an achievement of consciousness.

How do we have the unattended part of the discourse of a social system like a company? The answer, predictably, is to convene a social dreaming matrix, as has been done by a number of colleagues.

2.   In a consultation that I conducted using social dreaming, the first dreamer gave a dream:

> She is in the garden of a house she used to occupy. The garden is profusely overgrown. She feels that underneath all this wild boscage, there is a finer, original garden. Sometimes she sees the lineaments of it. She perceives what might be the garden when she goes to the top floor of the house for a bird's eye view.

This simple dream turned out to be the consultation. They were a set of people providing therapy for the underprivileged, and their founders had left them. They were doing good-enough work. Part of the nature of their work was to deal with unspeakable tragedy. Something of this came out in the consultation, as well as in the dynamics occurring between them. The working hypothesis we arrived at was that the nature of their work was such that it was difficult to keep hope alive.

3.   Marc Maltz and Martin Walker (1998) conducted a consultation and used dreams on-line—that is, dreams were put on computer by the participants via email. Maltz and Walker confirmed that social dreaming is a powerful tool for reaching the unconscious, or infinite, in organizations. There is always a tension between those who would want to interpret and those who are content to associate. Free association is open-ended, whereas interpretation curtails exploration. (Further examples of work in consultation can be found in chapters six, seven, nine, ten, and eleven.)

4. The sixth working hypothesis is: *the social dreaming matrix, when conducted in an organization, comes to contain the disowned aspect(s) of the social system.* This disowned aspect (e.g. "feminine authority") is symbolic of all the other disowned aspects of the system. If the disowned comes into the matrix, could it not become part of the discourse of an organization?

The seventh working hypothesis is: *the experience of the social dreaming matrix allows participants to tolerate the unknown, to be in doubts, mysteries, and uncertainties.* This is anathema in the company organization. Notice how when an innovative idea is produced, immediately a working party is set up to look at its feasibility. Very often I have the feeling that people in organizations are caught in acting-out the hallucinations of their bosses. A hallucination, I suggest, is a no-dream that can be controlled, managed, and manipulated.

Crick and Mitchison (1983) have put forward the hypothesis that all dreams are garbage, in an attempt to discredit the dream. Clearly, I am not of that view. We live out our lives in a materialistic and nature-controlling era, worshipping technology as the greatest of our gods. The dream, however, gnaws away at this by offering us each night a chance to question this, to pose existential questions of ourselves that relate to the nature of the lives that we lead.

Whatever exploration we make of our dreams, we have humbly to accept what Shakespeare said in *A Midsummer Night's Dream* when he wrote: "I will get Peter Quince to write a ballad of this dream. It shall be called Bottom's Dream, because it hath no bottom."

Dreaming is bottomless, but it is still a great adventure! It is bottomless because dreaming comes from the vast, timeless infinite that is the shadowland of our existence. From this mysterious shadowland has come all that we as human beings know, and have made, in our finite world.

I end with a final, and eighth, working hypothesis: *a social dreaming matrix is a transitional object, phenomenon, or experience and as such is the theatre of the infinite or the unconscious. The play in it is serious, for herein are the roots of our civilization and creativity.*

If the response to a poem is another poem, the response to a dream is another dream. I hope that, in reading this chapter, you will have responded with another, one much better than the one you have just read.

CHAPTER TWO

Social dreaming:
report on the workshops held in
Mauriburg, Raissa, and Clarice Town

Claudio Neri

S ocial dreaming is a method that focuses on dreaming with a view to understanding not the "inner world" of dreamers but the social and institutional reality in which they live. According to Gordon Lawrence (1998b), who propounded this technique, dreams contain fundamental information on the situation in which people are living at the time they dream. Social dreaming does not challenge the great value of the traditional psychoanalytic approach to dreams but tries to emphasize their social dimension.

This chapter illustrates some experiences conducted according to the social dreaming technique and draws some methodological, theoretical, and clinical suggestions from them. The first sections provide some practical information on social dreaming sessions and on how the method can be used to explore and improve the way an institution or organization works. Subsequent sections look at the origins of social dreaming and place it within a historical framework. The final sections offer accounts of some practical experiences.

The setting

Social dreaming sessions usually last one and a half hours. Each session should be part of a series, which can either be short or long. It is advisable to avoid having just one "crash" session, because the development of a process is an important part of the method. Such a development involves both the ability of the participants to function as a matrix and the dreams themselves. In fact, the dreams are connected to each other inasmuch as they are a response to the dreams told during the previous sessions (Armstrong, 1998a). The work scheme we have adopted generally includes three to five sessions, over a period of two or three days, with one or two nights in between. During these nights, new dreams come that usually refer to the group or to the situation that the participants are experiencing. Other work schemes may be worth considering, such as one or two weekly session over a period of several months.

The sessions can be conducted either by one leader, or host, or by a small staff, depending on the personal preferences of the leader. A factor that is often taken into account is the number of people that make up the group. Large groups usually require a staff of two/three leaders. At any rate, it is best not to have more than thirty to thirty-five participants in a group.

In our sessions, the leader and the participants sit scattered around the room or in a spiral-shaped formation. The space in between the people is left empty. The fact that the participants do not sit in a circle, as is customary in group psychotherapy, avoids members finding themselves face to face with the rest of the group. It therefore prevents each participant from being looked at and from looking at others straight in the eye. This, in turn, guarantees more privacy and a certain degree of anonymity.

The work in a session can begin in any given way. It can begin with the narration of a dream, with a contribution by a participant, or with a question addressed directly to the leader or to the group. There may or may not be a short introduction during which some basic information is communicated. In any event, the instructions given at the beginning of the first session should be few and concise. It is also possible to give the participants a written text containing some fundamental information, which they can read a week in advance. Yet another option could be to hold a preliminary meeting before the social dreaming workshop gets under way.

If the leader begins with a short introductory talk, this should explain that the participants are invited to share their dreams, make associations to the dreams told, and explore their possible social meaning. Lawrence (2001a) begins each session with a precise opening statement: "The primary task is to associate to one's own and others' dreams as they are made available in the matrix, so as to make links and find connections. Who has the first dream?"

The concept of matrix is explored in a later section; I wish to focus here on the notion that one can offer associations not only to one's own dreams but also to the dreams of the other participants. This notion implicitly suggests that dreams must not be considered as personal property belonging to the dreamer, but, rather, as something that is shared and that pertains to everyone. Furthermore, this notion establishes that dreams, associations, and thoughts (links and connections) are closely related (Hahn, 1998).

A few additional rules may help the session to proceed well: allow the individual participants to speak for not more than ten minutes; the leader should avoid answering questions that are put directly and engaging in a discussion with just one person. The purpose of these rules is to hold a discussion that gives everyone the opportunity to speak, rather than revolve around just one or two people or a very small group.

The work during the sessions

During the sessions, dreams are developed on the basis of free associations and also by resorting to the emotional and thematic "amplification" of the contents. Gaburri (1992, 2002), in referring to the traditional psychoanalytic setting and to the group psychotherapy setting, highlighted that free associations are stimulated not only by a train of thought or by what is said by the other members of the group, but also by the emotional atmosphere that is present and, more generally, by what is felt to be present during the session. This also applies to social dreaming. Images, dreams, and fantasies are then connected to one another through the contribution of all the participants. Light is shed upon how different dreams can have points in common. The sequence of the dreams that have been told is highlighted.

As a result of the way the work is conducted, a dreamlike atmosphere is produced during the sessions. The same idea can be expressed by saying that during the social dreaming sessions, dreams are dreamt a second time. It sometimes happens that a participant, while listening to the dream that is being told by one of the people present, thinks that he or she could have had the same dream. As they listen to the dream-telling, the people present may feel lost or instead may identify in unexpected ways. In this regard, I would like to describe something that happened during a social dreaming session that I attended, not as a leader but as a member of the matrix.

A woman was telling a dream in which *she was packing a bag for a trip or simply to leave the house. She put various objects into the bag—a lipstick, a pair of stockings—and then took them out again. She put them back in, replacing a few items. She checked that the bag was closed tightly. Then she put her hand inside it to retrieve something.* The narration of the dream went on and on with new details. The dreamer was becoming increasingly animated. It seemed that what she wanted to achieve by making these minor adjustments was packing the ideal bag. As I listened, I became increasingly impatient. I thought to myself: "No more!! No more about this bag!" Then I remembered the notion of "recognizing that a dream told by another participant could have been dreamed by me." I made a quick shift in perspective, asking myself the question: "It's clear that as a man I couldn't care less about this extremely accurate preparation. But what if I were a woman?" I tried to use my imagination. At that point, the whole process of putting things in and taking things out of the bag and packing it in the best possible way seemed extremely important, fascinating, and of great interest.

An aspect of the work that strongly characterizes social dreaming is the search for social elements that surface in dreams. It is a matter of understanding the way in which dreams and associations shed light on some aspects of the social environment and/or organization to which the participants belong by providing relevant images and other material. The work relating to this and to other aspects always consists in identifying the patterns rather than interpreting the contents of the dreams.

The matrix leader/taker sees to it that the rules of the setting are followed. He or she leaves it to the participants to make associations, find meanings, and identify allegories and symbols. The leader steps in to facilitate this work but does not volunteer interpretations regarding the group dynamics or the formation of sub-groups. His or her contributions are always based on what is evident. Especially during the first sessions, the leader may tend to clarify the social dreaming model to the participants, which is somewhat abstract and not always understood straight away. The leader's contributions usually refer to the dreams, such as: "Can we control our dreams?" or "Do dreams come on their own?" Sometimes a contribution may be aimed at establishing a connection between some elements of the dream and the overall discussion that has developed during that session or series of sessions. For example, if a participant dreams pieces of fabric, the leader may suggest that they represent the single contributions of the participants that eventually form a whole. In general, these are "guided associations" because they correspond to fantasies and thoughts that come to the leader's mind as associations, but, at the same time, they are geared towards clarifying a connection or an aspect of the way the group functions. The leader may occasionally encourage a participant to add some associations to a dream. Sometimes the participants in general may be asked to offer associations regarding a particular image or word that has appeared in a dream.

It should be stressed that this is a general description of steps and phases of a social dreaming session; each individual session, however, will have its own development and might not necessarily include all of these steps or may include others.

What is not taken into account

Social dreaming *cannot* have an established purpose, be it therapeutic or otherwise. Any pre-established purpose would distort the work and make it less effective; indeed, the work must focus only on the dreams, fantasies, and thoughts that surface and how they are interrelated. This does not mean, however, that there cannot be any therapeutic or other spin-offs as a secondary or side effect (Armstrong, 1998a).

Lawrence (2001a) states that in social dreaming, attention is focused on dreams and their interconnections, not on the dreamers and their relationships. Dreams are *not* ascribed to the childhoods of the people that tell them, nor to those of the other participants. Dreams are *not* used to highlight a psychopathological aspect of personality. Dreams are *not* used to draw attention to the personal and private relational life of the people present.

> During the second session of the workshop conducted at the Mauriburg psychoanalysis centre, a participant tells a dream: *I was going to the sailing club. A warship was moored to the pontoon, near the promenade. Some small sailboats and racing boats were also scattered here and there.* He goes on to add, "*It wasn't my club, it was my Dad's, which is in town. Although it's not my club, I know it well, because it's where I learned how to sail.*" As he is telling the dream, he remembers a second dream that is closely connected to the first one: "*I was talking on the phone with a friend that I haven't seen in years. I was saying to him, 'How can it be that you are not informed of what is happening?'* He explains: *'This friend is the person with whom I sailed in races.'*"

If this dream had been told during a psychoanalysis session, it could have been referred back to the childhood of the dreamer and in particular to his relationship with his father. One could have perhaps also hypothesized that the dream speaks of two aspects of the dreamer's personality, which are represented by himself and by his friend. Furthermore, the friend could have been considered as representing a distant aspect of the dreamer's personal analyst. One could have thought that the dream contains references to the psychoanalytic training of the dreamer and to his position as a student at the centre.

Instead, none of these keys for interpretation was adopted in the workshop. The associations of the people present focused on the image of the warship. Other dreams with similar images were told. A mosaic of images and associations was thus formed that revealed the impact that the war in Afghanistan was having on the everyday life of everyone present. In fact, at the time the workshop was taking place, the war had just started.

Matrix

Social dreaming originated in the early 1980s. At the time, Lawrence was on the scientific staff of the Tavistock Institute of Human Relations. In his capacity as Joint Director of the Institute's Group Relations Programme, Lawrence developed an approach centring around the concept of "relatedness"—that is, the ways in which the experience and behaviour of an individual reflect and are structured by conscious and unconscious constructs of the group or organization that are present in his mind. Together with Patricia Daniel, he then framed the idea of having "a group of people who would dream socially". In 1982, the first experiment was conducted, which was simply called "A Project in Social Dreaming and Creativity". The experiment lasted eight weeks. Weekly sessions were held, involving thirteen members from different professional backgrounds, most of whom, however, were familiar with the Tavistock study tradition. The sessions were called "Social Dreaming Matrices".

Lawrence (2001a) uses the word "matrix" to indicate both a "session (during which the participants offer dreams and associations)" and, more generally, "a place out of which something grows". He uses the word "matrix" in many circumstances where other therapists would use the word "group". According to him, the word "group" is associated too much with the idea of a certain number of people gathered in a room. Instead, he wants to shift interest towards what exists among the people, what is fed by their presence, and, in its turn, stimulates fantasies, thought, and dreams. Furthermore, the term "group" conjures up "group dynamics"; instead, he suggests that the latter be set aside in order to focus on the fact that being part of a matrix favours the ability to dream and to relate to others.

Lawrence borrows the notion of matrix from Foulkes (1964). Foulkes starts with the idea that the group is a whole: it is a living organism, with its own moods and reactions, and it has a characteristic spirit and generates specific atmospheres and affective climates. Referring to this idea of a group, Foulkes describes the matrix as something that is common to all of the members and has to do not only with the dimension of interpersonal relationships, but also and especially with the transpersonal and suprapersonal dimensions. All of the most important functions of the matrix stem from this definition. All verbal and non-verbal communications refer to the matrix. The meaning and significance of what occurs in the group depend upon the matrix.

Lawrence differs slightly from Foulkes in that he defines the matrix as a biosphere (a web that connects all living beings) and as a germinative organ (Vernadskij, 1929). I personally believe that the concept of matrix may be extremely useful for clinical purposes.

However, I am concerned by the fact the concept can be used in a very concrete way (as something that really exists and not as a concept) and at the same time in a highly metaphysical sense (as something that exists independently of the individuals that form the group). If the notion were to shift in this direction, its use would become an obstacle rather than an aid in understanding and studying the complex relationships between individuals and the group to which they belong.

Social dreaming in organizations and in professional associations

I now wish to go back to the origin of social dreaming and its subsequent development. In the wake of the first experiences at the Tavistock Institute of Human Relations, Lawrence and other researchers gradually developed the idea that in order to understand institutions better, it would also be necessary to take into account the dream life of the people that belong to them. They therefore employed the social dreaming method in various situations: business consultancy, refresher courses, and conferences.

One idea that underpins the use of social dreaming in these areas is that of the dream as a "container". In certain stages in the life of an organization, tension and conflicts reach peak levels. In these stages, it often happens that a great deal of energy goes into finding answers. Instead, it could be more useful to allow the questions present in the institution to develop. In order to do so, it is necessary to have an adequate container where the questions may be developed and that allows people to tackle them and work on them. Dreams can be such a container, and social dreaming the right technique (Tatham & Morgan, 1998; Ambrosiano, 2001b).

A second fundamental idea is that there are various different levels in the social and mental life of institutions, one of which is the level of dreams. We could say that the life of institutions, organizations, and professional associations is organized on three levels. The first level involves practical, administrative, and bureaucratic work. The second level has to do with vision, ideals, theories, and ideology. The third level is that of dream and fantasy life. The existence of the level of dream and fantasy life, for example, makes it possible to joke with co-workers and feel pleasure during work. It allows one to take what happens in the institution seriously, but also with a certain degree of lightness. The level (or dimension) of the life of the organization as a "place" where one dreams (or where the organization is constantly dreamt) is often lacking or inadequate. The inadequacy of the dream level stretches the distance between the practical level of the organization and its ideal-visionary level, to the detriment of both. The social dreaming method helps to focus attention on dreams and activates the dream level that should be present in all organizations (Lawrence, 1998a).

Another fundamental idea that underpins the use of social dreaming in organizations and associations has to do with the conflicts that can poison the life of these institutions. In fact, it is not one idea but, rather, a series of reflections, the most important of which involves the concepts of "uni-verse" and "multi-verse".

In an institutional group that is struggling with power issues (real or imaginary), the various people and subgroups in conflict try to control the way in which the others must or should think and act, in an attempt to persuade or to force them in various ways. In this "uni-verse", it is important to establish who is right and who is wrong.

Social dreaming does not help people to understand each other, but to understand— that is, to see the same dream (or the same issue) from different and even clashing standpoints. This is possible if one has in mind not a "uni-verse" but a "multi-verse". According to the approach suggested by Lawrence, all dreams have an equal right to come to light and to be considered real. This experience is a fundamental element of tolerance (Arendt, 1968; Arendt & Heidegger, 1998; Ettinger, 1995; Safranski, 1994; Lawrence, 2001a; Kaës, 2002).

At the third session of the Mauriburg workshop, a new participant arrives. He immediately begins to challenge the method. He boasts he is an interpreter of dreams. He then attacks the leader directly, maintaining that what the leader says is irrelevant. The other members of the group are irritated and try to oppose him, the only result being that the polemical tones of the discussion become even stronger. The session ends in this atmosphere. During the brief informal conversations at the end of the session, some participants observe that this member's behaviour is quite common in many of the scientific meetings and seminars of the centre. The fourth session takes place the next morning. The "disrupting" participant does not show up. Someone suggests they try to imagine what dream the disrupter would have brought had he dreamt and come to the session. Many share their fantasies and dreams. The overall picture reveals not a dream but an ideal that the absent member could have communicated. The ideal is not at all subversive and provoking; on the contrary, it is that of a motionless Psychoanalysis and a psychoanalytic Society organized in a strongly hierarchical and pyramidal way. After elaborating on the hypothetical dream-ideal of the "absent participant", many express a liking for that same person with whom they had previously been very angry. Some say they hope he will attend all the sessions of the next social dreaming workshop.

Social dreaming helped the participants to see the episode involving their colleague in terms of a dream or an ideal rather than in terms of roles, interpersonal conflicts, subgroups, or any definition of psychopathology. The colleague's "controversial" point of view was accepted, at least in part. Lawrence (2001b) defines this shift in perspective as a transition from the Oedipus vertex to the sphinx vertex (Bion, 1963).

Other possible uses

The social dreaming technique originated in an institution, and so far it has been used especially in working with organizations (structured groups that have set objectives: targets to be reached in work, research, or other areas). However, I believe that social dreaming can also be useful with groups comprised of people that are not personally acquainted or barely know each other. In this case, the common environment consists of sharing the same social reality, regardless of the scope and diversification this entails (Beradt, 1966).

In some situations, people who do not belong to the same organization or institution nevertheless have something very important in common. An example is provided by the people of New York who suffered trauma as a result of the attack on and collapse of the Twin

Towers of the World Trade Center. Another example consists of people who have been harassed in the workplace (mobbing). In these cases, the social dreaming technique could prove useful because it is a practice that is on the borderline between what is "therapeutic" and "not entirely therapeutic" and because it offers the opportunity to refer to and share events not as "facts of reality" but as "dreams that speak of reality".

Yet another example of people for whom social dreaming might be useful is that of immigrant men and women living in a country that is not their homeland. Immigrants have lost the world that was familiar to them, and they are faced with the task of building an image of the new social reality in which they are living. Dreaming and sharing dreams can help to build the image of this reality. Dreams, in fact, are a sort of interface between the individual and social reality.

In my experience with social dreaming, I have worked only with institutions and professional associations. Over time, I saw that by participating in social dreaming the members of these institutions experienced a sense of freshness and of greater and more accessible intimacy. People had the opportunity to recover—at least temporarily—a sense of wholeness and of being intimately connected. Also, as a result of participating in social dreaming, people were more open to becoming interested by common projects and to expressing feelings of gratitude and acknowledgement of efforts made by others. I believe that it is possible to ascribe these positive changes to some aspects of the social dreaming experience. During a social dreaming session, when a person tells a dream and other participants grasp it, offering their own associations or simply giving a sign of resonance through a facial expression or a bodily movement, the dreamer draws from this a sense of reality and sharing. During the sessions, people come into contact with each other on a level that is intimate and moving, if obscure. When I use the word "obscure", I mean to refer to a generative condition that is surrounded by scarce or total unawareness. This contact is obscure, but not massive or intrusive: it is the meeting of minds that dream together, of people who experience the shared lightness of joining in associative thinking.

The results I have reported lead me to think that the social dreaming technique could also be tested in situations different from those typical of an institution, such as with people who have suffered trauma or with immigrants.

Historical background

Lawrence states that social dreaming has a very long past and a short current history. There is nothing new in the construction of the material of social dreaming—dreams and free associations—but there is something truly revolutionary in the method and in the field of application. For many centuries, the close link established between the dream and its dreamer overshadowed the communicative functions that dreams have for groups or communities. From our contemporary perspective, it is probably worthwhile recovering this ancient approach to dreams (Selvaggi, 2001).

In many tribal cultures and in very ancient civilizations, dreams, like myths, were told and discussed during special collective gatherings. Since the members of the tribal group had so much in common in terms of symbols and language, they had the key to "reading" most of the meaning of a dream, of a tale, or of a traditional story. The role of their "experts" (who were, first and foremost, experts in rituals) consisted in emphasizing, clarifying, integrating, and elaborating on the dreams by means of poetic resonance, rather than "dis-enchanting" the story by offering interpretations and prophecies.

Through the interchange of dreams, it was easier for the members of the group to relate to each other and to attune their communication. This proved to be especially useful and beneficial in the areas of the life of the community where cooperation and interdependence needed to be fluid, harmonious, and timely. For example, hunting and fighting require the individuals to operate as a unit and to trust their companions completely. In fact, during these enterprises, the members of a tribe place their lives in each other's hands. Therefore, these activities require the ability to operate in a synchronous and complementary way. This can be facilitated by making adjustments in communication and relationships, which can be achieved by telling and sharing dreams.

In the urbanized world of the classical Mediterranean—Mesopotamia, Egypt, Israel, and Greece—the use of dreams has progressively pursued purposes that are different from the ones that I have described. Dreams have become messages conveyed by means of images. The language of dreams, which was previously transparent and capable of influencing the shared living of the group, becomes more obscure. A dream carries a message that is full of meaning, but it has to be interpreted in order for the message to be understood. Dreams are no longer a tool for unconscious harmonization within the group; rather, they shed some light on the fate of the dreamer.

Around the second century AD, Artemidorus Daldianus wrote a book dedicated to the interpretation of dreams, as did Freud many centuries later. Both Artemidorus and Freud develop hypotheses that lead to an "individual approach" to dreams. Furthermore, both take up the idea that the individual's conscious and unconscious are separate. Their approach requires the presence of an expert who is capable of deciphering the meaning, which has been ciphered by means of condensation and displacement. Experts in the interpretation of dreams must also know how to trace the day residue, to which considerable importance is attached in interpretation procedures. Artemidorus, speaking of the day residue, states: "A man will not dream about things to which he has never given any thought." Finally, both Artemidorus and Freud privilege allegorical dreams containing images that are arranged on various levels (cited in Murray, 1999).

Freud placed dreams at the centre of the scientific project of psychoanalysis. Dreams were considered especially in terms of the interpretations that made it possible to understand their meaning. Freud developed notions such as "censure" and "displacement" to explain the processes involved in dreaming, and in remembering and forgetting dreams. It was an extraordinary effort, thanks to which the narration and interpretation of dreams have become significant aspects of psychoanalytic work.

Over time, psychoanalysts of considerable standing developed Freud's theory and drew attention to two aspects that he had not taken much into consideration. Many psychoanalysts began to consider dreams not so much as distorted presentations of the dreamer's desires but, rather, as genuine and truthful representations of his or her feelings, desires, fantasies, and thoughts. It has also been highlighted that some dreams provide insight on a given aspect of the dreamer's personality and on what he or she is experiencing at that time in his or her life. Furthermore, emphasis has been placed on the importance that the feelings and thoughts contained in dreams can have on the dreamer's affective life.

Some psychoanalysts believe that dreams provide significant information on the fears, hopes and ideals present in the social environment where the dreamer lives. Adopting this standpoint, several Italian psychoanalysts—Riolo (1982), Corrao (1986), Vallion Macció

(1992), Ferro (1996), Correale et al. (2001)—consider dreams as an expression of a given situation (or of a given "ground"). Furthermore, they believe that dreams acquire meaning if they are placed within that situation (or "ground").

This way of looking at dreams is not very far removed from a perspective that considers it—as does social dreaming—not only as an expression of desires and fantasies, but also as a "special representation" of an individual's point of view on the community in which he or she lives and on the organizations to which he or she belongs.

Raissa

In addition to Mauriburg, we have held workshops in Raissa and Clarice Town. In both cases, the participants were members of professional associations. In Raissa, though, the social reality that was represented in the dreams and then discussed during the sessions was not so much that of the association but that of the broader social and political situation.

The Raissa workshop was attended by thirty-five participants: psychiatrists, psychologists, and social workers. Most of the participants were Israeli Jews; four were Arab Israelis. All of them belonged to an association that promotes dialogue between conflicting groups and communities: Israelis and Palestinians, Jews and Arabs, lay and religious Jews, and so forth. I ran this workshop with an Israeli colleague.

The organization itself is a group with a high degree of conflicts: its members are politically divided between left and right. After the assassination of Prime Minister Rabin at the hands of a right-wing activist, such a division became even more sharp and almost unyielding. "Leftist" and "rightist" participants had very different opinions on many important issues, such as, for instance, the peace process with the Palestinians and the fate of the Jewish settlers in the autonomous Palestinian territories. The *Intifada* and the recent kamikaze attacks in supermarkets, bus stations and restaurants fuelled strong feelings in all the people present. The fighting or warfare between Palestinians and Israelis was indeed the central theme of the social dreaming workshop.

At the beginning of the first session, I took the floor and briefly introduced the method. The session was characterized by a very fast-flowing and almost frenzied succession of dreams. One dream followed the other, the pace grew faster and faster, and the emotional involvement grew progressively stronger. At first glance, it might have appeared that each participant was isolated in him/herself and driven only by the urge to communicate by unleashing the dreams, emotions, and fantasies that had been far too compressed and kept in check until that time. One might have thought that the participants were unable to associate to the dreams of the others and could only bring their own dreams or nightmares to the group. Gradually, however, it became more and more clear that the dreams being told were actually associations to and/or the working through of dreams that had previously been presented in the session.

Some common themes came to the fore with astonishing force and were very evident to everyone present. Such central themes revolved around the feeling of being lost, of not being sure of one's way, the fantasy of being abandoned by one's parents and by people having authority, feelings of guilt especially towards one's own children. For example, the following dream reveals a participant's guilt feelings for the time and energy she dedicates to her volunteer work rather than to her daughter.

My daughter is shopping for clothes at the mall in Robinia. The woman who runs the shop takes 380 shekel from her purse and gives it to charity. My daughter gets very angry: she wants the lady to give her money back. The shopkeeper tells her that she can have it back, but that in order to get it she has to go to the "Left Wing Center" or to the city's "Religious school".

The next common theme is presented through a series of dreams centred around killings, threats, and danger, the wish to seek revenge, and a feeling of shame. The first session allowed the participants, who sided either with the left or with the right in Israel's politics, to discover and experience the existence of a common affective experience. Such a basic experience was revealed by the dreams, which had many similarities regardless of the political inclination of the dreamers. During the second session, they began a dialogue that entailed an intense and exciting analysis of themselves and of their

political positions. The third session focused mostly on the organization. This is where there was much disagreement. A great deal of
anger was vented, and the roles covered in the institution by some of
the participants were questioned.

While the workshops were in progress, I shared with the participants only the observations that were closely related with the dreams
and that I could express only as associations rather than as explanations. My general observations, *a posteriori*, are the following:

1. In the "conscious" (or "day") discourse of the participants, the
    division between Palestinians and Israelis was obvious. It was
    clear to everyone that Palestinians and Israelis were involved in
    conflict and probably in a real war. Different opinions were ex-
    pressed as to how to manage, how to "deal with" the conflict, but
    that was all. No one ever doubted that there was conflict and
    separation, that Israelis and Palestinians were clearly two oppo-
    site fronts.

    In the dreams, instead, the Palestinians appeared not just as
    enemies, but also as sons and daughters, servants, people who
    lend a helping hand, humbled and oppressed people, and much
    more. The novelist Abraham Yehoshua (1977) offers beautiful
    descriptions of these forms of closeness, intermingling, and inti-
    mate exchanges. For example, a participant told a dream in which
    a Palestinian was a genie. She swallowed it and a process that
    induced transformation in her began: "*A terrible genie came out of
    my mouth. I fought with it, then I ate it*".

2. The theme of the Nazis and of the Holocaust were present in the
    dreams, but the central drama that the participants in the work-
    shop shared was the conflict between Palestinians and Israelis.
    The current conflict overlapped and was confused with the terri-
    ble memories, the myths, and the whole collection of feelings and
    fantasies of Nazi persecution. The memory of the Holocaust also
    led the participants to make strong and conflicting identification
    with the Palestinian people.

3. In the dreams (in fact, not dreams but nightmares in many cases),
    time does not move in any direction. It does not go either forward
    or backward. It is not the circular time of myth. It is not the time of
    the *après coup*, which gives new meaning to the appearance of old
    events. Time in "nightmare-dreams" is repetitive and motionless:

it revolves around the same themes and fantasies and does not evolve. No action can be carried through. No action is recognized as having taken place. The same action is performed over and over again, or is followed by another action that appears to be its opposite but is actually identical.

During the sessions, my contributions focused especially on how time manifested itself in the dreams.

The image of a "dignified killer" helped to transform and overcome the repetitiveness of the killings among Israelis and Palestinians. A participant related an episode involving a pregnant woman during the Holocaust who overcame her passive attitude and killed a Nazi guard. Another participant commented that this had been possible for the woman because she was pregnant. She felt she was killing not just out of hatred, but also for a more valid and universal reason. At that point, another member of the group spoke about the feelings he experienced while on guard during the night, armed with a gun, because his family was in danger.

In certain situations, a person who wields a weapon or even a person who kills is not simply a criminal but a "dignified killer." A "dignified killer" is very different from a "professional killer". After having killed, the professional killer is clean and tidy, he has no bloodstains; however, inside him and in his victim, something essential has been destroyed. A "dignified killer" can preserve a little bit of honour for himself and also for his enemy. In fact, the counterpart of a "dignified killer" is not a persecutor or a victim, but an enemy. There is hope that eventually one may be reconciled with an enemy, though never with a persecutor. A "dignified killer" can accept the fact that he has killed. Facts really happen and are registered; time moves on, it does not coil up.

Clarice Town

The workshop in Clarice Town adopted the same type of setting and timing as that in Raissa. Four sessions took place. There were twenty-five participants, all members of an association of psychotherapists who have done training in psychoanalysis and follow a psychoanalytic approach. However, the members of the association belong to different schools and theoretical currents. Some follow self psychology, others draw inspiration from the work of Melanie Klein, others still belong to the Tavistock school. The decision to join in a single association arose because in the area there are very few psychotherapists.

The following dream told by one of the founders of the association, during the second session. "*I was jogging and was wearing shorts. I was much more fit than I have been in a long time and perhaps than I have ever been. I felt rather sexy.*" The narrator added, "Even though this dream may appear to be very personal, I think it refers to our association." Many fantasies arose. Someone recalled the "girls of Ashcombie Road", a street in Clarice Town known for its bars and prostitutes. Another participant said that in the early days, many years before, the atmosphere in the association had been much warmer. Everyone was more active. A third person described some images and feelings that were conjured up by the announcement that an Italian psychoanalyst was about to come to Clarice Town.

At this point, the discussion was being carried forward by only a few participants, the founding members. As I listened to their discussion I got the impression—which later proved correct—that they were making a decision without, however, referring explicitly to the matter they were deciding on nor to the fact that they were making a decision. One of the people belonging to the sub-group of the founding members suddenly asked someone else: "Do you remember when the supervisors came from Eudoxia?"

Little by little, through the contributions of four or five people, the whole story was told. Many years before, three "training psychoanalysts" used to come to Clarice Town once a month to hold supervisions and seminars, and, in a certain sense, got the association started. The psychoanalysts from Eudoxia worked and stayed in Clarice Town over the weekend, from Friday to Sunday. Some young women psychotherapists had been invited to dinner by them; later they went for drinks. Something inappropriate and not entirely acceptable had happened. The whole matter was never mentioned again. The psychoanalysts from Eudoxia involved in this questionable affair were never asked to come again.

Immediately after this old story was pieced back together, a woman, one of the members of the association who did not belong either to the sub-group of founders or to that of the youngest members, protested: "How could you keep this from us for more than ten years!" Another woman said: "Great! You've had your fun—what about us?" Yet another participant said: "Now I understand why sexuality and even the slightest mention of a friendly flirtation or physical proximity between us has been completely banished from the life of our association."

Methodological and clinical suggestions

- Dreams are extremely versatile. This can be seen in the fact that they can be used with excellent results both in the traditional psychoanalytic setting and in social dreaming.
- Dreams—as Freud (1900a) pointed out—express a desire, where "desire" is understood in the individual sense of the word. Dreams, however, also express a desire where the term is intended in its collective and visionary meaning, as expressed, for instance, by Martin Luther King: "*I had a dream. . . .*"

In group psychotherapy, special attention must be devoted to the possible conflicts among dreams. If a dream is the dynamic expression of a desire that has a social scope, a member of a group may be afraid of the dream of another participant because its manifestation may be seen as an obstacle or denial of the member's own dream, which he or she may not be able to express. One could also envy someone else's dream, and even more so a dream that is shared by others. An alternative to envy is the courage to express and share one's dreams (Lawrence, 2001a).

- Dreams are "the garments of our intimacy": they allow our innermost thoughts and feelings to be shared socially and to meet other thoughts, feelings, and people. This intimacy must be respected and welcomed. In some rather harmonious families, the family members are accustomed to telling each other their dreams and commenting on them in the morning while having breakfast, especially during the holidays or in the weekend. Psychotherapists who work with couples and families make a similar use of dreams.

The social dreaming method stresses the importance of telling and sharing dreams in order to favour the development of a good relationship among the members of a group. I also believe that in the traditional psychoanalytic setting, sharing the narration of a dream in a participatory way, prior to interpreting it or using it to understand, can be very useful to "fine tune" the relationship between patient and psychoanalyst (Friedman, 1999).

• The report on the workshop in Raissa shows that it was useful to compare the "conscious images" of the conflict between Palestinians and Israelis with the ones present in dreams. Perhaps it might be convenient to do something similar in the traditional psychoanalytic setting too.

• In Clarice Town, an "unknown element" that had surfaced only as a vague sign (the lack of vitality in the life of the association, as a result of which a request was made to organize the workshop) came progressively to the fore through a dream and subsequently took the form of, "lack of vitality = complete dismissal of sexuality from the life of the association".

The idea that dreams can have a problem-solving function is already present in *The Interpretation of Dreams*. In a footnote that was added in 1925, Freud (1900a) wrote: "At bottom, dreams are nothing other than a particular *form* of thinking. . . . The fact that dreams concern themselves with attempts at solving the problems by which our mental life is faced is no more strange than that our conscious waking life should do so; beyond this it merely tells us that that activity can also be carried on in the preconscious. . . ."

Tagliacozzo (1992) and Fosshage (1998, 2001) have highlighted the fact that when a new configuration surfaces in a dream this may be an indication that the dreamer is seeking a pathway to evolve in analysis and in life. Social dreaming reintroduces the debate on the cognitive function of dreams and in particular on the cognitive function of telling and sharing dreams (Bernabei, 2001; Friedman, 2000).

• In social dreaming sessions, the meaning that a dream has for the dreamer remains in the background while attention is focused on its social meaning. In the group psychotherapy sessions, the two approaches to dreams do not rule each other out; on the contrary, they acquire cognitive and emotional significance through the connection of one to the other. Also the method is different: it is best to go from the personal meaning (or "group" meaning) of a dream to its social meaning and then back in the other direction. This to-and-fro movement should be repeated several times. However, social dreaming can be extremely useful in understanding the way a group works, which in the context of psychotherapy is something that may remain unexplored as a result of the commitment to the individual participants (Neri, 1998).

CHAPTER THREE

Dreaming the future

John Clare

If Heaven I cannot bend,
Then Hell I will arouse.

Virgil, "Aeneid", Vii 313

Dreaming the future

For twelve months a group of people meet in a room and share their dreams. Many of the dreams are violent; some are about a forthcoming catastrophe that cannot be averted. There is a sense of powerlessness, for politicians are remote, inept, and preoccupied with presentation. Despite the sense of impending doom, these social dreamers take pleasure at the freedom of expression in a discourse with comparative strangers. They are surprised at their facility to think together. Then one day, almost a year after they began meeting, the towers of the World Trade Center are attacked by terrorists, there is international alarm, and people start to talk of apocalypse now. The dreamers continue to dream (presumably like everyone else), but there is no sense of surprise in their dreams. It is as if they have known all along the inevitability of this catastrophe, which kills over 3,000 people and begins a war against a Third World country.

In fact, it seems that they have been dreaming about this disaster for most of the previous year, calmly and with patience and friendship. In their dreams they have been "thinking", and when the dreams are scrutinized it appears they have all along known something that was unavailable for thought.

This social dreaming matrix took place in London, meeting once monthly and consisting usually of ten to fifteen people. Most participants had never met before and did not belong to the same institution, or occupation. It was a disparate matrix, in that dreamers did not share a common activity that could become a focus for dreaming. Each dream-telling matrix lasted ninety minutes and was followed by a thinking section of one hour. This was in part an ongoing piece of research to find out what type of discourse would develop over and beyond the associations to the dreams. It was not clear what kind of thoughts the first section would spark off. The thinking function gradually developed its own changing dynamic, without ever being specifically defined or elaborated. Part of my task in this chapter is to examine possible uses of this component. As well as sharing and associating to our dreams, how can we think about them and what can we do with these thoughts?

I shall begin by highlighting the key dreams in sequence and discussing associations that arose both in the matrix and in the thinking section. I then explore the potential of a predictive capability in social dreaming and the practical implications of the dream as premonition.

MATRIX 1
The first dream

In examining over a year's social dreaming, a chronological overview is a useful way to glean themes and patterns of relevance.

The first dream, short and stark, was of *a white blank mirror with a lurking Nazi presence*. This produced rapid associations of "thought" police, war criminals in Belgrade, Orpheus in the Underworld, the First World War, fear of being unknown, of being tortured, of being undead. These themes reoccurred in the months to come.

The second dream was of *a large ferry turning in a harbour while the dreamer's luggage was left on the quay*. This created the thought that dreaming together could be a brilliant but dangerous manoeuvre, a taboo practice especially related to the idea that the prophets were dreamers. Also expressed was a sense of absurdity in trying to be containing in such a dangerous world. Another dream was *of being on a ferry and seeing a speedboat bombing down the Thames en route to a football match*. At that stage there was no sense of how significant the idea of bombing was to become. There were associations to fear of crowds, racial prejudice, the knifing of a young man at the Notting Hill Carnival, ethnic cleansing.

In the next dream, *a dreamer gave therapy to a girl called Cassie, stating that he needed objectivity not hostility. The girl hurried away uncertainly. Then, as he closed the door of a huge house, the door bent into an arc from top to bottom. It was difficult to shut, as there was no key. Upstairs was a builder/architect, who was also a navvy. There was a flash of light from a mirror, or a glint of steel, as he walked down a steep straight trench towards the monolithic foundations of a building made for Richelieu. It was uniform and regulated.*

With hindsight it is possible to see that most of the key themes of this year-long matrix were present in this first session. These were:

- mass murder and impending danger, which could not be contained;
- a war of racist persecution;
- a sense of powerlessness in the face of danger;
- the difficulty of constructing a container, a boat, a ferry, an ark, a place of refuge;
- the need for a space for objective reflection rather than a blank mirror;
- fear of descent into an underworld of chaos and bombing;
- the possibility of dreaming's being a portent, a Cassandra-like prophecy;
- the ominous shadow of the First World War, the "war to end all wars";
- the notion of a work group, able to use the dream like a builder/architect/navvy;

• the problem of finding new ways to think, other than in the straight lines of convention, uniformity, and compliance.

Such varied images of violence, determination, and impotence were present amidst the pleasant introductory paraphernalia of the opening session. Of course, with hindsight it would be easy to select a version tailored to fit subsequent events, but in fact these specific themes recurred in the dreams, rising in intensity each month, as public services deteriorated and world affairs pushed nearer to the abyss. To summarize some significant events of this period:

1. In Britain, BSE, foot and mouth disease, train crashes, flooding, NHS crises, and escalation in Northern Ireland, despite the peace initiative.

2. Tit-for-tat assassinations in the Arab–Israeli confrontation.

3. In America, George W. Bush "wins the presidency" amidst accusations of cheating.

4. The proliferation of trivia and celebrity hubris grew in the media as part of Hollywood's fantasy depiction of "reality" and with cult programmes such as *Big Brother* and disaster films like *Titanic*.

5. In Asia, the nuclear stand-off between India and Pakistan.

A final thought from the first session was the fear of amnesia and the idea that if we lose our dreams to the unconscious, the vast and formless void, then the abyss awaits us. That if we cannot make it in the Overworld then, like Orpheus, we may slip down into the Underworld. This concern persisted throughout the programme. Perhaps the fear was that, as ordinary people, we were destined to be like Cassandra, aware of the danger but unable to change events.

MATRIX 2
The disaster movie dream: a warning

Among other dreams about urban terrorism and a mugging to steal a mobile phone, the following dream was reported:

THE BEE-WARE DREAM. *I was in a disaster movie. A man is walking towards me wearing on his head a busby made of a swarm of buzzing bees (a buzz-bee). His head is alive. Someone says "Oh! It's the latest thing, it's called bee-ware." And then I go into a room and there's a pig's head on an anvil. Men batter it to pieces and just the ears are left. I put these on. Next, there's a flood plain with a typhoon coming. The atmosphere is black, angry. I feel "I've got to get out of here!"*

The imagery of this dream anticipates many of the themes ahead. The need to beware coming violence to man and beast—the slaughter of over 2,000,000 animals in the foot and mouth epidemic had not yet happened; the importance of reverie (his head was alive); the necessity of humour (this dream caused much mirth); the fear that those in authority would make a pig's ear of things; issues of concern, about which we had bees in our bonnets; an apocalyptic dread of bad weather of Shakespearean dimensions; and a growing sense that dark forces were making the world too dangerous to survive. One participant said: "What's coming out seems subversive, but we don't seem able to read the portents: we don't know how to read the gore to find out what will happen."

There was the suggestion that the thinking component of the meetings was a form of amplification, like a spreading tumbleweed of ideas blowing about to suggest links between dream thoughts. Participants voiced uncertainty, the fear of a shared hallucination, the sense that we were just "blind mouths", to quote a phrase from Milton, in the face of CJD disease and the spread of MacDonald's fast food. The feeling developed that there were omens and that there could be a danger in dreaming, not because of internal/personal material but through the idea of external portents. Indeed, in just the way that Freud located the latent content of the dream in the individual's unconscious, perhaps the latent content in social dreaming is outside us, in the social arena. This idea of impending jeopardy persisted and became one of the foci for the thinking section. Thus the dreams stood as signposts, symptoms, omens, or clues broadcast from beyond and available for scrutiny and exposition. This is an idea almost akin to reading the runes. Originally the rune was a mark of magic significance, a character of ancient Greek alphabets used to forecast the outcome of a situation. The *O.E.D.* defines runes as small stones, pieces of bone etc. bearing such marks and used as divinatory symbols; also, a spell or incantation. Perhaps the runic quality of objects in dreams can be used as a form of research into the social meaning, or latent content, to be gleaned from the busby, the pig's ear, the anvil, the flood plane; to act as another way of reading the dream.

Empty clothes and high-rise attack dreams

Two dreamers had dreamt of clothes without people inside them:

DREAM 1. *I get a phone call from Oxford to say my daughter has disap-peared and her empty clothes have been found, left standing up, as if she was still in them. The clothes are ginger coloured. I feel alarmed at this news.*

DREAM 2. *I'm in a room with my wife, we are in a labyrinth, there is a fun-fair outside, I must stay conscious. The door slams, I feel very frightened. Then there's a figure in front of me but it's just clothes, just breath, a spirit. Stretching in terror, I woke up, my heart pounding.*

This image of emptiness, a figure with nothing inside, is in sharp contrast to the depth and substance of many other dreams. Vacuity was an ongoing motif redolent of a narcissistic consumerist culture reflected in the "dream" of advertising copy, the cult of celebrity as "creative art", and the postmodern gloss of surface and fragmentation glimmering in the empty dreaming mirror of the TV screen. In the late capitalist world, the cult of celebrity reduces the human figure to commodity and mere image. Photography and advertising strip eve-rything away, leaving only appearance, with no feelings or inner depth. There is no longer the notion of the subjective, of an internal world with feelings and expressivity. In Frederick Jameson's phrase, there has been a "waning of affect", emotion is dissipated, with noth-ing inside and nothing to express (Jameson, 1984, p. 77). The hermeneutic model with latent, manifest, and repressed content is redundant. The anxiety of the empty-clothes dreams could be seen as the realization of the death of the self in a late capitalist world, the emptiness of the narcissist who constantly needs filling-up to quell the sense of dread. Van Gogh has been replaced by Andy Warhol, Prozac is on hand to stop any unwanted feelings, death anxiety abides in a world devoid of myths to negotiate the very idea of dying, and artists repeat the past in order to try to resurrect the sacred in a godless world. Of course, a society in which individuality and autonomy have been dissolved by organizational bureaucracy and technological mass reproduction has no use for the idea of the dream as the manifestation of a greater reality, either inside us or "out there". Repeatedly, the free expression of the matrix prevailed as an antidote to this postmodern gloss and superficiality, suggesting that the dreaming process itself could be a counter to this deadening of the self.

It was after this that the first lucid "warning" dream appeared:

THE HIGH-RISE DREAM.   *I was with a wise companion and others in a high-rise building in London. I was talking to a man who was outside the window strapped to a black, flapping contraption, which looked like a parachute blowing in the wind. I tried to help him. Suddenly the building began to move and swivel as if blown by a turbulent wind. Very scared, I shouted: "Is this an earthquake?" "No," they shouted, although no one could say what it was. The man "flying" outside risked death but disregarded the danger. My wise friend said, "That's what they do—there's nothing you can do about it."*

A high building was being attacked, the man outside had no fear of death, others could not understand what the destructive force was, and there was a sense of powerlessness in the face of danger. To read this in retrospect gives a chilling sense of what was to come on 11 September 2001.

MATRIX 4
Violent dreams: a paradigm for conflict situations

At this stage the matrix began to speed up. Skipping through the material, the associations ricocheted from dreamer to dreamer, mirrors reappeared as people, and a synchronicity developed as one dream reflected another. While these were unremittingly violent dreams, there were clear attempts in the material to grasp and communicate key underlying concepts.

THE HIPPOPOTAMUS DREAM.   *I was underneath a motorway and had to escape through an underpass. There were pillars and concrete troughs, and I was jumping over trenches. One was an animal trap. Stuck between the channels, I was terrified and I was attacked by a hippopotamus.*

It had no teeth, a bit like a tortoise. I was negotiating my way through a zoo armed with only a paperknife. I was so scared I woke up.

New technology appeared as both exciting and scary. There were repeated anxieties about mobile phones, information technology, the use of the Internet, and the inexorable speed of social change and loss of traditional forms of communication. Things were going too fast. This was reflected in the alacrity of dream thoughts, as weeks went by and the matrix went hyper, hurrying on to the next technological landscape.

Associations to the hippopotamus dream pointed to a sense of defencelessness in a world of labyrinthine threat. What was this toothless horse in the river? It seemed to stand for a sort of external id threatening to overpower us, a hell where things go too fast and technology is all-pervasive and where we are terrified of being sucked in by some external force that we cannot control, the toothless mouth of the voracious hippo of cyberspace.

Similarly, a dream of *a monastery in which people sat around looking more like mirrors than people* led to uneasy thoughts of alienation, blocked communication, Perseus and Medusa, a mistrust of certainty. In "La stade du miroir", Lacan (1949) identifies this stage in human development as a point of alienation, in that the mirror shows a total unity that cannot be touched. One's own body is other than the self. The mirror creates a unity that reveals a lack of being, where realization lies in another or imaginary space. If people facing one another are mirrors, this posits an idea of the gap, the ineffable, the infinite. One image reflects another, which reflects another, and that in turn reflects another, and so on without end. This is similar to the realization that the world will continue endlessly after one's death and life will not exist forever. In this tableau, something is missing that makes us what we are. The dream is both our essence and our absence.

Each of the nine dense dreams in this matrix featured violence. One of these will serve as an example:

THE TOWN VS. COUNTRY DREAM.   *In a town there was going to be a fight between the hard, cynical metropolitan rationalists and the country people, who were mainly 65-year-old pixies in pink fleeces and wearing dreadlocks. I was on the side of the cosmo-rationalists. There was a pitched battle in which we killed a child, so they got on their mobiles and phoned the IRA for back-up. I wanted to get out, so I escaped to the edge of town. Suddenly the IRA arrived and put a pitch-fork into my chest, and I could not get away.*

There had been several dreams of attempts to escape attack and then of being violently pinned down. These dreams were felt to be a way of accessing something crucial about violence. Through the creation of a paradigm for various conflict situations, dreamers discovered the existence of shared ideas, common to many dreams. For example:

- The notion that injustice or brutal defeat leads to the formation of violent counter-ideologies of which terrorism is the prototype. ("Bloody Sunday" in Northern Ireland in 1972 would be an example.)

- The fear of difference (men vs. women, town vs. country, inside vs. outside, natives vs. foreigners, dreamers vs. non-dreamers).

- A sense of powerlessness in the face of things getting out of control.

- The existence of mirror-image paranoia.

- The realization that violent situations were not conducive to thinking.

However, in the thinking section the idea developed that dreams were a way of thinking, of organizing chaos, of making structure and boundaries, of making the space for research.

The synagogue dreams

The synagogue was a recurrent object in the dreams, as was the monastery, church, temple, or theatre, each of which to some extent represented the matrix. As a meeting place for the exchange of dreams and ideas, the synagogue or theatre was a fertile milieu in which we were all "agog with sin". It provided the safety of a frame where free-ranging research was possible without censure or ridicule. Out of this environment came a liberating idea that the matrix is an attempt to "go native" in order to experience the real, to detect things that are actually happening of which we are not aware. As someone put it: "A place where you can just leave it to the dreams. The freedom here is that we do not police one another's rationality." However, there was also the contrary idea that it is dangerous to trust anyone, anywhere. This may reflect the tension between a desire and a fear intrinsic to modern societies. I would suggest that the rarefied experience of free association peculiar to social dreaming—the communal telling of dreams—is the antithesis of this paranoid state of mind, a willingness to reveal apparently psychotic parts of our selves in order to counteract the rational madness of our conscious thinking. This idea of "going native" could mean, in the current conflagration, that an American dreamer might be able to dream about "why we are hated", a question repeatedly asked in the aftermath of the World Trade Center disaster.

MATRIX 5
Reading the runes

Participants continued regularly to dream other more nurturing and inclusive dreams, which helped foster a collective identity of belonging, acceptance, and connection, almost as a counter to the violent images but at the same time enabling the difficult dreams to be dreamed. This reaffirms the point made by Gordon Lawrence that if we are "a dream that dreams", then like the Aboriginals we can dream ourselves into existence (Lawrence, 2000b, pp. 218–219). Opening ourselves to the dreams of others we become part of their dreams and we of theirs. Members were able to trust their dreams, which then in turn produced further dreams in others. This is close to Harold Bloom's point that "The meaning of a poem can only be another poem" (Bloom, 1973, p. 94). The more that people in the matrix valued and talked of their dreams, the more creative, amusing, portentous, and profound their dreams became. The aesthetic of the matrix was such that dream moved seamlessly to dream. As one member put it: "This is about pleasure, like the joy of seeing a shoal of fish turn over and catch the light. It leaves a trace, it's an aesthetic."

Each dream, whether sinister or benign, made further dreams possible. This enabled the outpouring of disturbing images, which could then be explored in the thinking part of the matrix. As one participant put it: "We are involved in a narrative of symbols." This session in particular threw up ominous signs with myriad connections. It seemed that we were reading the runes, picking up signifiers and symbols, and passing them around in a fast-moving hermeneutic search. Perhaps a selection of the dreams will give a picture of this process of uncovering.

DREAM 1.   *I was in the U.K. on a bus. I got off and waited for another near a block of flats. Now I was in Israel. Then I went to a doctor's house and my brother was there. He was confused and talking about the future. I returned to England. Now I feel very uncomfortable.* (A bus in Israel had recently exploded in an attack by suicide bombers.)

DREAM 2.   *I was at home in bed asleep. Part of the floor had come away and was tilted, and I could see the floor below. The basic structure looked solid; it just needed shoring up.* It was during an earthquake in India.

DREAM 3.   *I'm searching for a woman, and I fear I won't have the gravity she has. I come into a temple and there are many symbols on the floor. She runs from symbol to symbol, and I'm running after her to get her to notice me. She stops, and through the roof we can see great black, bruised clouds, like cauliflowers. It opens into a vision—the head of a sperm in the sky, with a wriggling tale. President Clinton is playing the sax, and I get a great feeling of support when the woman puts her arms around me.*

DREAM 4.   *It was like that Ken Russell film,* The Devils. *There'd been a disaster, and I was in a makeshift mortuary surrounded by young couples. We had to tidy and arrange a corpse, a nasty one. It was Pompeii-like with twisted hands, yellow and shrivelled. I had to lift up an arm onto the slab, and I had to wash my hands. It was nauseating.*

DREAM 5.   *I was at my shop, trying to get into the inner sanctum, but had lost my key. Then I found the key and it was purple.*

DREAM 6.   *I was in my home, it was dark, and I heard a rattling sound. A duck flew out of a little window and in its bill it had a black bird. There was earth on the floor, and there was a black cat. Also I was attacked by a Jay and thought my neck had been criss-crossed in the attack.*

DREAM 7.   *There was a baby with a deformed spine. It had come out of the womb damaged. I ran with him and saw a black dog coming towards us in a tunnel.*

DREAM 8.   *I was taking some black cardboard to China to an artist, but it was all going to be stolen.*

DREAM 9.   *The sea had two colours. It was blue on one side, brown on the other. You could float on it and it would support you.*

It is an ominous list. Buses attacked by terrorists (a weekly reality), a tilting structure (the world was becoming increasingly unstable), a disaster creating a corpse (earthquakes, train crashes, hospital failures were increasingly commonplace), a deformed baby (the fear of what might emerge from this mayhem), a divided sea (the great divide between the First and the Third World). All of this accompanied by the traditional motifs of dread and doom that we expect to find beside the witch's cauldron—black cats, black dogs, black birds, black clouds, black cardboard, this last perhaps the fear of our very own fragile defences. At the same time, in the midst of this mayhem, is a benign object, a purple key. Purple, it was noted, is a sacred colour, the colour of high rank as worn by a cardinal. This key was to be used to enter the inner sanctum. This struck the matrix as an item of much wonder and hope. Perhaps it represented the search for words of wisdom to provide authority in the face of danger, a way out of the psychotic tilting house. Perhaps it is the dream that serves as a key of enlightenment, a tool with which to think. This could happen only if the unthinkable psychotic thoughts could be dreamed about, the trauma that consciousness avoids at all costs. Hence in this session it was noted that the thought of death, and the possibility of talking about it, was emerging. In a post-religious environment, where death has become taboo, this is no small achievement.

Despite their sinister nature, these dreams were welcomed and greeted with interest and curiosity. Thus the transference was to the dream and not the dreamer. The dream became an object that could be used creatively. In a very real sense these were not destructive dreams. They were, to use Winnicott's term, transitional objects; tools in the negotiation of reality, which the dreaming matrix unwittingly takes on (Winnicott, 1971). As one participant said: "We are a nomadic community where dreams are the only solid things." I took this to mean that in a group of relative anonymity, where most members inhabited separate lives outside the matrix, the dreams gave a sense of shared meaning and sanity in a society of rapid social change and instability.

MATRIX 6
The democracy of the dream

The theme of creativity carried through to the next matrix. Members focused on the actual process of social dreaming as an alive and spontaneous exchange, often surprising themselves. They celebrated the intellectual and aesthetic pleasure of the discourse, connecting thoughts and ideas through literature, art, religion, humour, television, sport, and so on. Everything is grist to the mill of the matrix. Some notes taken from the thinking section will hopefully give the flavour of this dialogue in the work group:

> "This is like a *meze* meal. We get the pleasure of the click when one dream produces another. It's not the dreamer but the dream."

> "Yes, it's the democracy of the matrix. We are interpreting one another on an equal basis. There is no hierarchy, no dream is better than another. Social dreaming is a great leveller, and it negates the dangers of difference."

> "Yes, the intimacy created is so interesting. We share something primary, which I suppose is the dream. It's more than good manners and conviviality—it's the irrelevance of difference, and the matrix is the breeding ground of dreams, the mingling: it makes us stronger."

> "Thinking is as intimate as the dreaming part. This is about communication. It doesn't matter how much intellect or life experience you have, because a dream is a dream. I thought when my partner had a dream, is this bed part of the matrix? That's what makes us the same, the dream."

> "We merge. There's a lack of individual specificity. This is a medium for meeting. We are equal and it's a tool for thinking. My subject as a teacher keeps coming through. For example, when ideas from the Bible come up as dream material, people use it. They atomize, split it up, and deconstruct it and therefore come up with new ideas. This is why this intimacy is so interesting and so indefinable."

> "There's a tribe in Thailand who believed that the people they dreamed were chosen to carry a message from the whole of the community."

Participants were interested in what made the experience pleasant, uncompetitive, and different to normal group interaction (e.g. work, the family or the therapy group can each be inhibiting milieus). The telling of the dream creates relatedness. The dream is inviolable, an object to be used, and in this way the process is therapeutic. The matrix is thus a container and promotes a method by which to practice what one dreamer called "radical ambiguity". In the words of Marshall McLuhan (1967), the medium is the message. The key to the experience *is* the experience itself. That is, if "we are a dream which dreams", then it is the *activity* of sharing the dreams that produces more dreams, and this in itself means we find out more of who we are and what we can be. As one member put it: "The dream is special statement, a sacred document. It can seem like a message, it's a text, the dream points the way."

Society torn apart

MARRAKESH DREAM.   *I was in Marrakesh. I felt spat out of this dream, it was so horrific. It was like the closing sequence of the* Silence of the Lambs, *with Hannibal Lector wearing a Panama hat. I melted into him and was torn apart from the tips of my toes to the top of my head, by sharks that had suddenly appeared with grappling hooks. This was ministered by a pair of archons ripping my flesh. It happened moment by moment; hooks came through my head, and I was condemned each time to forget this process. But I did repeatedly forget it about every thirty seconds. It felt quite ordinary, as if just part of the natural order of things, as if this is just what happens. The sharks just tore me apart. They were like pure forces. There was no morality attached to it. Fear reaches up from the normal to the metaphysical, resting, remembering, forgetting, repeated on and on until I thought I'd go mad.* When I woke up I felt, "Can I cope with this?" It was not from outside but inside me. I'd been to Morocco alone, and it had triggered off old memories of not knowing the rules as a child.

The telling of this dream was compelling, traumatic, quite unnerving. Associations were to purgatory, Botticelli's drawings of Dante's Inferno, Sisyphus being punished in Hades, an overstated malevolence where the manifest world is evil, the descent into paranoid schizophrenia, the alienation of feeling alone and a stranger in the world, the "unbearable" pain of childbirth, the shark as an ancient "perfect" creature beautiful in its purity but terrible. One dreamer related this to the social order, "all these things like GDP, tobacco in Third World countries, all that hypocrisy. But this may be about to change—you were not eaten but just torn apart." It reminded others of the foot-and-mouth crisis and the hypocrisy of farmers who talked of "poor little sheep". "Yes, it's like the mouse-trap theory of God. He pretends to be caring, and then we die."

Another member suggested that the dream could have been a tool. "Just as Jonah was swallowed by the whale but then thrown up. The experience was a tool for Jonah to find what he was supposed to be doing. He's the victim of a ship in a storm swallowed up by a city on the Mediterranean. Like the dream in Marrakesh." After all, it was suggested, the dreamer had had to go to a Third World country in order to have the dream.

> DREAM OF GROWTH.   I dreamed about social dreaming. *I was in a huge space at the RSC or the National Theatre. I saw many scenes and photos of landscapes with bright lights. A woman appears and says, "I don't like those two photos." A character like James Hillman appears. I show him these scenes and he says, "Oh! No, 'growth', I hate that word, you can't use that."*

The response in the matrix was to relate the word "growth" to cancer. There was great antipathy to the idea of economic growth, which was felt to be out of control in a world of inequality and globalization. Society was seen to be in danger of being torn apart by uncontrollable forces. This sense of disintegration was both inside and outside us, in that the dream, though an illusion, was our imagination enabling us to contact what was real, through the "unreal" and playful aesthetic of the dream discourse. While there was no conscious understanding developing, there was a sense in the dreams of an idea growing in the night, thoughts reminiscent of what Christopher Bollas refers to as psychic genera, which are conceived and gradually take shape in the analytic dyad (Bollas, 1992). However, in this matrix, there was a reference to enlightenment with the following free association to the clarity of the dreaming experience:

> ". . . Hitting the light; like when you enter Marrakesh. It was like hell. Marrakesh by Scorsese. Very live. I thought, 'So this is life.' It

made me appreciate London when I got back. I felt less disgruntled about this social order when I got back. It had seemed like something on the tipping point."

". . . My association to this is balancing, as long as I can use my vision to control balance. I need this link with the outside world. My inner ear. I love the moment when I come back from holiday and see my flat afresh and love it. I also get it before a period, premenstrual awareness, absolute clarity. A shift, a turning around in consciousness. An illumination."

MATRIX 8
A big bang

There now appeared two dreams of catastrophe in a market place, where forces of rebellion were gathering. One of these dreams, which though violent, has a strangely optimistic ending.

The market place was very busy, full, humming. I was in a square, which was full of soft witchetty grubs. Suddenly a steel-headed snake forced itself into the square like a battering ram. It had steel jaws. Its slackness squashed the grubs, which then exploded, killing the snake. This gave a sense of freedom for me.

There were two other dreams, the second about the future:

DREAM 1.   *Animals rush into a valley, this is war. A centaur arrives and tries to talk. Then there's a big bang.*

DREAM 2.   *Entertainment involves live car crashes; a car is run over by a truck. Gene Hackman appears and says menacingly, "You're time is coming. Oh! Shit, I've let that slip." The dream continued with anxiety about the increasing menace of the corporate collective mentality.*

The ensuing associations to these ominous dreams entailed apocalyptic images of nuclear disaster and fear of the corporate mind, which is unable to think, a totalitarian state in which ideas are fenced off, symbols not allowed. There was the idea of a centre (centaur) that will not hold. The message in the third dream had been "Your time will come." How close this dream scenario was to the coming terrorist attack in New York, with a (World Trade) centre that quite literally did not hold, an attack in a "market place" from the gathering forces of rebellion, a big bang, a tragic disaster that undoubtedly gave a "sense of freedom" to some people in the Third World. The unthinking corporate state is a key motif, as is the totalitarian stance of extremist Muslim fundamentalism, enjoined by the thought that "underneath, something was happening". Despite the speed of associations, playfulness, and a mood of conviviality, we seemed to be dreaming the Underworld to find what was to come.

MATRIX 9
The end of the world

DREAM 1.   *I was in a shop in Romania, where I found, behind a glass counter, books on Jewish eschatology, which told of the end of the world.*

DREAM 2.   *I am in hospital about to have my nose cut off in exchange for another, and I wonder whose nose I'll get back.*

DREAM 3.   *I'm in an aeroplane, and a voice says: "Ladies and gentlemen, welcome to your flight, we will be flying at 800,000 feet and at 90,000 miles per hour." Passengers were annoyed at arriving too fast. Something was taken away from them—they were going too fast.*

In the matrix the view was that the nose was about knowledge—that is, what someone knows (nose) and that we need to trust our intuition, our "basic sense of smell", which conveys danger. It was felt that we were ignoring what we were being told, that there were messages that we were not reading. Most of the session concentrated on the creative speed and communality of the matrix, and yet hidden clues were not picked up. Green foliage in one dream lead to the Dylan Thomas poem, "The Force That Through the Green Fuse Drives the Flower", which carried on to a green shrub (President Bush), which in turn went back to the colours black and green, the cobra hidden in the grass—a hooded serpent, magical and dangerous in the dark. Despite these clues, to miss the significance of Rumania (literally to rue mania, to regret madness) and eschatology (concerned with death, judgement, and the final destiny of humankind), suggests that this snake in the grass felt far too dangerous to pick up and examine. Perhaps the matrix was whistling in the dark. Growing tension in the Middle East, combined with a president in the White House with a poor grasp of English and scant knowledge of world geography, was cause for serious concern. At this point in 2001, it did seem that events were moving too fast, and the response of most people, including social dreamers, was to avoid thinking about any coming crisis. We told ourselves we were missing something vital, but we did not manage to think it through. What of course did happen at the end of this dreaming programme was the devastating attack on the World Trade Center on September 11.

Summary: the dream as premonition

Just as a dream may compensate for deficiencies in the individual's personality and warn of the dangers in his or her present course, social dreams have a similar role in the external world. The dream can be a warning. There is no magic in this. Individuals have longings for dangerous adventures, and political and religious groups demonstrate similar traits. Dreams may announce certain situations long before they happen, but this is not necessarily a form of precognition. Many crises have a long unconscious history. Step by step we move towards disaster, but what we fail to see consciously is visible in our dreams. This is as true of nations as of individuals.

In this dense resumé of nearly a year's dreams I hope to have charted the escalating trajectory of violent dream material. This, I would suggest, reached its *dénouement* in the cataclysmic events of 11 September. From the warning notice (bee-ware) in the disaster-movie dream near the start, through the high-rise building that wobbled out of control, through war and division, to the psychotic and violent dreams and then to the explosions in a market place followed by the big bang, it would not seem too far fetched to suggest that members of this matrix had been dreaming for months about the coming disaster. Presumably they were not the only people dreaming this conflagration. Indeed, Hollywood disaster movies had for years projected these images in myriad features from *Godzilla* to *Towering Inferno*; *Silence of the Lambs* appeared in several dreams. One member of the matrix, watching television in an airport on 11 September, believed he was watching a Hollywood film of a twin-towers attack until someone told him it was real and happening live, there and then. The disaster movie had become reality. America had been "dreaming" this for years.

This chapter is not a thesis about magic, or clairvoyancy; nor is it about the chosen few, the new-age beings of a sci-fi world in which people with special powers can foretell the future. The work of Charlotte Beradt in prewar Germany shows that Jewish people were dreaming of their fate a long time before the "final solution" (Beradt, 1966). The suggestion is not that people were dreaming of something they could not possibly know in advance. It is rather that their dreams revealed ideas that were too traumatic to be held for any length of time in consciousness; notions that could not be thought, or spoken, or remembered, or held onto. The specificity of the imagery in the dreams is remarkable but the wider context of a growing crisis was also being dreamed. The escalation of politico-religious and economic difficulties was clear. We dreamed and talked regularly of the Middle East crisis, the dangers of cultural relativism, terrorism, fundamentalism, American foreign policy, the mass murder of both humans and animals. The particularity of objects and place is similarly no mere coincidence. People knew that the World Trade Center had been attacked before. The American embassy in Nigeria had been bombed with heavy casualties. The threat of Muslim suicide bombers was common knowledge. The dreams named things. The detail of thing and place was impressive. It may be surprising that dream imagery included an attack on a market place, a high-rise building threatened from the sky. People dreamt of attackers who had no fear and were impervious to dialogue, a wounded centre, an attack by terrorists from the country on cosmopolitan city-dwellers: the psychosis of being torn apart in a third world country, the phrase "Your time is coming". Of course, this was dreaming about the future, but it was a future that lay dormant in the present.

Dreaming the real

Perhaps, when someone dreamed about the psychosis of being torn apart in a third world country, they were dreaming about reality. When New York sustained that terrible attack, it found out what people in third world countries had been experiencing for years (sometimes as a result of American foreign policy). America now discovered the real, which was hitherto always out there, somewhere else, or as the "problem" to be solved by Star Wars, John Wayne, or Superman. The Twin Towers attack was the future happening in the present, the disaster movie come true in the here-and-now. This is the opposite of Plato's conception of the simulacrum—the identical copy for which no original has ever existed, the memory of a perfect past. Instead, we have a clearly described future that is glimpsed but is deemed unthinkable and therefore quickly banished from consciousness. Perhaps we could call this the "premonacrum".

In *The Interpretation of Dreams* (1900a), Freud stated that "A dream is a (disguised) fulfilment of a (suppressed or repressed) wish". Could it be that after decades of sci-fi fantasies, war films, media bombardment about ruthless, cunning, cruel barbarians who are always outside and threatening, America got what it unconsciously longed for—contact with the real? Slavoi Zizek emphasizes this point when he suggests that the threat of American vulnerability was always libidinally invested. "The unthinkable which happened was thus the object of fantasy, America got what it fantasized about and this was the greatest surprise" (Zizek, 2001, p. 2). He suggests that the World Trade Towers stood for something quite unreal—the centre of virtual capital, of financial speculations disconnected from the sphere of mental production. Thus the impact of the bombings is accounted for by the background of a borderline that separates the digitalized First World from the Third World "desert of the Real". Living in an insulated, artificial universe has created the notion that some ominous agent is threatening destruction from outside. As Lawrence puts it, the more we deny tragedy, the more we bring it into being, because somebody somewhere is having the kind of psychotic thinking that generates tragedy (Lawrence, 2000b, pp. 208–231).

I would suggest that in the dreaming matrix this is precisely what was being dreamed about; in the expressionistic nightworld of the unconscious, people were having the American "Dream" of the unreal and also the psychotic Third World nightmare of the real. This is the essential conflict of the postmodern psyche. The absence of myth in contemporary society means that we have no way of negotiating the tragedy (death, misfortune, illness, loss) that is part of the human condition. Death has become a taboo subject, and, amidst this psychic anomie, "we are left alone with the myth that we can live without myth" (Lawrence, 2000b, p. 215). Increasingly adverts replace the dream, Hollywood simulates myth, soap opera fakes real life, celebrities stand in for the hero. The death of tragedy means we inhabit a Macbethian state of anxiety, faced with the choice between our own avarice and aggression, or the abyss of meaninglessness in a late-capitalist society. It is like Shakespeare's play, in that the dreadful vision we get from identifying with Macbeth mirrors our own fate. It is as if the witches had predicted our own terrible end in a terrorist state, which could have been avoided and which we knew about all along. "Macbeth" reveals a heart of darkness with which we find ourselves identifying, just as in the dream we encounter the worst aspects of the other, which is actually ourselves. These are thoughts that elsewhere are unthinkable. They subvert the normal rules of conscience and replace life with ambition at all costs. If the United States remains in this nihilistic and paranoid position, it may, like Macbeth, be destined to repeat "surgical operations" from which there is no recovery. Perhaps this is the abysmal "tipping point" referred to in the dreams.

Five working hypotheses of the disparate matrix

The first hypothesis of this chapter is: *when something ominous is happening in a society, it may be impossible to think about what it really means.* Instead, individuals will dream the knowledge, the "unthought known" (Bollas, 1987), but since dreams are mostly treated as the junk mail of our psyches, to be put straight into the rubbish bin, the essential key to that knowledge is thrown away without reaching consciousness. This is despite the body of evidence to suggest that dreams are a vital part of our intuition, our creative intellect, our humane caring aesthetic, our bodily thinking, our psychic genera, our self-knowledge.

The second hypothesis is: *encapsulated in our dream is a vision of the future which we already know.* That is, in global terms, we have unconsciously detected from all available information the inevitably tragic consequences of the late-capitalist hegemony—the global economy, pollution, fundamentalist religious groups, totalitarian thinking, absolutist foreign policy, the dehumanization of language in order to conceal cruelty and oppression, international terrorism. We "know" what is wrong and we sense what is going to happen, but this knowledge remains unthinkable, available only in our dreams.

The third hypothesis is: *social dreaming can be a way of delineating the experiences of people at the margins of human existence.* The dream may be a method of "going native", of contacting the further limits of experience in situations where oppressed groups reach extreme levels of despair. The communication of what is real in other cultures may entail traumatic and psychotic ideas, which the matrix helps to process. I would liken it to the profound cultural apperception engendered by contact with the art or music thrown up by any people who write, sing, or paint about loss and rejection, sadness and joy. The gypsy groups of Rumania, the township musicians of South Africa, Aboriginal art, the blues singers of the Deep South are examples that come to mind, and there are surely many others. This looking outwards, this dream of an alternative *Weltanschauung*, is perhaps more typical of the disparate matrix where participants are not connected by occupation or shared interests.

The fourth hypothesis is: *the unrehearsed freedom of the matrix as a process can promote a sense of human solidarity.* Social dreaming is a buffer to anomie, an antidote to the emptiness and isolation inherent in narcissistic, consumerist societies. Lack of hierarchy and competition creates a climate of democracy and the acceptance of difference. Extending and elaborating the self via dreams can create a sense of relatedness. Telling the dream leads to a mosaic of associations that connect us to others. We project ourselves into the future by trusting the dream and discovering how it relates to social the environment.

The fifth hypothesis is: *the freedom of expression in social dreaming is based on contingency, the absence of certainty and finality.* Its modus operandi depends upon flexible forms of exchange, spontaneity, and playfulness, even when the material being conceived is dark and horrendous. Members give themselves up to the unknown vicissitudes of the dream telling, blindly and with no purpose. This can lead to the discovery of new metaphors. The contingency of the matrix, exposing ourselves to chance, means that one dream may lead to another, recreating the way we talk, what we want, who we are. Adam Phillips refers to the "acknowledgement of contingency" as one aim of the creative life (Phillips, 1994, p. 20). Here we open ourselves up to unknown possibility; we wait to see what happens. In this way social dreaming is about relinquishing control and realising that our emotional life is new at every moment. The process is as crucial as the material. It cannot be completed because there is nothing to complete.

Conclusion: the dream as prescription

An essential part of living is the reclamation of tragedy in order to face the reality that we will all die. Only if we can acknowledge death can we rebel against it in order to live a creative life. If we can also see that the dreaded monster out there, glimpsed through a glass darkly, is actually the mirror image of ourselves, then perhaps there is a glimmer of hope.

In his paper on language and social dreaming, Francis Oeser (1998) suggests that we carry within us knowledge and skills that uniquely the matrix encourages us to utilize: "Dreams can illuminate what we feel, can often inspire what we ought to feel" (p. 76). He ends by quoting Edgar, in King Lear: "The weight of this sad time we must obey, / Speak what we feel, not what we ought to say."

The life and work of Samuel Beckett could be seen as an exemplar of the "tragic position." He described his work as "the attempt to fail better", not as a quest for happiness necessarily but as a search for what is real. It was the darkness of an inner world, which Beckett referred to as "my most precious ally" (Knowlson, 1996). In a very real sense, Beckett realized that there was no cure for life, and his project became to express and articulate the suffering and bleakness of twentieth-century existence.

If dreams can be potentially transformational, or prescriptive, what might we do with this idea? As Zizek observes, in the days following the Twin Towers attack, people dwelt in the unique time between trauma and its symbolic impact. How will Americans now respond? Will they decide to fortify their "sphere" of unreality, or to risk stepping out of it? If they stick to the "evil axis"—the idea of an external threat—then they risk further paranoid acting out. Alternatively, if they step through the fantasmic screen into the real world, then they could move from, "A thing like this should not happen here" to "A thing like this should not happen" (Zizek, 2001, p. 2). September 11th produced a crucial question for the American conscience. Some people began to ask, "Why do they hate us?" thus opening a possible dialogue of self-reflection, a possible dream, a potential conversation about ourselves in relation to the other. Thus could be developed a different vocabulary and the creation of metaphors in which we are seen to share the same kinds of experiences as others. In his passage on Orwell, Richard Rorty (1989, pp. 71ff.) notes that in *Animal Farm* and *1984* the novelist sensitized us to a view that the rhetoric of "human equality" has been used by intellectuals of different persuasions to defend the commonplace cruelties of communism and capitalism alike. Orwell gave us an alternative perspective. Instead of answering the question "What is to be done?" he suggested how not to try to answer it, because our previous political vocabulary was no longer relevant. What we need now, as then, are new scenarios, different metaphors, new dreams—not to stand for an existing idea but as new creations in their own right. In social dreaming it does not matter whether the truth is subjective or whether it relates to external reality. All that matters is that you can say it without getting hurt. This is the essence of free association.

> What matters is your ability to talk to others about what seems to you to be true, not what is in fact true. If we take care of freedom, truth can take care of itself. If we are ironic enough about our own final vocabularies, and curious enough about everyone else's, we do not have to worry about whether we are in direct contact with moral reality, or whether we are blinded by ideology, or whether we are being weakly relativistic. [Rorty, 1989, pp. 176–177]

There are some societies in which the sharing of dreams is illegal and risks imprisonment. The freedom to dream and think together creates the circumstance where "me" merges with "we", and then "we" extends to "them". It is the freedom and contingency of the matrix which can generate a sense of solidarity. This idea is not inevitable, but perhaps it is worth pursuing. It is not about some basic inner or external truth but about the irrelevance of religious or racial differences in the face of pain and humiliation. It is the ability to think of people different to us as being just like us.

CHAPTER FOUR

Not two and not one

Alastair Bain

The first social dreaming conference in Australia was held in September 1989 at Janet Clarke Hall, University of Melbourne. Gordon Lawrence was the director of the conference. Suzanne Leigh Ross (the author of chapter five) and I were on the consultant staff, together with Susan Long and Ann Morgan.

In 1991, Suzanne Ross and I decided to offer a social dreaming programme for the public. In fact, the matrix turned out to be a network of people connected in some way with myself, with Suzanne Ross, or with the Australian Institute of Socio-Analysis. The matrix met for twenty-three 90-minute sessions, with reflection sessions every three or four weeks, and there was a one-day event during the year. Eighteen members participated in the programme for all or part of the year. When we began, we were thinking that it would be similar to a group experience, with a time limit that would mark its ending. However, it did not develop that way. The matrix seemed to have a life of its own, and it continued in 1992 with four of the same members plus two new members who joined during the year. We found that the matrix was viable with as few as five members. In 1993 two participants who had been in the matrix since it began continued, two participants who were in the 1991 matrix re-joined, one participant from the 1992 matrix re-joined for part of the year, and there were two new members. The primary task of the matrix was: "To associate to one's own and other members' dreams, and to make connections."

While this chapter concentrates on some of the experiences of the Australian Social Dreaming Matrix during 1993, it should be emphasized that what is reported has grown out of an evolving experience of social dreaming in a matrix that continued in the same format for three years. Other experiences that have been formative in our approach to social dreaming include: the Spa conference in Belgium in 1991; for me, working as a consultant to a matrix that formed part of AISA's Advanced Consultancy Programme in 1990 and, in 1993, working on an experimental social dreaming/action research project, directed by Gordon Lawrence, for the William Alanson White Institute; and, for Suzanne Ross, co-directing the social dreaming matrix with Gordon Lawrence at the International Group Relations and Scientific Conference held in Australia at Lorne in August 1993. Our two chapters in this volume on our experiences in the Australian Social Dreaming Matrix are complementary and represent different facets of the matrix. This would seem to be appropriate. Growing a crystal is the closest picture I can get to the "making" of the matrix. A crystal in its growth is subjected in its interaction with the environment to pressures and to chemical processes that give it colour, and so forth. A crystal is multifaceted with a core, and, like the matrix, one can look at it or look through it. (See the social dreaming poem below, "Back to the Present".)

Social dreaming as a threat to ordinary awareness

I have found it a struggle to write about social dreaming. One of the difficulties is that social dreaming is about exploration and "making"—making "what" is not clear, but making all the same. It is not an analytic approach to the meaning of dreams, and there is a danger, which we have deliberately avoided in Australia, of premature conceptualization. During the Lorne International Group Relations and Scientific Conference, a member of a matrix (fresh to social dreaming) asked on several occasions: "But what is the conceptual framework within which we make sense of social dreaming?" It is a seemingly reasonable question, but it is one that precludes experience without preconception.

Dreams in psychoanalysis are regarded as the dreams of a patient, and "meaning" is usually sought in the dynamics of transference within a two-person relationship. The nature of the interpretation will depend on many things—among them, an interpretative framework that includes the assumption that the dream is a dream of a patient. This approach has its own rationale and value. While psychoanalysis provides a valuable container for exploration, it is limited to a two-person field and it has a specific vertex for exploration. The vertex and the held draw boundaries as to the observable. Similarly, in analytic psychology Jung developed theories about the collective unconscious and how dreams can be interpreted according to a theory of archetypes. As with psychoanalysis, the interpretative framework provides a background that is "known" through which what is "unknown" (i.e. the dream) is understood. In psychoanalysis and analytic psychology the focus has tended to be on the individual rather than on the illumination and generation of what, for want of a better word, I will call "us".

Currently social dreaming does not have an interpretative framework. The meaning that arises comes not as the result of analysis but through what is "made" by dreams, associations, and connections within the matrix. The focus of social dreaming is not the "I" of the dreamer. Frequently this shift in focus is difficult to make for therapists and analysts during their early experience of social dreaming and for people who are strongly attached to the notion of "It's my dream". The shift in social dreaming is away from ownership or possession of a dream and one's ego connection with it, though indubitably a dream is dreamed by a dreamer and dreams have individual significance. The shift is analogous to Bion's "thoughts in search of a thinker": dreams in search of a dreamer.

Joshua Bain, my son aged thirteen at the time, after hearing some of the experiences of the 1989 social dreaming conference, remarked:

"I dream therefore I am."

To build on this:

"We dream therefore I am.
I dream therefore we are.
We dream therefore we are."

I have found it difficult to hold on to detailed memories of social dreaming. I found that when I read the dreams and associations of the matrix that was part of AISA's Advanced Consultancy Programme I *recognized* the dreams and associations as having taken place during the programme, but when I thought about what dreams were dreamed and what was said about them *before* reading them I was blank. It was as though nothing occurred, there were no dreams and no associations, and it was as though nothing that had taken place was remarkable. On reading the dreams and associations, I noted that there were a number of remarkable events.

This experience led me to ponder the question: if dreams and associations are so quickly forgotten, why? Are we dreaming and making connections in a way that is "not allowed"? And if "not allowed", what is the agency preventing this? Or, to put it another way, if we were "allowed" to dream and remember, what would that "threaten"? And what is it that is threatened?

If this is approached from the standpoint of social defences, one knows that groups and organizations are defended in various ways from the experience of anxiety (cf. Menzies, 1970; Bain, Long, & Ross, 1992). Thus, what can be heard, taken in, and acted on is partly a function of the systemic defences of that system.

In everyday life we live by generally unquestioned notions of time and space. Time goes forward from the past to the present to the future, and space has three dimensions. Relativity theory, quantum mechanics, and experiences through meditation, prayer, and so forth notwithstanding, this is the "common-sense" way individuals perceive and act in space and through time. As an individual, "I" perceive that "I" experience or act in a space, and that time elapses as this takes place, or "I observe" that events that seem to have nothing to do with "me" (i.e. occur outside "my" space) affect spaces and take place over time. My identity "I" is based on this premise that time is linear with an arrow to the future, and that transformations in space may occur during this linearity.

My hypothesis is that social dreaming threatens the fabric of this "common-sense" awareness of space and time. It is actually difficult to remember the events that occur during the social dreaming matrix, as they seem to reflect space–time realities that are different from one's life outside the matrix which is patterned on "common-sense" assumptions about space and time. The "struggle" to write about social dreaming is, in the main, the "struggle" to write about these realities. For me, social dreaming is about discovering a new identity as human beings, which is not based in "I". "I" is there, and "us". Not two, and not one.

Social dreaming poems

I have taken the approach that one way of communicating what goes on in social dreaming is to present some of the dreams and associations from the 1993 Australian matrix in the form of poetry. Thus the notes of dreams and associations taken down by Suzanne Ross and myself during sessions have been distilled into social dreaming poems. The distillation is of two kinds. First, not all the dreams and associations in a particular session have been used; second, the dreams and associations that are used have themselves been distilled. The social dreaming poems are based on four sessions: 5 May, 12 May, 8 September, 10 November.

The two May sessions were held in a large room above a bookshop on Rathdowne Street in Melbourne. This had been the setting of the matrix 1991 and 1992. The matrix moved to a room in the Astronomer's Residence, Royal Botanic Gardens, for the second half of 1993. The sessions in September and November took place there. All sessions took place early on Wednesday mornings. The dreams that form the social dreaming poems were dreamt by six members of the matrix, three men and three women. The associations in the social dreaming poems are made by the members of the matrix and the two consultants.

The Second Coming (Session 5 May)

DREAM 1

> Carnations.
> A cracked angel offered me a
> mirror. To show me the world.
> I looked.
> It cracked into shards.

Association: "The beast slouches towards
Bethlehem
To be born."

DREAM 2

Hospital. A blackboard.
Scrapped. Broke a bit off,
A bit more,
And more,
until none left.

DREAM 3

Frank Lloyd Wright house.
North by North West.
Conference,
Higgledy, Piggledy.
Staff? Members?

Association: Tears. "Falling Water."
Frank Lloyd Wright House.

DREAM 4

Water falling
From
A Conifer.
Splashing
Clear blue sky.
Dew
at top.
Rivulets.
Torrents.
Soil is not washed away.

DREAM 5

Christenson is coming.
Signs?
Helen.
A Christmas tree on Helen's
palm.

Association. A little conifer.

Cat: presence (Session 12 May)

DREAM 1

> Heart transplants
> for cats.
> Criteria?
> Cat I have
> Does not fulfil
> criteria.

DREAM 2

> Dreamed I woke up.
> A presence.
> It's the cat.
> I don't have a cat.
> A black cat.
> A beautiful animal.

Association: A black cat
on my doorstep
For a week.
Thinks I'm a witch.
Association: An unwanted black cat
Inhabits our backyard.

DREAM 3

> My tongue had been taken.
> Lots of blood.
> Father (who's dead) there.
> He felt it's okay.
> Tongue frozen.
> "Has the cat got your
> tongue?"

DREAM 4

> White T-shirt
> Imprinted
> From lying on a wall.
> Address and message.
> Next morning couldn't get it.

DREAM 5

> *Letter fluttering.*
> *For ages*
> *From sky.*
> *Message: "Shut up!"*

Association: Presence.
  Presence—Cat dream.
  Presence—An absent member
  (of Matrix).
  Presence—writer of letter.
Association: Egypt. Cat. Deity.
  Domestic-cat-ed.
Association: I feel the presence of a cat.
  Creepy.
Association: I put my cat down recently.
  Every time I go to speak,
  It feels as though
  It's got my tongue.
Association: Vagina dentata.

Back to the present (Session 8 September)

DREAM 1

> *A genius.*
> *Encyclopaedia Britannica*
> *He knows where.*
> *Right page every time.*
> *No index.*

Association: Genii–us.
Association: Index.
  Forbidden books.
  Catholic Church.
Association: Chattopadhyay story.
  A computer factor analysis
  of all opinions about God:
  "God is
  An echo
  of a rumour"

DREAM 2

> *Sea.*
> *Tunnel*
> *In*
> *Ocean*
> *Drive or walk.*
> *Going somewhere.*
> *There—not there.*

Association: Time tunnel.
Dr Who.

DREAM 3

> *Tunnel*
> *to*
> *Centre*
> *of Earth.*
> *Young Man and Old Man*
> *Dead.*
> *Up*
> *From*
> *Centre:*
> *To see what lovers are doing.*
> *Old Man's wife with another.*
> *Accepts*
> *Back to*
> *Centre.*
> *Young man's wife*
> *with another.*
> *Not accept,*
> *Stays.*
> *Time Passed.*

Association: Orpheus.

DREAM 4

> *A village*
> *on way*
> *To somewhere.*
> *A to B.*
> *House in village*

on hill.
Car backing
back
    to house.
    Someone
    Threw bomb in.
    Exploded.
    Ill. Cold.

Association: Back backing.
Reversing.
Wrong way around.

DREAM 5 (*TELLS DREAM BACKWARDS*)

In bathroom.
Back of house,
with two men.
Bathers on.
Beautiful house.
All glass.

Association: Look at glass.
See reflection
or see through.
Association: Matrix.
Look at
or look through.
Association: Paradox.
Association: "Paradox for Windows" (computer program).
Association: Philip Dick.
S.F.
Counter clock world.
Time running back.
Corpse
Coming alive.
Time tunnel.

DREAM 6

Postmortem room.
Body sits up.
Moral dilemma!

Association (from 1992 Social Dreaming Matrix dreams)
Dream: *"Roll call of dead"*.
Dream: *"Helping*
corpses
walk
Into Chapel."
Association: Time is
an echo
of a rumour.

Space and time (Session 10 November)

DREAM *1*

Spaceship
Revolving
Around
a round shape.
Gap.
Door numbers.
Door.
Ribbons.
No. 33.

DREAM *2*

I am
In a building.
Outside
A Space Capsule.
Port Hole in it.
Suspended.

Association: Outside and
Inside.
Association: Dreamed
My reality.
In
Car Park.
Parked
No. 33

Dream 3

> *Time is known*
> *when*
> *Two elements*
> *Are*
> *Connected:*
> *Beta and Greta.*

Association: Jigsaw
At end
of
Matrix.
Association: Egypt. Pyramids.
Boomerang,
Spin.
Association: 33. Flip a 3.
8
Flip 8
∞

CHAPTER FIVE

The science, spirit, chaos, and order of social dreaming

Suzanne Leigh Ross

In 1989, I was invited to be a staff member on the first Australian Social Dreaming Conference directed by Gordon Lawrence. Since then I have been involved in social dreaming in a variety of ways: a matrix member at the Spa conference in Belgium in 1991; as a co-consultant to a long-term matrix with Alastair Bain, from 1991 onwards, and as co-director of the social dreaming matrix with Lawrence at the International Group Relations and Scientific Conference in Lorne, Australia, in 1993.

Through these varied experiences across task, role, duration, membership, and focus of the matrices, I have become increasingly convinced that social dreaming is not new; it has a very ancient base in many cultures. For the Australian Aborigine, "In the beginning was the dreaming" (Lawlor, 1991, p. 13). This ancient connection has been suggested by many, including Lawrence himself. Our experiences from a long-term matrix parallel the archetypal aspects found in many writings of past cultures alongside the theoretical parallel, which I feel confirms this position.

Unfortunately, our "sophisticated" Western society has lost touch with not only the intrinsic importance of social dreaming to a harmonic evolution, but also the ability to engage wholly and creatively with our collective dreaming.

It is through Lawrence that social dreaming has been rediscovered, so that we may, as T. S. Eliot wrote, arrive where we started and know the place for the first time. Or similarly, as one of our matrix members dreamt, "*I arrived on the same platform after a journey but in a different space.*"

Although social dreaming has a long past, its modern tradition and form as envisaged, practised, and shared by Lawrence is quite young. This is similar to psychology in that: "it has a long past but only a short history" (Sharpe & Ross, 1990, p. 5).

The attitude one brings to social dreaming would seem as important as the rediscovery, the structures, and the "work of it". Lawrence's "way of being" is congruent with social dreaming itself, a way that is spiritual in nature and transcends the individual. Like the Australian Aborigines who have no word or concept for accumulation of possessions, he has willingly shared his idea, invited union in its development, and encouraged independence in its growth, innovation, and modification. He has modelled reverence for creating a sacred and playful space that fosters delight in discovery.

In Lindsay Clarke's novel, *The Chymical Wedding*, Edward says: "However varied our dreams, they all have the same punchline. It is: WAKE UP!" Lawrence has challenged us to wake up and has provided us with a matrix in which we may relearn our lost dream abilities.

In a moment of stuckness

Alastair Bain and I took a weekly matrix for three years involving around seventy sessions plus five single days of associated activities, such as dialogues, drawings, and experiential exercises.

This chapter has proved quite difficult to write as, although social dreaming is in one way "sweet nectar", there is rather a lot to digest, a situation familiar to A. A. Milne enthusiasts. I am referring, of course, to the time when the Bear, or the pair in this case, goes "visiting and gets into a tight place".

Pooh Bear, having gone down into Rabbit's hole (the unconscious), eats large amounts of honey (three years of matrix dreams), and finds himself unable to get out. He is stuck, with half of him outside the "whole" (waking time) and half of him inside the "whole" (dreamtime).

Christopher Robin informs Pooh Bear that he will be his old self again, in order to negotiate the space, once some time has passed—that is, he has a space–time problem. In the meantime, "Pooh" asks to be read a "Sustaining Book such as would help and comfort a Wedged Bear in Great Tightness".

The following pages involve a small selection of the unusual, exciting, and sometimes frightening experiences in our three years of the Australian matrix. Stories are woven around these examples with an invitation to dialogue regarding these or any other "plausible enough" stories.

Shifts that pass in the night

There were a number of shifts over the three years, two major ones being:

• Dream ownership
• Dream cast and role

Dream ownership has moved from the individual through a number of expansions towards a more global experience. Originally, members were cautious about sharing what they saw as their personal property. Concerns ranged from the fear that one's dream was not "socially important enough" to "Be careful, that's my unconscious you are talking about." As the first year progressed, the anxiety reduced and members loosened the restrictions regarding their own sharing of dreams and how they would allow themselves and others to associate to dreams. The next expansion involved two members bringing the same dream to a session. In this dream, each one was trying to find their way across Indonesia's countryside using an old map. They were trying to cover the types of terrain found away from the main roads and cities. The sharing of similar dreams and associations, as in this case, also occurs within family groups. The matrix seemed to be developing into a "dreaming family" who were still, perhaps, using old maps in unchartered areas.

Around the same time, a phenomena we named "double-dose or no-dose" appeared. This is probably the matrix equivalent of valency; the matrix needed a "nightmare", and one member was having the nightmares on behalf of all. At one session, she exclaimed: "I'm sick of having nightmares for everyone; someone else can have them for a while and I'll have some other type of dream". This aspect continued quite strongly until the middle part of the second year, and there was then only the rare appearance.

A mid-year expansion of membership occurred in the second year, and with it we saw our first evidence of what I would call "dreaming across the boundary". The consultants agreed that there would be a couple of sessions between deciding someone could join and their first session. The rationale was that the matrix members and the new person needed time for "dreaming in". One member imagined the new member would be a "well-rounded, grey-haired woman", in contrast to her dream where "*she had dark, wavy, shoulder-length hair; was young and attractive, wearing modern black clothing*". She later exclaimed: "*She was exactly as I had dreamt her to be, even wearing the same clothes.*" This resembles Ullman, Krippner, and Vaughan's "dream telepathy" (1973). They state that perhaps their most basic finding at the Maimonides Medical Centre was the scientific demonstration of Freud's statement: "Sleep creates favourable conditions for telepathy."

The members, aware of these unusual occurrences, were increasing in their acceptance of new ways of dreaming, sharing dreams, and associating to dreams. The dreams and associations led to questioning: "Does membership of a particular religion or cosmology limit one's view?" The following dream was offered:

I dreamt the whole matrix was out in the ocean diving from an old wreck—an old galleon. Alastair found a treasure, a metal rectangular object with a tiny hole. When he looked through this, he saw something special. He saw more looking through the tiny hole than the larger one—it seemed to work the wrong way around. I don't know what he was seeing but it was something different.

The immediate association from one member was: "The Kingdom of Heaven is through a narrow door." Jung wrote about our dreams being "the small hidden door in the deepest and most intimate sanctum of the soul, which goes into primeval cosmic night." The final destination, he continued, was one of wholeness—that is, freedom "from the shackles of the ego".

This marked an end of the dream-possession struggle that occurred at times in the first year, the debate being: "Does the dream belong here or in the therapy room?" Members said that they selected which dreams would go to which venue, or even which portion of the dream. Although to some degree, this continued to occur, the "story" I have for this new way of seeing is called "quantum dreaming". There was a new freedom to allow oneself to share, associate, and connect as the "spirit" moves one, in either venue and often with the same dream. From quantum theory, we know that an electron may be in this orbit (venue) or that orbit, depending on the "energy". For some reason, it is never in between—a quantum leap. Members of the matrix were now "quantum dreaming", without being too fussed about orbits or the dream/venue problem.

This shift reminds me of my first year at school. I walked there each morning with my brother, who is five years my senior. The fifteen-minute walk, along sandy tracks, was a major treat, for he would answer the never-ending "number" questions that fascinated me. I remember asking him the answer to wonderful questions like "What is 86 plus 42?" He would reply with magical-sounding three-digit numbers I had never heard of. Finally, I asked the macro question involving the two biggest numbers I could name—I excitedly waited for the answer. "What is 100 plus 100?" His quick reply was 200!!!—surely not, how boring, how simple, how disappointing!

Quantum dreaming has redressed this disappointment. I recently read *Quantum Healing* (Chopra, 1989) in which Chopra discusses duality with Maharishi. He speaks of the need for duality and unity—the need for contradictions and the fusion of polar opposites into one whole. He suggests that "without duality, unity has no substance", demonstrating this with an ancient text meaning that "This is full, that is full" and that two fullnesses complement each other.

> There is one hundred percent diversity and one hundred percent unity, both performing their work at the same time. That is the nature of the work of creation—this is true reality. To us, one seems real and the other unreal. The reality is that both are real at the same time. [Maharishi in Chopra, 1989, p. 228]

So I suggest that the same dream can be fully and creatively used in the therapy or analytic context as well as the social dreaming context.

A 100 plus a 100 does make 200—it's so simple, so exciting. Yet for a year or two the matrix made it so complicated.

By the third year, the "dream ownership" had shifted again to "themes in pieces". The dreams and associations were more like jig-saw puzzles, with each member having a piece—collectively they made a whole picture. One such session could well be a story of a "cat attack". There were six members present, and three had powerful cat dreams:

> — A dream involving vague criteria for which cats would be allowed to have heart transplants. The dreamer's cat, with whom he had a difficult relationship, did not qualify even though it was a beautiful domestic cat—one of the stated criterion.

> —A dream about a beautiful black cat, after which the dreamer awoke with a strong sense of the cat's presence at her back—so present that she had to remind herself that she didn't have a cat.

> — A dream in which the dreamer's tongue was removed, there was a lot of blood, both fear and comforting about communication loss and a strong association on waking: "Has the cat got your tongue?"

Associations were generally of a negative nature—for example, pending disaster (cat scans, catastrophe, offel/awful), psychosis (cata-tonic), and the occult (witches, cat worship). There had been three associations regarding real-life experiences with cats the previous week; none of these people had been cat dreaming:

- an unwanted black cat inhabiting a backyard;
- a member grieving as the family cat had been "put down" that week;
- a black cat sitting on a consultant's doormat all week.

The presence of cats at this time seemed to enter the space of the matrix. The only member who had not been involved with cats in either dreams or reality that week said "Me-ow!", to indicate he was hurting. He said he was uncomfortable, and it felt creepy as he felt the cats' presence in the room, right then. At this stage, I felt I could see a black cat in the room—moving around the spaces between the chairs.

So, of course, one is left with many questions: Are we going mad? Is this coincidence? Who let the cat out of the bag? Was a consultant,

Suzanne, "cat-napped" by the matrix process? Did it actually happen, and, if so, what does it all mean? Themes after this, in general, ran over a series of sessions, the major ones all relating to "doubles", mirrors, twins, and making the already pregnant pregnant.

The anxiety in the matrix stayed heightened for a number of weeks until the session when the dream below was offered. It is interesting to ponder what it means for a consultant to enter the matrix illusion so deeply as to "see the cat". Did this dream prove "she had lost it", or was it necessary for the "seeing" to precede resolution?

As soon as I woke up I had a sense of resolve. It was a dream about the matrix—Suzanne had gone deep into the jungle to map out the coastlines of South America. She was wearing magnificent midnight blue with suns, moons and stars over it. She came back and said she had found what she was looking for—The Poetry. She turned to me and said: "I know you like poetry and _____ likes it also." She presented it to the matrix. The poetry was the missing bit, and it felt resolved between male and female.

This dream seemed to hold a resolution of opposites including male/ female (yin/yang), in/out (coastlines in the centres of jungles), and sun/moon (light/dark). Another matrix member commented on feeling quite fragmented and on the edge and yet part of the whole. So we also had the opposites of whole and fragment.

The resolution in the "jigsaw dream" where fragmented or missing pieces made up a whole was followed by mild anxiety. This seemed to relate to this "whole" creation and involved a definite shift from the individual to the collective. The dreams and associations centred around a fear of being hung for drug trafficking. Social dreaming was being equated with drugs—both producing altered states of consciousness.

Terrence McKenna suggests: "To my mind, the Divine Imagination is the source of all creativity in our dreams, in our psychedelic experiences, in the jungles, in the currents of the ocean. . . . Psychedelic experiences and dreams are chemical cousins" (Abraham, McKenna, & Sheldrake, 1992, p. 16).

Another example was the desire to venture no further—"the bear won't eat us if we lie down and stay still".

However, in the final session for 1993, we seemed to make one last shift—from a whole jigsaw to something resembling Benoit Mandelbrot's fractals or David Bohm's holograms. I have a slight tendency to use fractals, as the previous dream involved coastlines and these are often used to exemplify the concept of fractals—fractional dimensions. It is also interesting to note that "fractal" comes from the latin *fratua*, meaning irregular, "but Mandelbrot also liked the word's connotations of fractional and fragmented" (Briggs & Peat, 1989, p. 90). Both fractals and holograms suggest that a part of a phenomenon represents a microcosm of the whole.

The final session showed some indication of this possibility, as all the dreams presented had a similarity in structure. The dreams were all stories of separations and of successful or "transitional" connections with the consultants or members of the matrix.

—Attempted meeting with Suzanne unsuccessful, so a package was left to be handed on to her.

—Two female matrix members in a spaceship had to connect with a wall via ribbons with the assistance of a third (male) matrix member.

—Church—people walking past the door—Alastair is gruff, however, some children with altar gifts of bread and wine were encouraged by him to enter.

—Suzanne left a pram so people would know of our presence (in a psychiatric hospital).

—Time is when two elements come together Beta and Greta (pronounced Greater).

—Docking of spies; passing of information by coming together and apart quickly.

Perhaps this is not a fractal matrix—it may simply be that the matrix had a two-month break. However, it is a possibility. The psychiatrist Montague Ullman's research indicates "that even the structure of our dreams may be fractal . . . the dream 'story' contains repetitions of the dreamer's central concerns. Reflections of these concerns can be found in both the overall 'story' and in its finer and finer details" (Briggs & Peat, 1989, p. 110). If this is true individually then it may also be true in the matrix orbit.

Another possibility in the final session is an attempted link with Bion. It is interesting to think of the associations to the Beta/Greta dream—no one associated to Bion's beta-elements. Is it possible that following the catatonic/occult/catastrophic "cat session", a Greta (pronounced Greater) container was needed. At matrix level, the beta-elements of dreams, dream thoughts, and myths, aspects of personality by a sense of catastrophe, needed to "dock" with a Greater container than we would usually conceive. Perhaps the "G" stands for Gaia—Mother Earth—where "mother" is usually enough, at the matrix level. This working story will sustain the stuck bear for the moment at least, until a better story comes along.

So, in summary, the move progressed from personal imprisonment of dreams to a global or Gaia dream matrix (see Fig. 5. 1).

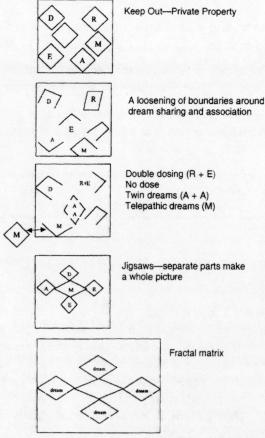

Keep Out—Private Property

A loosening of boundaries around dream sharing and association

Double dosing (R + E)
No dose
Twin dreams (A + A)
Telepathic dreams (M)

Jigsaws—separate parts make a whole picture

Fractal matrix

Figure 5.1.   The shift in dream ownership

Another type of shift was in the dream cast—that is, who was allowed in the dreams and what roles were allowed. In the first sessions, no member dreamt of any other member; in fact, in an early session, it was said that "if anyone dreams about me, I'll leave the matrix." Men at this stage were rarely allowed in dreams; in fact, they often had to cover their faces with beards or face flannels. By the middle of the first year, the consultants were present in the associations: members who had left the matrix were thought to have been eaten by the consultants after fattening-up in the matrix. By the end of the first year, Alistair and I, as consultants, had appeared separately in dreams and, in the second year, as a couple. The consultant couple was in the form of associations to dreams of circling storks and nesting chooks—that is, we were no longer seen as parents who eat their babies but ones who produce and nurture. Consultant–members matrix relations are worked out at dream level.

Members slowly appeared in each other's dreams—as did members and consultants together. Finally, there were matrix appearances—that is, "the matrix was . . .". The shift is best portrayed by the move from absolute horror that someone might dream about you to the situation in our last session for the year. A dream was recounted involving the matrix membership—the question was asked by one member, "Was I in it?"—with the addition, "It's not a question regarding feeling left out or envious—simply one of curiosity" (did curiosity finally kill the cat?).

Your space or mine? Our space

The matrix space, as I have experienced it, involves science, spirituality, and play. As such, it has connections with Eastern philosophies; Aboriginal cosmology, the new scientists, and writers like Andrew Samuels, Theilhard de Chardin, D. W. Winnicott, and obviously Jung.

Winnicott has spoken of his excitement, as a young lad, on reading Darwin's *Origin of Species* to discover that scientific method accepted gaps in knowledge as "potential spaces" to explore, work, and play. He argued that in playing, whether child or adult, we are able to be creative and use our whole personality, potentially leading to discovering the self (Davis & Wallbridge, 1983). This "potential space" is neither inside the world of dream and fantasy nor outside in the world of shared reality. It is a paradoxical "third place" or a "place of illusion", partaking of both these places simultaneously, thus transcending the me–not me boundary. In *Playing and Reality* (1971), Winnicott writes of illness through separation from creativity, estrangement from dream, and loss of contact with the infantile experience in the merged state if we hold too closely to objective reality.

Samuels (1989) describes his concept called "imaginal network", which also has some similarities to matrix space. The word "imaginal" comes from Corbin's (1990) *Mundus imaginalis*, which is a state of being and perceiving without evaluating, a place populated by unconscious fantasy and archetypal imagery. To this, Samuels adds the word "network", with its connections to threads, wires, or nets alongside its newer meanings including systems, grids, links, maps, relationships, and less rigid boundaries (Samuels, 1989, p. 40). Images, according to Samuels, have the capacity to generate more images, this is our experience of associating to the dream in matrix orbit.

The "meditative silences" during the matrix are also important times where images form and later bubble into matrix life. Silence seems more easily accepted than in group work—members and consultants have learnt how to listen to the spaces.

The matrix space also shares some aspects with the modern science. We have the wave–particle paradox, for example, as discussed in the Introduction. Members became very comfortable about many associations and connections, as they held "it" being both this and that. Space was no longer three dimensional and time no longer linear; in fact, they were not even separate entities—we had space–time.

In the second year of the matrix, it became evident that the female members were having dreams and associations relating to space, whereas the male members had dreams and associations related to time. One female sketched during and after sessions. She shared one drawing, which involved a sea of sperm and an egg with a space in the centre. It was only after she finished that she realized the space she created was the drawing, and she called it the unborn child, the foetus being very clear.

This "allocation" also seemed to apply to the consultants. Where I have imagined the cat in the spaces between the chairs, Alastair had been objectively watching the "movie". During a series of sessions when Alastair was actively involved, as were the other males, in the time issues and particularly time going backwards, we had a reversal of the cat experience. I felt like I was watching an interesting movie, while he became partially blinded, not being able to see anything except people's mouths moving, and he was unable to say this during the session. It reminded me of the "blind architect" dream at Spa (Lawrence, 1991) and of Theilhard de Chardin's letter speaking of "an almost 'blinding' perception of the two poles of my thought and of my action" (de Chardin, cited in Duggan, 1968).

Theilhard de Chardin was highly motivated to bridge the gap between science and religion (or spirituality) which, he wrote, were "the two conjugated faces or phases of the one and the same act of complete knowledge" (Chardin, 1959, p. 285). We are again challenged with union or collision: did a consultant lose sight of his task, or was this in the service of the matrix task? The resolution of the space–time split occurred in two forms: a dream and a poem. A female member offered the dream:

> I dreamt I was joining the matrix, and instead of there being only a few people there were hundreds of people. They were holding hands and forming a shape. I became elevated in the air and could see the shape was an eye. In the second part of the dream, I was circling the earth sitting on the wings of a time-bomb. The earth looked beautiful from space, but the bomb focused in on the matrix. I got off before it blew up.

The poem had been written prior to this (not that we worry about the order of time these days). In our final session, a member was exploring the difference in viewing her dream from within versus outside it; she explained one aspect, saying, "I dreamt it before it actually happened, but that's not an answer, because who knows about time and space in regard to a matrix." She was exploring combined time and space issues. Returning to the poem, it seemed to contain some of our concerns about reversal. One set of associations had involved writing parables backwards, and this poem, which offers an alternative way of conceiving the creation, was the resultant container.

> Adam,
> Having lain with Eve
> Dreamily touches her rib,
> And creates God.

And, for Einstein, space and time did collide, giving us four-dimensional space–time.

Rupert Sheldrake (1991), one of our modern scientists, has also given us "morphic resonance"—the transmission of formative influences through or across time or space. Matrix experiences associated to this include a member who had missed two sessions. He returned to the matrix after no contact with members and offered, as the first dream, a dream that was a logical progression of the previous week's work. Similarly, after the Lorne conference, a matrix member who had no conscious knowledge of that conference dreamt the obvious next dream, thus dreaming matrix members from the conference back into this matrix.

Sheldrake (1991) sees the universe as evolving and that "laws" of nature may do the same. Evolution, he argues, is the interplay between habit and creativity. Sheldrake connects with Jung's "collective unconscious",[1] as he suggests that "One model for this creative process is dreaming." This leads him to posing questions like: "Is there a kind of Gaian dreaming . . . is she awake on the side in the sunlight and the side in darkness dreaming? At night, are plants, animals and whole ecosystems in some sense in a dream state? What form would a Gaian dream take?" (Abraham, McKenna, & Sheldrake, 1992, p. 15). Perhaps some of the answers to his story, from the human side, are found in the following matrix dreams and activities that involve a human/plant/animal connection.

—*Trees growing out of a woman's stomach.*

—*A Christmas tree held in a member's palm* (the whole world in her hand).

—*"I dreamt I was planted in the earth . . . was standing like a tree, my feet were planted covered with soil."*

—In an experiential exercise where one member was sharing his experience of social dreaming, we were asked to find a flower and basically understand it from its experience.

—*"I dreamt I was partly human but had huge wings. I had claws instead of feet and could walk along fences."*

This latter dream was sketched; the sketch resembled a drawing entitled by Jung's term "Individuation" that accompanied a poem by Gavin Greenlees (in Drury, 1979), which the member had not seen.

From the Aboriginal cosmology, their boundary between dream and reality is not dualistic as is ours. "The Aborigines refer to the inseparable relationship between the actual and the potential, the conscious and the unconscious as the light and dark faces of the moon—both are always present." (Lawlor, 1991, p. 41).

Suzuki (1956) when explaining the difference between the Zen position and psychoanalysis states that the latter, when studying a flower, would analyse it to the point where all that remained would be a collection of abstractions, not the object itself. The Zen approach "is to enter right into the object itself and see it, as it were, from the inside. To know the flower is to become the flower" (Fromm, Suzuki, & de Martino, 1960, p. 11).

Chaos and order

It would seem that the ancient peoples, the new scientists, and Eastern philosophies are converging. The ancient people considered that chaos and order were in an uneasy harmonic tension. In most cosmologies, the primordial state of chaos or nothingness was there from the beginning. The ancient belief in the "oneness" of the universe has been given credibility by scientists like David Bohm. The work of Poincaré and those who have followed suggest mirror worlds of chaos and order. They are separate, as a head is from the toe, but both are part of the body. With chaos and order, the relationship is more circular—that is, violent order being disorder (chaos) and, similarly, extreme disorder being order. They are the same but different, as are twins. An object and its mirror reflection are also the same but are opposite—such as chaos and order, or perhaps science and spirituality.

Like Theilhard de Chardin, Karan Singh suggested (at the ITA Global Conference in Prague in 1992) a union of science and spirituality. Singh said that both were quests for truth, "science on one hand goes out into the very heart of matter" while "spirituality goes inward into the mystic heart within us". Both are manifestations of the Divine: if the Divine is manifested outward, it is also manifested inward.

It is difficult for the Western scientific mind to accept that something is at the one time the same but different, or that an atom behaves like a wave and a particle. The "'sustaining story" here is to hold in mind the joke that my brother told me when I was seven years old (I didn't trust him with numbers after his "200" failure!). This joke has, to this day, remained my favourite and in some way is relevant to our matrix at the moment:

Q: "What's the difference between a duck?"
A: "One of its legs is both the same."

My current "working story" is two sets of twins, or two sets of mirrors reflecting the reflection. One set involves chaos and order, the other science and spirituality. Mirrors and twins were a major theme through the matrix years, and specifically during its final six months.

In 1992, when asked to draw their experiences of social dreaming, one member drew herself in front of a mirror looking at an image of her back. Another member said he had dreamt the same thing. Seeing ones back requires two mirrors. In 1993, dreams about mirrors involved having an offer to view the world in a cracked mirror and seeing oneself, visiting a building with mirrors all around while searching for people behind the mirrors, and, finally, seeing one's opposite-gender sibling standing in the mirror and leaning towards you, separate yet connected. These all seemed to be pointing towards something that is the same but different. It is tempting to link this to the many references to mirrors in psychoanalytic, spiritual, or scientific literature or to myths like Narcissus; however, this "doubling" is fairly fresh material and has not yet "run its course".

The other doubling in dreams has involved pregnancies, and the doubles often have Asian links. If Australia were to expand to a more global mentality, it has been suggested that Asia is our nearest neighbour. Another association is that of yin/yang. Some examples of the twins dreams are: the matrix being given Chinese twins, which were fossilized, and a new set of Chinese twins was found (opposite gender); feeding Romulus and Remus; four babies including Siamese twins joined at the head; a lady in a twinset; being pregnant with twins; making a pregnant woman pregnant again; having sex with a Chinese pregnant woman; and a dream involving two houses, two friends, and two fish. Again, it is tempting to link this material to literature on true and false self, conscious/unconscious, and the many myths and legends across cultures involving twins/siblings. The International Conference at Lorne included a moving opening address about Cain and Abel.

There is an Indian painting based on the "union of irreconcilables"—that is, the marriage of fire and water. This painting is very similar to the apparatus used in alchemy. If past experience is a guide, these dreams will continue in the matrix, not unlike making a saturated solution in junior science classes. Eventually a "seeding crystal" or "strange attractor" will cause crystallization or order. The dreams will have come full term, and the situation will be clearer.

The role of the "twin" consultants at times has been like identical twins, fraternal twins, mirror images, and shadow boxing. In the first year these positions seemed to align along the outward/inward pair. This involved creating a facilitative environment to venture inward to the spiritual centre for dreams and bring them out for sharing and associating at the personal and then wider level. Our task seemed to be managing and balancing between science and spirituality—that is, inner and outer. (See 1-3 in Figure 5.2.) In the third year its emphasis was a different line, the line between chaos and order (2-4-2 in Figure 5.2), the need to allow enough creativity without too much madness—that is, the containing line. I believe that, at times, Alastair and I did this together, whereas at other times one of us moved right over into "chaos" and the other needed to lean right out to "order" to achieve a balance. At other times we simply used "interpretations" (attractors) to achieve the same result. I have to admit we also experienced chaos/order conflicts.

Models and muddles in the middle of a matrix journey

A tentative working diagram for the present matrix experience involves the twin mirrors of the outward science/inward spirituality and chaos/order. Each of these is circular and hence it is actually like a globe with a line of zero longitude and zero latitude. This is represented in Figure 5.2, which has been drawn two dimensionally to simplify understanding.

The science–spirituality line is the start of the creative matrix process—the fishing line. We have to let down a fishing line of chaos and infinity to bring ideas out.

There are negative forms of each of these, all which happened during the matrix: for example, A+ negative is the non-sharing or "personal property" of dreams; A* negative is attacking associations, non-associations, abstinence, or "association interruptus"; Z* negative may involve premature birth, miscarriage, or abortion of the matrix work; Z+ negative involves the inability to make connections and evolve or mutate individually and collectively. The consultants' task is to balance the boat of chaos and order during this entire fishing (fishy) experience.

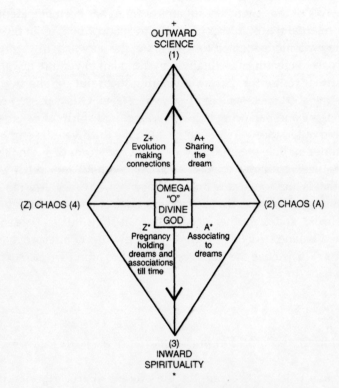

Figure 5.2.   Twin mirror worlds:
the art of fishing in a balanced boat

The journey (1→3→1) begins with dropping a net from the outward rational conscious world (1) to the unconscious, spiritual archetypal world (3) to catch a dream. The return journey to (1) involves holding and remembering the dream. The direction is then clockwise around the diamond.

• 1→2 (quadrant A+) Sharing the dream in the matrix.
• 2→3 (quadrant A*) Associating to dreams, listening to spaces, union of opposites.
• 3→4 (quadrant Z*) Holding the fertilized eggs (dreams and associations) or "saturating the solution".
• 4→1 (quadrant Z+) Birth, crystallization, making connection with the outer world. New habits may form—evolution.

Fission, fusion, and futures

The final session for 1993 contained dreams and associations with single and double "3s". One of these associations was to Christ's death at the age of 33 and another suggested that joining two 3s made the infinity sign. We can talk of the "threefold unity of forces" across many teachings. Examples include the balancing and complementing of the two (Yin and Yang) with the one (Tao), the trinity of supreme deities in Indian mythology: Brahma the Creator, Shiva the Transformer, and Vishnu the Preserver. Gurdjieff (1999) formulated his Law of Three, the affirming, denying, and reconciling or equalizing forces in everything, and we have the Holy Trinity of Christianity, with the Father, Son, and Holy Spirit. In recent matrix dreams, there are the trios of sun, moon, and stars and also of plants (often trees), animals (mainly cats), and humans. So as well as double pairs, we have multiple threes.

The following fourteenth-century poem by a monk in China, a country whose ancient culture knows so much more than we do, was written to accompany a Zen ink painting; it holds many of these symbols:

The Four Sleepers
Old Fen-Kan embraces his tiger and sleeps,
All huddled together with Shih-te and Han-shan.
Their great dream reaches infinity
While the frail old tree clings to the bottom of the cold precipice.

[Barnet & Burto, 1982, p. 46]

Note

1. Jung's collective unconscious is an obvious connection to social dreaming; however many dream groups still focus back to the individual, which a matrix avoids. (For an interesting discussion on archetypal psychology and the personal/collective unconscious focus, see Samuels, 1989, p. 168.)

CHAPTER SIX

The discovery of social dreaming

Laura Ambrosiano

Traditionally, we think that dreams are private, that they are the personal expression of intimate experiences that take place inside the individual mind. We hold on to this hypothesis even when, with Bion, we question these spatial definitions and consider the mind as a function that goes beyond the psychic borders of an individual, a function that develops from the dynamic relationship of container–contained, maternal reverie–child experience, group–individual.

The interpretation of the dream is linked to our way of conceiving subjectivity; the theoretical transformations of the notion of subject transform the way in which we comprehend and interpret dreams. The psychoanalytic orthodoxy defines the internal world of the subject as its privileged observation nucleus and sees the dream as a distorted representation of the ambivalent and conflicting desire (Freud, 1900a).

The studies on object relations describe the internal world as the stage where the objects relate to each other, and the privileged observation nucleus moves on to the analytic relationship. From this point of view, the dream is regarded as an expression of thoughts on the vicissitudes of the relationship between patient and analyst, on the potentialities of transformation, and on the difficulties and deadness that the patient is undergoing at that moment.

From these considerations the focus of observation is neither the object nor the subject but the space between them, the shared field, which generates emotions and unthought thoughts that are waiting to be welcomed into the mind. Next to thoughts that are born in the shared field, other common points of reference that exist before the meeting are present: for example, the group to which one belongs and its mentality offer ready-made meanings in both the patient's mind and the analyst's (Ambrosiano, 1999; Eisold, 1994). Inside the psycho-analytic group cure, the dream told during the session is greeted as the bearer of fresh meanings that refer to the emotional life of the group as a whole, to the emotions, difficulties and problems that the group is busy dealing with at that moment of its history (Friedman, Neri, & Pines, 2002).

In conclusion, for a vast area of psychoanalytic research, therefore, the meaning of the dream cannot be received otherwise than in rela-tion to the context in which it is told; it comments (in the internal world) upon the transpersonal experience of contact within a context (one has only to think of the contributions of Ogden, Bollas, or Ferro, to mention but a few). In this sense, the dream is understood as an activity of transition between the intrapsychic and the outside world; it expresses the connection of one individual to another, to the envi-ronment, and to the social world. It is an apparatus to capture mean-ings, which regard a context cohabited by a set of individuals who share the mentality, values, tension, and fear towards the complexity of reality and the incompleteness of our representative capacity. Law-rence (1991) maintains that he did not invent social dreaming but discovered it, exactly as we can say that Freud did not invent transfer-ence but discovered it. I would like to discuss this hypothesis by presenting experiences from a workshop and, subsequently, propos-ing some theoretical conclusions.

The Rome workshop

The workshop took place in a university and was organized by the department of psychology, spurred by a common interest in social dreaming. The participants were about 250 students of the faculty, divided into six groups. Seven matrixes were held over three days. In his opening presentation, Gordon Lawrence introduced the theoretical basis of social dreaming, which animated a plenary discussion.

In the first matrix, after a few moments of bewilderment, the participants tell some of their recurring dreams that they believe to have a fully individual meaning. But, unexpectedly, the dreams reveal some common aspects, which can be gathered into two themes. In the first one, we have dreams of exploration of submarine places, abysses shot through by rays of intense light, labyrinth-like houses in which the rooms are intertwined, old cities, underground cities, and so forth.

Dreams of bodily transformation belong to the second theme:

—*I had water in my head, and inside there were fishes. I had to be careful as to how I moved in order not to make them fall.*

—*I dreamt of a famous man who had his head split open and inside there were dead, rotten fishes.*

—*I was pulling out of my mouth long, green, never-ending intestines. . . . I looked at myself in the mirror and I was completely green.*

From the narration of the dreams, various associations spring out: progressively, the fishes are connected to the fish-thoughts that are in the head, unknown, alive—dead, strange—a bit scary—they raise the question of whether it is important to let them live, of whether we can explore together this unknown world. From the starting cues we are under the impression that the focus of the dream is on the container–contained dynamic. The social dreaming is represented as a labyrinth-like house or an underground city, an unknown and disquieting container. In a parallel way, each participant sees her/himself as the container of disquieting contents.

As in an M. C. Escher drawing, nothing is as it appears but each element can join others in mysterious ways in a game of continuous returns. The participants seem to start playing with dreams in a Winnicottian way. Little by little, they start telling last night's dreams:

—*There was a tiny little child, a baby, with a big head, and he could already speak very well.*

—*I was at the foot of a mountain, I start climbing, it was hard. Halfway up I find a person who says: I'll help you climb.*

The matrix gets animated. It is starting to develop in the participants' minds and promotes exchanges; they speak of sharing and brotherhood, but, anguished, they ask themselves: What are we doing here? Are we raving, are we dreaming? Are we trying to fall asleep here? Someone says, "It's like being on the beach, when you all gather around a fire and each one tells a story." Despite this attempt to improve things, the anguish grows. What are matrixes? Are they cages in which we are locked up?

The wavering between curiosity and paranoia brings to attention immediately afterwards the scenery of the war in Afghanistan, which began right at that period. Two other dreams:

—*I was running with a baby in my arms in a town in ruins, we were being followed, I put the baby in care of a couple who could save him, I gave them a letter which the child could have read once he grew up.*

—*The war and children theme spreads in several directions of meaning, orientated, it seems to me, by the fear of the container dissolving under bombs.*

One dream that seems to want to reassure describes pregnant women, but *"they had open bellies in and out of which the babies jumped as they liked, they could go back into the belly when they wanted to."* But if the matrix is an open belly, where can we find reliable borders? The matrix is not a group, the dynamics are not analysed, there are no alliances, there are no roles, we don't even know each other's names, to lose your name is like losing your identity, it's like being in a concentration camp where the first thing the Nazis did was to cancel names; Lawrence is not interested in the single individual, he's interested in dreams, but what do our dreams have in store for us?

In the fourth matrix, a particular dream captures the attention. It is told by an older student, visibly different:

I'm ashamed of my dream. It's linked to yesterday's dreams, to the war. *I dreamt that I was in Afghanistan, a desert landscape, military trucks and tanks, I was travelling with an army the nationality of which I didn't know. I was worried because I hadn't informed anybody at home. We were marching along the coast and some soldiers were bathing, which was a bit of a surprise to me, then we arrived in a big city and two guys robbed me, two occidentals, European guys. I'm disorientated and confused and I try to join my convoy but I can't find it any more . . . I am*

*against the war . . . in the dream I don't react . . . but I was also comforted
by the fact that the thieves were European.*

The matrix discuss animatedly on the fact that in front of death, we
are all equal, human beings of the world; when people die, we cry for
the dead, for all the dead; there are no goodies or baddies, there aren't
people on our side, like us, it's impossible to say: which side are you
on? and then, perhaps there isn't an Afghan, there is something
greater than us; to immerse ourselves in these feelings, as in the
ocean, is frightening too.

As a coordinator, at that moment, I share the frightened bewilderment and dismay. I feel like a faceless woman, invisible under a
burkha, surrounded by people, the participants, who I don't see entirely, whose names I don't know; I don't have an interpretative
function. Then I think that that very morning I bought some little
Afghan trinkets to give as presents to friends—some little boxes, and
a ring with a little mirror exclusively used by Muslim women to look
around under their burkha.

Without the container represented by the name, the professional
role, the membership, one feels without definition, anonymous. Anonymity comes to mind as a scary feeling that overwhelms when we
cry for all the dead without gathering in coalitions. The name masks
personal identity, but some add that the name is a mask, a pole that
marks an artificial border; others object. However, behind a name
there is a whole family history; without a name, one feels naked, yet
to be naked is to be free, to look for something unknown—*nuda
veritas.*

This the first dream of the fifth matrix:

*Walking around my town, I could see builders building a primary school.
I was with my father and he was saying the workers had not received a
salary for three months, but I was happy because I was thinking: how
nice, in this way, we'll put all the children in there.*

This dream seems to suggest the image of a container adequate for all
the children, anonymous and naked, or swaddled very tightly, which
had previously populated the dreams of all the former matrixes.

But the workers do not receive their wages. The wait for interpretations that can explain is frustrating; they seem to think that the
explanation is the salary, which acts as the recognition of the accom-

plished work. They ask themselves: what is the aim of such a work, what experience is this?

— *"We were all sitting at a table in a bar. We had to look for something, then one of us shows a parchment, and we wrote one word each on this parchment."* (This seems to represent the invention of language, which Freud indicates as being the first creative contribution of the masses.)

—*I was at a friend's house, a beautiful one with new furniture . . . but, after a while, it didn't seem to me so new anymore; on the contrary everything looked old. Her grandmother arrived and she was carrying big red lilies, and the house immediately became nicer . . . the lilies were like Japanese paper flowers which, once put into water, take different shapes . . . or different colours."*

—*Someone, a man perhaps, a foreigner phoned my parents to tell them that I was pregnant, I said: no, it's not true, I'm not pregnant. I was anguished, then I thought that perhaps it was true, that perhaps he was right.* Perhaps, little by little, we were all pregnant of dreams that were not ours but were leaving in each of us some small fertility seeds, without losing the shape and the colour of our differences.

The aim of the matrix, they say, is that everyone puts something in, as when you throw a stone into water and the waves open up. The matrix is like something in expansion that widens up on its own; each person can only throw a stone—an experience one wished would never end. "But these professors steal our dreams":

—*Some burglars broke into my house and one of them was definitely G. Lawrence . . . our professors did it on purpose so we would become a group, during the lesson then will something carry on?*

—*A man who was completely burnt was following me . . . he was as red as fire . . . the doctor takes notes with a red pen . . . sex is red . . .*

—*I was making love with a boy I like . . . also betrayal is red . . . red is also the colour with which they marked our mistakes at school . . . red is the red thread for us . . . the doctor is a kind of common mother . . . red is the traffic light, it's the signal to stop, the end, the separation.*

We take leave of one another affectionately, still lost, happy.

Comment

The participants seem committed to facing ambivalent feelings towards the ongoing experience: one moment they feel used and robbed, one moment some character appears to offer help, distress then shoots through the field—they feel locked up in a labyrinth with no exit, immersed in the immensity of the ocean, they are nameless, undressed, in a space that expands and promises that new things can be gained.

The underlying questions seem to evoke the sense of a growth journey, understood as an itinerary during which you set up borders between you and the others, in which you define your own name, learn the elements of the delivered knowledge to succeed in passing the exams and becoming adults. The participants seem to describe their commitment in an itinerary of development but also in a growth as an adjustment that can make them become newborns-speaking. The wise suckling baby described by Sàndor Ferenczi (1913) can be seen as the metaphor of a personal evolution that seems to require giving up one's own tiny, fragile, and touching aspects, which have to be swaddled very very tightly.

This perspective is all the more significant if we think that the participants are students in a basic assumption of dependence, committed to learning what is conveyed to them from the outside as an indispensable tool for their development, and that they expect to be judged, during their studies, on this degree of leaning.

But the same questions also seem to let the adult condition be imagined as a common work, in which each gives his or her own contribution to be integrated to the others': writing on the parchment. This tension develops a genetic anguish: what will be born out of it, what will the product be? And how specific will the offered contribution be? How long will each person's personal contribution survive?

During the matrixes the dreams seem to offer metaphors to receive and contain these torments, to put them under a new perspective. The perspective that progressively seems to emerge is that it is possible to grow, thanks to something that comes from the inside, something shapeless of which one is pregnant, perhaps without knowing it.

The matrix, they observe, is a place where something is born.

During the experience, I am under the impression that the matrix enables a (little and timid) trust in the existence of an internal world and in the psychic work to come forth.

The dream register, figurative or pre-symbolic, is rooted in an emotional dimension that expands and never lets itself be entirely caught by the linear speech; for this reason, it causes excitation, bewilderment, and fear.

The emotions arise from a pre-symbolic and pre-individual mental level (Gaburri, 1992); they indicate potentially fresh comments on the ongoing experience, on the environment and the bonds which it generates. The emotions give birth to ideas-children, which pertain to the group; fear also spreads that these ideas-children could lead to catastrophes and unveil painful connections or links with the most unsettling aspects of the experience.

The associative thought is often avoided because we are afraid that it might establish connections that would make us face the painful and traumatic aspects of the experience, which we try to avoid through splits. With splits, we can set up ways of denial, like revolving doors, at our disposal to avoid the central dimensions of fear. The group mentality organizes these splits into beliefs and ideologies that offer to the individual single and linear explanations of past and future events, inasmuch as the mentality is set up also as a system of prophecies—"Things will go on as they always have . . .", "Anyway, nothing really changes", and so forth.

The individual, spurred by the need to belong, collaborates and unconsciously complies to the mentality set by the group; in the latter, he finds a container, borders, a stability—"people like us".

In the name of these needs, the individual is ready to submit (relatively) to the common thought and to sacrifice (relatively) his or her individual thought. But at the same time, each person also feels an intense a need to single him/herself out and thus tries to emancipate him/herself from the collective mental condition—the mass, as Freud (1921c) defines it—and renders him/herself available to unpredictable dimensions and to unexpected meanings. The group evolves in a discontinuous way, swaying continuously between its consolidation in mentality and ideology and the transgressive function of the mystic and of the freely associative thought, a function that enables us to *be aware* of new connections, to be taken by surprise by fresh connections.

In a similar way, the individual evolves by establishing a bond with common sense while trying at the same time to get some spare space for him/herself in his or her mind, some openings for new ideas.

The dream highlights this internal dialectic, creates containers that make it bearable, offers intermediaries between the individual and the group, between the need to belong/contain and the need of individuality, between the collective mental condition and the expansion of one's own specificity (Ambrosiano, 2001b), or, as Bion (1992) says, between narcissism and socialism.

The experience of social dreaming seems to me to lead us to the heart of this dialectic, offering the opportunity to pause on this conflict ridge. It rouses in each individual the impression of getting lost and of losing one's own specificity in a dimension of meanings that tend to appear ocean-like.

The discovery of being pregnant of ideas-fishes unknown to ourselves, which do not belong to us as individuals but *emerge* on their own, transforms the idea of subjective growth and of sharing and spreads trust in the possibility of learning through experience. The dreamlike condition that progressively takes place approaches the unconscious as a generative dimension of the mind. The internal world and the unconscious work can be felt as a tonality of trusting wait instead of a paranoiac suspicion.

Free association

In social dreaming, dreams are not seen as bearing meanings but connections, links, and bonds (Lawrence, 1998c). The mind works by finding connections through the freely associative thought. But the mind also needs to set borders to its explorations, and it therefore puts up an opposition to the connections that arise and tends to limit the indefinite (not infinite) potentiality of meaning.

The mind operates denials and splits that simplify events and offer quite reliable systems in order to sustain the impact with experience. The group organizes its culture also on these denials and splits, which are organized into mentality (Neri, 1998). Mentality has the aim of enabling the exploration of the world but also of protecting the group and thus ensuring its survival. The individual is called upon to answer to both aims: to keep well connected to the mentality of the group the individual belongs to, by collaborating to consolidate the acquitted culture, and to transgress that mentality to allow space for personal and group development.

The main aspect of the proposal of social dreaming consists in helping a freely associative thought. The dream offers a figurative language to help this type of thought. The associative thought is not inside the epistemological deconstructionist orientation inaugurated by Freud in 1900 and based on his research on dreams. While interpreting dreams, Freud would offer different hypotheses of meaning, implying that others could have been guessed, that other hypotheses of interpretation could have arisen from other possible connections between different elements of the dream.

Free association appears when you start to lose your own train of thoughts because the birth of other thoughts breaks up the continuity of conscious thoughts, and then the coherence of the speech breaks down and reveals new and diverging lines of thoughts that describe something known unconsciously but not thought. We think of the dream of the marching army related by one of the dreamers.

The dream told in the matrix of social dreaming is re-dreamt by the participants, and, through free association, we can catch a glimpse of new possible meanings, giving us the impression that the dream expands in time and space. In the work of free association, the problems, difficulties, even anxieties are greeted not as undesirable but as signals of something that is emerging, something new, heavy with expectations and possibilities that go around in the group.

The associative thought, because of its apparent chance happening itself, of its digressive characteristic, modifies in a drastic way our point of view on the events. These processes allow us to be hit by what Bion (1963) defines as thoughts without thinkers, to change the peak from which we observe events, to feel unexpected moments of identification with other peaks and points of view, to emancipate ourselves, if possible, from the sectarian thoughts and from the compact ideologies that put the mind to sleep. Free association put us in contact with something unknown that concerns us, and this contact, in itself, modifies our way of thinking of ourselves and keeps the tension towards knowledge alive, even when it means facing painful macro-social or historical events that concern us all.

The suspension of the interpretative function

The mentality consolidated by the group produces a thick network of interpretations on the meaning of these events and offers categories to find one's way in the search for meaning to establish exchanges and relations between individuals and to draw borderlines as to what is true and relevant. These interpretations are temporary, changeable, and malleable enough to comment on the experience and communicate with the others, but they can also be transformed into strong signals of belonging, in totems (Bollas, 1999), in protocols that rule the search for knowledge. The individual's mind is permeated and organized by the interpretations offered by the mentality of the group to which the individual belongs.

I retain the suspension of the interpretative function to be the core element of the technique proposed by Lawrence. If part of the staff and the participants to the matrix abstain from interpreting, it actually produces a dreamlike atmosphere, which permits new associations to be picked up. The meaning—or, rather, meanings—arise from associations, and from them they widen towards other connections, passing over the usual denials and splits, passing over the discussion of identity itself, in terms of continuity and personal compactness of role and professional function. As Neri observes (2001) in his introduction to the experience of social dreaming in Italy, the individual during the matrix has the impression of getting lost, of identifying with the others in an unexpected way. The interpretation, in this context, can be seen as the group mentality trying to impose its order on the emerging material. The interpretation can be seen as a defence against the anxiety of free association. It obstructs the destructuralization of the dream. The matrix is a rare reflection space, one that can be difficult to experience, in which participants experiment with thought as transformation.

At a time like ours, of experts and super specialists, of returns to strong ideologies, of ethnic and religious matrixes, each of us risks, from our own professional summit, to find ourself like the character of a cartoon who walked around the streets with a ream of paper in his hand shouting: "I have a lot of answer here—who has any questions?" The emphasis on the dimension of the cure has implied, ever since the origins of psychoanalysis, the risk of catalyzing the analyst's attention on what is already known, on the theories that revealed themselves useful in the past, and on reducing the cognitive tension—

the capacity of psychoanalysis as an instrument to explore the functioning of the mind.

In my experience of social dreaming, this suspension of the already available answers has been the most precious aspect. On a personal level, I am grateful to Gordon Lawrence and to Claudio Neri, who gave me the opportunity to feel in a direct, immediate, pervaded by curiosity, and distressed way (the woman wrapped in her burkha) the core of the negative capability that Bion, in his writings, highlighted so much.

Negative capability is the way in which Bion reformulates the Freudian notion of neutrality. This reformulation underlines the core of the analytic functioning of the mind as a reverie resource. Negative capability preserves the mental space of the reverie, through a (always partial) suspension of memory and desire—that is to say, a (partial) suspension of the competence of our theories to organize (clinical) events and a suspension of the pressure that the acquired knowledge and metaphorical fruit of group consent exert on the mind. The lack of negative capability excludes reverie, which as we know, excludes listening to the child on the caregivers' part or on the analyst's part when in contact with the patient. In these circumstances, adults are unable to mediate the meeting between the newborn and the shared culture, as they themselves are its concrete spokesmen (Gaburri, 2002).

It then seems that the child is brought up by the group, inasmuch as it is brought up by adults who have not obtained a minimum degree of individuality and separateness with regard to the group and to its theories, which, like prophecies, foretell the meaning of the events. They do not perceive the differences of which the child is the bearer and they do not offer the child the elements for its individuality.

The child then finds itself living in an affective universe that is unsolvable and incomprehensible outside the prophecies that sustain the group mentality.

I would like, in this respect, to introduce a literary passage that in a paradoxical way comments on this discussion. It is from Durrenmatt's short novel *The Death of the Pixia* (1985). In an almost surreal key, Durrenmatt describes a dialogue between Tiresias and the Pixia (the prophetess). Tiresias discusses with the prophetess this passion that men have for prophecies, yet they do not realize that prophecy tellers are organized by the group and express its mentality.

The two interlocutors seem freely to associate myths and narrations. As soon as he became king, Laio seduced (or was seduced by) his sister-in-law Ippodamia who gave birth to a daughter who became a priestess condemned to chastity, the Sphinx, while Ippodamia's father, out of revenge, emasculated Laio, who therefore could not have begot a son with Jocasta. Menesthus, Jocasta's father, had paid the oracle so that he would predict the prophecy that should have prevented Laio to beget an heir, so that it would be Creon, his son, who would succeed to Oedipus on the throne of Thebe. And then how is it possible to believe Oedipus to actually be Laio's son—Laio himself doesn't remember having intercourse with his wife, he didn't like women; as to Jocasta, it was a well-known fact that she had had intercourse with other men during her marriage. And perhaps Oedipus wasn't even Jocasta's son—the Sphinx, having just given birth to a son after having been raped under Laio's eyes, swapped babies, saving hers and giving Jocasta's son to the lions to be eaten up.

A roundabout of hypotheses and fantasies is the one described by Durrenmatt, which populate the mind of a child brought up by a group, which happens to live in an affective universe that is unsolvable and incomprehensible. Tiresias confesses to the prophetess to have always known everything about incest and the rest, but by then, he says, there were the children and the marriage had to be saved:

> that gentleman Creon, so devoted to his sister and to his brother-in-law, who nevertheless, given his vision of the world, if he had come to know that his brother-in-law was also his nephew . . . would never have been able to accept such a thing, would have kicked Oedipus off the throne out of sheer devotion to the common sense of morality. And we would have had to put up with a totalitarian system, as in Sparte, where they kill handicapped children at their birth, see heroism as civic duty . . . blood at lunch and dinner. . . . [p. 50]

That gentleman Creon, in Durrenmatt's story, seems the expression of a flat mind reduced by common sense and by the notion of a linear truth that is at the origin of sectarianism and ideologies. Creon knows what is true, what is fair, what is moral. Creon does not exert any negative capability, his mind is saturated with interpretations supplied by common sense. Tiresias, the fortune teller who pretends to be blind in order to be listened to, does not know the truth, he has in mind different hypotheses that give to the events a particular meaning, each time bringing to evidence different aspect. He comments:

"Irrelevant stories do not exist, everything is linked to everything else. Whenever something is changed, the change regards everything . . . with your prophecy," he says to the prophetess, "you have invented truth" (p. 48). The suspension of the interpretative function enables linear logic, even the one produced by our non-linear psychoanalytic theories, to fall.

In the matrix of social dreaming, the feeling that some thoughts are *diverging* or incoherent, or irrelevant, or beside the point, dissolves and blurs, each thought speaking strongly of the emotional halo that experiences produce. When these speech categories dissolve, there is also a lessening of the search for *alliances* between individuals, of the running into sub-group positions that express the defensive need for delimitations and artificial and rigid borders, which lead to racism and *integralism*.

It is not by chance that in Durrenmatt's story, Creon, the just, is the tyrant who rules with an inflexible, and therefore bloody, justice.

On the other hand, the suspension of linear logic produces distress, a sense of loss, and insecurity.

Our students were very curious and uncertain as to this type of work. Every now and then, they went back to looking for linear explanations that would not change the order of the world: "Perhaps the professors have hidden goals", "Perhaps it's another way to judge us", or "They're making us do work for free" (i.e. producing interpretations from which they'll learn), or "They study us, they're doing an experiment. . . ."

The oceanic feeling

Armstrong (1998a) observes that the dreamer gives voice to the dream inside him but that it is not only his. Lawrence's hypotheses (1998a) consider the dream as a possibility to pick the individual's unconscious connection to society. The hypothesis that I propose is that the individual mind works on the basis of both individual factors and cultural consensual factors.

The presence of these two factors enables us to imagine two mental dimensions: the oedipal dimension, which expresses a tension towards individuation and separation; and the mental dimension, which we could define as pre-individual, not neurotic, not governed by affective ambivalence but by emotions not yet represented and shared. I do not think it is enough to define one as progressive and the other as regressive, inasmuch as both are structuring for the mind: one in the sense of individuation, the other in the sense of empathy and exchange.

The development of the mind actually feeds on the dialectic, sometimes conflicting, between these dimensions; the suspension of this dialectic interrupts or hinders psychic life. Dreams can offer a comprehension of this pre-individual and consenting mental space—that is to say, not only of the internal world of the dreamer but of what lies between individuals in the biospace. The ways in which an individual lives and considers his or her experience reflects and are organized by conscious and unconscious buildings of the group and of the organization to which he refers and belongs.

The notion of social connection in general is understood at different levels of meanings: at a first level, it refers to conscious exchanges and collaboration; at a second level, it refers to the unconscious sharing of mentality, ideals, and ideologies, to the social bond understood as fruit of the individual's introjection of the common sense of the group; at a third level, the connection leads us to consider a transpersonal nebula of emotions that punctuate the experiences and the events of the shared universe.

This last level of meaning of the notion of connections leads us to the "oceanic feeling" that, in the period between the two world wars, constituted the heart of Freud's debate with Romain Rolland (Freud, 1930a).

While Freud thinks of the organized masses—today we would speak of the basic assumption groups, like the church and the army—and disputes Rolland's hypothesis, the oceanic feeling in the latter's thought indicates a sense of *original connection*. Freud is afraid to face this oceanic connection; he fears that it would lead him to betray his new research path, and he declares himself an earth man, not equipped for sailing on the deep sea (Freud, 1936a). The disorientation that seizes Freud in front of the Parthenon, as he tells Rolland, expresses very well the dismay that the oceanic dimension of identity produces in us, as the experience with our students demonstrated.

In 1931, Rolland answers Freud:

Your amiable dedicate opposes with irony the earth man to the oceanic man. This opposition does not happen only between two men but in a man himself, in me. . . . The strangeness is that this vital feature is actually so impressed in a thousand of these earth men's minds who know nothing, as far as most of them are concerned, of any ocean. [in Vermorel & Vermorel, 1999]

The oceanic feeling describes a known tension to plunge into the shared universe, to "feel with", to participate and mix; it is at the basis of the possibility of sharing and of understanding each other. An (always relative) understanding of the other rises from a field thick with regressions, projections, personifications, and constructions, which, through the free game of doubles, of identifications, intertwine the borders of identity. The earthly mental dimension fears these intertwinements, opposes them, fears sailing and change; it takes up a defensive position by asking questions like who said what, or, what does this mean to this person. It looks for static, clear-cut borders, and in this it keeps *on this side* the processes of separation and mourning.

The oceanic dimension constitutes an active, unavoidable, and not ignorable component of normal psychic life. It orientates the mind towards the shared universe, putting at its disposal empathy and intuition like bridges towards relationships with others and towards knowledge; it puts at the mind's disposal that "mysterious attraction linked perhaps, in a way or another, to the knowledge of all our differences" that Freud writes to Rolland about (in Vermorel & Vermorel, 1999).

The oceanic feeling is articulated on the one hand with the group mentality soaked in egalitarianism and on the other with the oedipal tension that tries to differentiate itself, to obtain a personal specificity. The mentality is used to guarantee the survival of the group. The oedipal deviation allows a peculiar configuration endowed with specificity and originality to emerge from the psychosomatic endowment. This articulation constitutes the life of the mind, and it roots it in a conflicting dialectic.

Freud and Rolland (poetically) describe it as the articulation between the earth man and the oceanic man, but in their debate the contrast between the two dimensions leads in the end to the inside of the same individual and of the same group, as an internal conflict.

The oceanic connection is different from the egalitarian consent promoted by the group mentality; it arises from the common root and from the common fate, notwithstanding the differences between individuals, their sexual, ethnic, religious diversities and their affective ambivalence because it places itself on another level. But this mysterious attraction of man towards man has, for Freud as for each of us, elements that echo our nostalgia for fusion, and the egalitarianism of the group in basic assumption seems to lead it back to a regressive register.

Fusion itself, fantasy of immediate correspondence, of spontaneous sharing, is an indispensable ingredient in all relationships; it is able to preserve the bond. [Neri, 1990]

Besides being a fantasy of avoiding the object relation, as it has often been interpreted, fusion is also its forerunner (Neri, 1990). It expresses the need to contain the emerging self; its failure produces a catastrophic sense of fragmentation and an anguish of non-existence.

The failure of the search for unison introduces the mind into a dimension of non-belonging and, together, of non-individuation, a dimension in which the connection seems lost and individuality is felt as an explosive break. The vicissitudes of fantasy and the need for fusion give a dramatic importance to the course of characterization; in fact, they put at stake the fear of losing oneself or the fear of losing the connection, the dread of exposition without the mediation of the self to all the suggestions or of narcissistic isolation (psychotic). So that the fantasy of fusion remains available in the mind, in a transitional way, we need to feel we can "re-emerge", to echo Freud.

A good experience of fusion could allow the individual, in this orientation, an opening towards the project of characterization without giving up the oceanic capacity of unison and sharing. The oceanic feeling could describe a bond that is created beyond the differences but without avoiding them, not assimilable *tout court* to the regressive fusion or to the mental condition of the mass described by Freud (1921c). But as articulated as the categories we use to operate these distinctions can be, we are dealing in any case with schematizations that do not spare us the bewildered dismay that the oceanic connection produces in us. The borderline between the two dimensions is of a subtle and iridescent quality that is different to define on a theoretical level. The oceanic dimension leads us to conceive of the mind as a much larger space than what we define as identity or subject, a space that extends to include the other, as species, culture, and consensual mentality. From all this we are led to think that the individual emerges from the culture and the group, and not vice versa.

As is known, on the epistemological level it is not possible today to draw clear demarcation lines between object and subject, reality and illusion, inside and outside. Besides, Freud himself intertwines these notions in all his works, blurring and making the borders less clear cut, even beyond his conscious intentions. We just have to think of the uninterrupted reflection on transference love; Freud never concretizes a strict distinction between identification and object love, and neither does he profess to disentangle the problematic connection between the two dimensions. Lawrence's social dreaming has, to my way of thinking, the advantage of bringing us into contact with these mental territories—and, in that sense, it is a discovery, not an invention.

CHAPTER SEVEN

Relationship and relatedness between the elementary school as a system and its violent parts

Hanna Biran

During a period of six months, from January to June 1997, I directed a workshop under the aegis of the Israeli Ministry of Education. I met once a week with a group of professionals, eight of whom were educational psychologists and the other eight educational consultants. They represented sixteen different schools from the central districts of Israel, mainly from areas experiencing economic and cultural stress. The professionals willingly chose to attend the workshop in order to enhance their skills in dealing with violence at school. Eight people, from each discipline, were selected in order to enable a dialogue and mutual learning. These two professions are crucial for schools, and a lot of pressure from both teachers and parents is put on them. The primary task was to explore the phenomenon of violence in schools and to find new ways for dealing with it. The primary task was defined before the beginning of the workshop and was sent in a letter to all participants.

The workshop methodology

I worked using four dimensions for exploration and dialogue:

1. The process in the group here-and-now.
2. Presenting participants' reports on events from their work at the schools, in order to analyse the material in the group. (One event was presented in each meeting. The order of presenters was prearranged.)
3. Using participants' drawings, in which they were asked to express their experiences when confronting violence at school. The group members were asked to share their associations by the drawings.
4. Using participants' dreams. In addition to the event, the participants had to report on a dream they had had during the week that preceded their presentation. The aim of the workshop was to find links among the dreams, the drawings, and the events, in order to understand the unconscious processes that occur in the schools' systems.

The working hypothesis was that unconscious processes that occurred at a school had strongly affected the relationship between the school as a whole and the violent parts of the school. In the workshop we also tried to discover common denominators among the different schools, in order to reach deeper understanding of violent phenomena.

The longer the workshop continued, the more we discovered that dreams constitute a substantial reservoir for understanding processes in schools. The appearance of the dreams, and the ability to remember them, are connected with the fact that a dialogue concerning each dream was held at the workshop. These dialogues facilitated and contributed to the emergence of the dreams presented later in this chapter.

The idea to work with dreams came from Gordon Lawrence. My method for working with dreams was also substantially influenced by Lawrence's social dreaming matrix. His unique working method allowed me to find the relationship between the dream and the institutional insights. Lawrence wrote:

> Social dreaming starts from the premise that there are dreams in
> search of a dreamer in much the same way, as W. R. Bion postu-

lated, that there are thoughts in search of a thinker. Dreams, therefore, are not just the private property of the individual but can exist to be shared with others. In so called "primitive" societies people made use of their dreams to illuminate their waking life and to help them solve the problems of living as well as answering the spiritual puzzles with which they were faced. From past social dreaming programmes it has been learnt that dreams do illuminate contemporary life in institutions such as commercial companies, do make manifest that unconscious processes present in societies, do give indications of what may happen as dreams limn the "shadow of the future care before", to borrow Bion's phrase, and do shed fragments of transcendence. [personal communication 1994]

This chapter is based on four examples out of the sixteen that came up at the workshop. I would like to introduce the connections I have established in each case between the dreams and the school as a system. Following these cases, I discuss the common denominators in the ways in which the different schools confronted the different cases.

Example 1

In one of the schools, a special education class that contained the highest concentration of violent kids had been moved to the basement of a separate building outside the school's grounds. During the process of exploration it became clear that, unconsciously, the psychologist took upon himself the role of a police officer whose duty it was to encapsulate the violence, outside the school's premises. His self-perception as a "cop" was created by expectations indirectly transferred to him by the school's management, which was eager to get rid of violence in the school.

The psychologist's way of talking about the class, which had been moved outside the school, gave us the impression that this class was distanced from the "mother-object", and that this school had no parental, sustaining powers that could—or would—sustain that class as an integral part of the system.

The school is located in a mixed neighbourhood, and the children studying there come from families in distress, as well as immigrant families, including Russian immigrants and a large proportion of Ethiopians. The class that had been moved to the basement included the "lowest of the low". On top of the feelings of discrimination that the school children felt *vis-à-vis* the Israeli society generally, those children had once again been discriminated against. The group that was distanced was that of the "Ethiopians" or the worst cases of "special-care" children in the school.

At the workshop, the educational psychologist brought up an event in which he had observed a lesson at the class in order to advise the teacher later. The lesson was in religious studies, and the subject was "Joseph and his brothers". The lesson dealt with the chosen and loved son, and unconsciously it caused unrest that led to a violent outburst of the children against each other. The teacher did not have the tools to help the children find the contact between the lesson and their own emotional experiences.

Following his observation of the class, that same night the psychologist had this dream:

I am inside a room where guests are arriving. They are coming for my wedding. I am sleeping in a bunk-bed. Wearing a track suit, I am not prepared to receive guests. Relatives whom I have not seen for twenty years are coming to my wedding. My father comes and kisses me. They are bringing me wretched gifts, ugly flowers, ugly utensils, which break the moment I touch them. No one brings a cheque. All the gifts are useless. I have no wish to mingle with the guests. I run outside, feeling guilty.

Through the dialogue and the associations that came up in the group we assumed that the room in the dream represented the dreamer's self, the place where he rests, dressed casually. Into this self, when he is the least prepared, are brought the "gifts" given to him by the school's system. It is important to indicate that in the story he heard that morning—the story of Joseph and his brothers—there is an emphasis on the beautiful and valuable gifts that Joseph receives from his father, Jacob. The psychologist's father in the dream brings him no gift. This is also the existential situation of the children in the class. They are children without care, without "gifts", who are exposed to economic and cultural want.

Incidentally, several other points in the dream are connected with the story of Joseph that was taught in class that day. The meeting with relatives whom he "had not seen for twenty years" correspond to Joseph's meeting with his brothers after many years of separation. The brothers also carried gifts with them when going down to Egypt.

The father's kiss corresponds to Joseph's reunion and embrace with his father, Jacob.

In his dream the psychologist identifies with the deprived children, but he also experiences the gifts given him by the school. The school entrusted to him children who are like useless objects. They are like breakable and valueless parts of objects that he has to protect. All these experiences are running around inside him, in his innermost territory. He cannot stand it, and he leaves, feeling guilty. Even consciously he is engulfed by guilt, being unable to deal with the problem of the violence on the one hand, and with the vulnerability and fragility of the children on the other. The school made him "wed" those weak, useless aspects, but he is not up to the task. That day he leaves the class with a bad feeling of guilt. With the same feeling he leaves the room in his dream.

The final conclusion of the discussion in the group was that the school's defence mechanism was an attempt to encapsulate the violence, and the psychologist was sent to keep it separate in the basement and silence it as much as possible. The psychologist identified with the system's demands so strongly that he really believed that his role was to contain the violence inside the class like a policeman. In this role he failed, and this brought about the feelings of incompetence and failure.

We helped him understand that these children must find alternative means for channelling their violence—for example, open discussion of their feelings following the story of Joseph, the chosen one. We also made it clear that the school as a system cannot shake off its responsibility and send the psychologist, without any support or backing, to keep the violence at a safe distance from it. It was also recommended to him that he should suggest that this class would study at the main building and not outside the school. Another advice was to break up the class and integrate the children in different classes rather than keep them together in a special class.

Example 2

A woman psychologist introduced the following event at the workshop. During one of the breaks a third-grade boy, aged about 8 years, pushed a girl classmate on the floor and threw himself over her. Many children crowded around them, their number increasing gradually as children from all classes came and cheered the "couple" on. Following the agitation and the sexual excitement, violence had broken out among the children.

The school's principal and teachers responded with alarm and with fear of losing control. The couple who was the trigger for the event was beginning to undergo stigmatization. The event was continually discussed at the faculty room and was at the top of the agenda for a long period. The adults had classified the event under the titles of both sex and violence. The 8-year-old boy and the girl were dubbed "the Rapist" and "the Easygoing".

Discussing it at the group, we came up with the hypothesis that the dramatization of the event and the constant dealing with it constituted a kind of pleasure for the faculty members, and that it was used for the channelling of their own wishes and fantasies. The jargon they were using ignored the generation gap and was more suitable for the adults' world, rather than that of children.

Following this working hypothesis, we found out that different rumours were being circulated at that school and that there was an atmosphere of secrets regarding alleged flirtations among the faculty, as well as between teachers and parents. Through the denial of the children's tender age, the school turned the event into a drama, which channelled the unconscious passions of the adults. In this way they created a camouflage, and also used the children as a trigger to act out their own needs.

On the day she made her presentation to the group, the educational psychologist brought a dream she had had following the event at school:

I am with a group, and there is a guide who tells us where to go. I realize that the guide is my husband (who is in fact a tour guide). He assumes responsibility for the trip. He explains different things to us. He cares. He has knowledge and is willing to share it with everyone. We walk for a very long time. We find ourselves on the outskirts of a Wild West town. We walk through a huge warehouse full of furniture. Everything is painted in bright sunshine-yellow. I then notice that the whole town has been painted in the same colour, and so were our clothes. Everything was painted in the same uniform colour.

Through the dialogue and the dream's associations we tried to look for connections between the event and the dream, in order to help the psychologist find new means for working with the system. The dream had given us the clue to the fact that the psychologist had been over-absorbed in the school's faculty. This is something that happens when an all-engulfing event occurs. In such cases, it is difficult to observe from a distance. The psychologist had lost her own unique mantel and had become a part of a uniform system. It was hinted in the dream that the school's faculty had lost the ability for observing a complex situation, and that everything was coloured in the same colour. That event, which occurred during the school break, had spread out and coloured the whole system.

We tried to decipher the meaning of the yellow colour, which in the dream was connected with the sun. We thought that when the light is too strong it is blinding, just as the sun may blind, and then it is impossible to see the variety of possibilities and colours. In the dream the psychologist invites an external masculine authority to show the way; someone who knows and cares, because the group itself had lost the ability to see and to know. Our conclusion was that the child who was dubbed "the Rapist", had in fact coerced the whole system to study itself.

We advised the psychologist to present to the faculty the ideas that had surfaced at the workshop, in order to create some kind of relaxation, to keep some distance and rediscover the rules that will create order. This was necessary since the system was threatening to turn into the "Wild West". It was hoped that the discussion with the faculty and administration would help discover the dream's "furniture warehouse", or the range of possibilities that existed for treating the system and bringing it back to its senses.

One of the results of the discussion with the faculty, and the bringing up of working hypotheses, would be to free the children of all that was projected on them, and to avoid a one-dimensional, all-engulfing reaction. Another would be to give the faculty members different individual roles, according to their abilities and qualifications, in preventing violence and to train them to use varied reactions when violence reappears on the playground. We believed that developing diversity among the faculty members, and the ability to view a situation from different angles, would lead to a different way of dealing with the problem of violence.

The bright colour of sunshine that painted everything in the dream reminded me of Bion, when he says that when the light is too strong it is impossible to see. Bion (1973) writes, referring to Milton:

"He could not investigate 'things invisible to man' while he was blind with the brilliant light of facts" (p. 104). Bion then adds: "Would it be better to blind ourselves artificially so that the dark should be so pervasive that any very faint object will show up—like the expression about looking for a black cat in a dark cellar without any light" (p. 105).

Example 3

An educational consultant told the group of a recurring event of violence in one class. The event always started the same way: one child, who was constantly restless, would tear up the working sheets of children who got better marks than he did. He could not cope with the frustration of getting a mark lower than 100. He was obsessively busy comparing his and other children's marks, and was in the habit of shouting: "I cannot bear anyone getting a better mark than I." Whenever marks were given for tests or working sheets, the class turned into chaos.

The educational consultant said that the boy's family background was problematic. His mother was handicapped, and an elder brother was retarded. The family expected the boy to compensate it for the handicap and retardation, using unconscious messages. The boy happened to be in the class of an ambitious teacher who was strong on achieving, marked every paper, and wanted to turn her class into the best in the school.

The boy could not face failure in living up to the family's or the teacher's standards. The teacher usually knew when the violence was going to break out in class, but she kept on handing out marks while anticipating calamity. It was never explained—neither to her nor to the boy—what the unconscious dynamics were that would make him violent. Instead of processing the relationships and the expectations and demands that he had internalized, he was sent for art therapy, to find some outlet for himself through it. The art therapy required that he should be taken out of class. This therapy was in the non-verbal tradition, and it did not touch the truly painful spot, which required dealing with the wound itself. The educational consultant was the one who had initiated the art therapy, while she herself avoided treating the child. A day before presenting the case at the workshop, the consultant had had the following dreams:

The time is 6:30 a.m. A consultant from a different school arrives at my home and tells me about a third consultant. She tells of a serious case of violence at the school of the said consultant. I listen to her and then have a chat, drink coffee, and go to school. Later, in another dream, *I return home from our workshop and take a shower. Once I'm out of the shower I see my grandmother (who is no longer alive) washing dishes. This is very unlike her, since she was a kind of "prima donna" who never washed dishes herself.*

The discussion and associations of the dream in the group helped us to shed light on the events at school. The dream brought up associations that had to do with distancing and sterilization. The distancing was expressed in the dream through the event at a third school, which the consultant never sees or takes part in. The grandmother also represents distancing to a third generation. We thought that the consultant's need in her dream to take a shower immediately after our workshop represented the aspect of the system that wanted to clean up and avoid the dirt. The system found it difficult to touch the violence that the child had been trying to express in his own way; while the class was studying, he left for art therapy.

But the dream had also given its dreamer an answer. The "prima-donna-like" aspect, which had never touched the dirt, was called upon to change its ways and touch the dirty dishes. The grandmother, who in life had never washed the dishes, in the dream did what she was unaccustomed to doing by touching the dirty utensils. The consultant, who had kept her own distance, was asked by her dream to go out and do the dirty job. It is important to indicate that psychologists and consultants consider it a "dirty job" whenever they have to give feedback to a teacher who has done something wrong and must be told about it. There is a great fear of being critical towards the teachers. In our case, for example, it was necessary to guide the teacher to avoid handing out marks with such frequency.

Example 4

An educational psychologist painted himself running in a drawing. At work he had created a method by which he was always available to immediately answer any request by a child or a faculty member.

This man had emigrated to Israel many years ago from an English-speaking country, with the wish of "saving the state of Israel". All those years he has worked in a social context, and even now he works at a school for an underprivileged community. At school he is personally involved in any event of violence, breaking it up and separating the fighting children even with his own body. During breaks he often sits in the faculty room, in case any of the teachers need him suddenly. The rest of the break time he spends in the playground, sitting on a bench and holding talks with the children. His tactic is one of "putting out fires". He does not coach the system to deal with violence on its own. When problems recur, he deals with them himself. During the work with the group, his wish to belong, to be a part of the Israeli society, was exposed. His ability to be available at any moment and solve any problem endows him with the feeling of belonging. He arrives at school each morning with a schedule of meetings, but he never keeps those prearranged meetings. There are always some urgent problems that require his immediate intervention. He has no yearly work programme, and since he is always answering immediate needs, he finds himself running about constantly.

In the discussion, we brought up the possibility that he, perhaps with some other school staff members, constitutes the aspect of concretization for the system. This is the aspect that has no space for discussing problems in a more abstract way, or for finding deeper solutions. He represents that method of the system that deals with the symptoms, but does not investigate the problem's roots.

The assistance he provides on the issue of violence is a temporary and local one, without the insight that enables the system to deal with violence more effectively. In the area of violence, the system remains static, on the same spot, and has to "invent the wheel" time and again. Through a dream he brought to the group, a new possibility was created for looking at the system differently:

I am shown an apartment under construction, and I decide to buy it. This is going to be a beautiful and tidy place. I am shown on the draft plans a gadget called "Ingo". It is a pipe system that, if a baby falls in, it is not lost, it can be found. When the apartment is ready I'm going to live there but the plan has been spoiled. The apartment is not as beautiful as it was in the drafts. There is a strange family there, and a door leading to another apartment. All these were not in the drafts.

The dream brought him face to face with distress, with his home being invaded. Also, there is a wide gap between what he planned and the realization of his plans. The babies who fall through the pipes and are found again were interpreted by us as the beginnings of new things that constantly fall through and he finds himself having to restart all over again. The pipe system absorbs the ideas with which he had started to work, and, instead of development, he finds himself going around in circles.

The dream and its processing through the discussion with the group made it possible to separate himself from the aspect of concretization, and to begin working with a plan that includes limits and may assist the system to discover powers within itself. We helped him release himself from the role of the "saviour" and enter a role with limits and order, so that he could coach the system into dealing with the causes for the disease and separate itself from the pattern of "putting out fires".

Discussion

This experience, which I went through for six months, brought about a serious dilemma for me. I was invited to the project due to my work on social and political violence, a subject on which I had published several articles. But the violence of children at school was a subject I was not familiar with, other than through the media, since the subject has become a major issue world-wide.

The following thoughts constitute for me some questions that have not yet been answered.

• The psychoanalytic method of dealing with organizations allowed me to investigate at the workshop the complex occurrences that take place at the encounter between the inner world of the role holders and the external reality at school. Dreams, events, and pictures make it possible to penetrate the processes that occur when the internal and external collide.

• Every person has an individual interpretation of his or her role, which is influenced by his or her internal world. However, the system is the element that dictates the possibilities for the individual to express him/herself, as well as the limits of this expression. The systems with which we have dealt were viewed by us as full of anxiety, and even helplessness. All violent phenomena are, in my view (Biran, 1998) and in Bion's language, "beta-type elements" that did not undergo transformation into "alpha-type elements". It means that they have remained in crude form, with no way of expression through feelings, dialogue, metaphors, and so on (Bion, 1962). The systems do not know how to make this transformation possible. In fact, they react with alarm, with the wish to get rid of the phenomenon or with the expectation for a magical solution and deliverance.

• The anxiety-filled system pushes its psychological-consultant role-holders to "give answers", "be a saviour", "be the cop", and so on. It pushes them into doing, thus blocking the possibility for creating a space for investigating and thinking. Bain (1998) explains that organizational awareness and organizational learning will happen only in some conditions. The essential conditions are commitment and involvement of the management and interdependence among three dimensions: individual, group, and organization. These variables create an organizational container that is crucial for organizational growth. In the workshop outlined in this chapter, I have had difficulty in assimilating the learning into the schools because of the lack of these conditions. The paradox lies in the fact that the system stops only when a catastrophe occurs. In the lulls between the outbursts, the system does not really prepare itself for the next wave. The consultant is required to think when there is no time to think, and the management refuses to think together with him over systematic solutions while it is still possible to do so.

Can the expansion of consciousness of the role holders create any change? Can a role holder make a whole system think and function differently? I am full of doubts on this matter. The external reality contains powers much greater than the professional's insight, and they are the ones that threaten to swallow him or her up or castrate his or her potential.

Through the process at the workshop, I was able to identify the following forces:

1. The context in which the children live is full of social violence. The media is saturated by it, and, in such an environment, paradoxi-

cally violence becomes more and more legitimate and a part of everyday life. Can the professional role holder challenge such a massive social context? The school is not an isolated island, being a part of a larger system. A violent social environment also vibrates inside the playground.

2. Concepts of the education system such as authority, punishment, hierarchy, and so on have undergone substantial changes. Authority is not as clear as it used to be in the past. The education profession has gradually become more feminine. School principals are women who are trying to adopt more pluralistic and open systems of values. The distance between teacher and pupil has become much smaller. The punishment system has become less menacing. Parents are constantly involved in school life and complain of the teachers daily. Teachers feel that their hands are tied, literally, due to their inability to exert punishments, and they feel abused by the children, who are backed by their parents.

The social change in the system of values, and the transfer from a severe hierarchical system to an open and more democratic one, are favourable changes. But they create a problem once they are imposed on communities that are not yet ready for these changes—communities in distress who lack the tools for internalizing the change are in need of clear limits, clear hierarchy, and a more substantial generational gap. Such communities feel safer with a more traditional structure. They are not ready yet to internalize an open educational system. Zagier Roberts (1994) writes that such a process of change has an impact on the boundaries between subsystems within the organization and also on the boundaries between the institution and its external environment. The boundaries turned out to be vague and, as a result, the primary task also blurred. For the organization to be effective again, it has to redefine its boundaries and its primary task very clearly.

Perhaps these communities are in need of an external framework to direct them. They should have guidance, as they are not mature enough to do it for themselves. Returning to systems with clearer regulations and limits is not suggested here as the ultimate solution, but as food for thought. In the dialectics between rigidity and openness, perhaps a new kind of synthesis is required today. This could be a structure that will have freedom but will operate inside clear frameworks.

Conclusions

We discovered that different schools use different defence mechanisms against violence. These defences are in fact inefficient, and they include encapsulation, dramatization, sterilization, and concretization. We also found five common denominators among all schools. These common denominators arise because institutions that deal with the same primary task and belong to the same organizational and cultural area behave in a similar way. Bain (1998) coined the concept of "system domain" and argues that "part of the difficulty in modifying the social defences within a particular institution is because they are an expression of system domain fabric and are not 'stand alone' institutions".

The five common denominators are:

1. All systems react to violence with panic and confusion. Administration and staff find themselves in distress and shock when facing violent outbursts from children. As a result of the panic, the different systems try to bypass the problem or to cover it up.

2. All the systems cope with the symptom, but not with the unconscious processes that cause it.

3. All the systems regard the problem as a local one, not taking into consideration the reciprocal relationship among different parts of the system.

4. In all systems there is no integrative plan that includes staff meetings and brain-storming. The professional person is sent alone into the lion's den to bring solutions.

5. Dilemmas that arose during the workshop leave open the questions on issues such as authority, limits, or hierarchy. The hypothesis is that children will feel more protected, even from their own violence, in a system that contains them and keeps them within clear laws and frameworks. At the moment, the term "authority" remains vague and the term "limit" remains unclear in all these school systems.

CHAPTER EIGHT

Childreamatrix: dreaming with preschool children— or, bootlegging dreams into the school years

Ron Balamuth

The impetus for starting a social dreaming matrix with children came after participating in a social dreaming matrix led by Gordon Lawrence. I could not have anticipated how radically my understanding of dreams and dreaming would change. Over years of listening and telling dreams with patients and colleagues, psychoanalysts accumulate many procedural assumptions. I entered the matrix believing that dreams are very much a personal creation, an individual idiom, and an expression of a person's essential self, a bit like a psychic fingerprint. For me, it crystallizes the dreamer's preoccupations, the conscious and unconscious life into a summary image or narrative. While I was attracted to Jung's formulations about the collective unconscious and its expression in humans' dreams and waking life, I could not find immediate application to those notions in my clinical work. The next three days of sharing dreams with my colleagues in the matrix were like a gradual process of relaxing the grasp of the old analytic convictions about dreams. Most supportive of this process of surrendering and letting go was the gradual appreciation of the life of the matrix, a grouping that becomes like a sensitive and intelligent instrument of thinking and finding connections. The difference between interpreting dreams and associating to dreams may appear subtle on the page, but in the dream matrix it made all the difference for me and for the other analysts and therapists. There was no need to be more clever than the dreams nor than the dreamer. As we gradually let go of our habitual analytic algorithms, a new appreciation of the aesthetic coherence of the matrix was shared, leading to feelings of joy in discovering new meanings.

I spend many hours in my practice working with young children and their families. I conceive of my clinical role as an attempt to restore the capacity of parents and children to be creative and imaginative together. That is especially true with preschoolers on the cusp of entering school. This is an important dialectic juncture for the young child. I feel that the work of the early childhood teacher and child analyst needs to be at times subversive. How much of the child's unique way of being in the world through his or her senses, experience, and actions will he or she need to sacrifice to become part of the group, part of the culture? The child is not a reluctant participant in the process. On the contrary, in their desire to "grow up", children are often even more eager than their parents and teachers to translate their analogue world into the digital and binary world of the adult. I often think about my role as an attempt to undermine the oppressive squeezing-out of creativity and playfulness that the transition into the unyielding, constricting world of school may entail for children and parents. As one 5-year-old boy told me when I asked him about what he thought about his transition into first grade, "I have to play all the time this summer and use all the toys from when I was little. Next year is going to be all work!"

I think about dreams sometimes like Trojan horses. If we can only fill them with the world of imaginings, flights of fantasy, and the spirit of curiosity and surprise, we may sneak them past the guards at the gates, into the school years. There they can live and serve as antidotes to the "bookish" form of knowing that kids cling to in the early years of school. My hope is that like the proverbial pea under the princess's many-layered mattress, the dreamatrix will continue to disturb the sleep and preserve the link to the child's earlier holistic way of being and learning.

My interest in dreams as a transitional phenomenon between objective and subjective reality goes way back to my own childhood. From when I can remember myself, I was always interested in "middles", "hybrids", Minotaurs, sphinx, and the like. I was passionate about the elusive point, equidistant from each polarity, that is neither hot nor cold. I recall, as a young child, hours spent by the light switch searching for that intangible and, for me, magical place that is neither light nor dark but something altogether different. Just like the wardrobe in C. S. Lewis's *The Lion the Witch and the Wardrobe*, or the more recent platform number 9¾ in J. K. Rawlins's *Harry Potter* stories, that space opens into a world of magic.

Winnicott's (1951) description of transitional objects and transitional phenomena is a natural bridge connecting "reality" and "fantasy", in an amalgam called dream.

> The transitional object and transitional phenomena start each human being off with what will always be important for them, i.e. a neutral area of experience which will not be challenged. *Of the transitional object it can be said that it is a matter of agreement between us and the baby that we will never ask the question "Did you conceive of this or was it presented to you from without?" The important point is that no decision on this is expected. The question is not to be formulated.* [Winnicott, 1951, pp. 239–240, emphasis in original]

Preschool children are still interested in origins. As Freud so accurately captures in his classic paper "On the Sexual Theories of Children" (1908c), the child is a persistent seeker. Thus, the question "where do dreams come from?" is right there on the tip of the child's inquisitive mind. In his recent book Paul Lippmann (2000) recalls when his 5-year-old daughter asked him, "where do dreams come from?" and she answered her own question: "She pointed to her eyelids, but than said, 'I think sometimes they come in the window'" (p. 119). Lippmann's daughter is not particularly distracted by apparent contradictions. She allows dreams to come from the inside and the outside, from that space in which the "question is not to be formulated", to use Winnicott's words.

Freud has reclaimed parapraxes, hysteric symptoms, and dreams as meaningful phenomena, as originating in the individual's psyche and its conflicts. The downside of this discovery is that

> The modern citizen seems somewhat shy and hesitant in elation to dreams. The knowledge that dreams come from within seems to increase one's alienation from them. With personal authorship comes increased personal responsibility and occasional guiltiness or even shame whether in the dream's images or in interpretation. A more imaginative, mystical, religious point of view about the origins of dreams may have permitted a greater feeling of familiarity and closeness with one's own nightly mental produc-

tions, as though one could feel closer with less personal ownership. [Lippmann, 2000, pp. 124–125]

Young children may be relatively free of these constraints. It is conceivable that young children are immersed in a social dreaming matrix. They make links and find connections to their dreams and to their thoughts so long as the adults provide a safe container for such a process. The childreamatrix[1] described in this chapter is potentially such a vessel for this process. As an extension to Winnicott's dictum that "there is no such thing as a baby" alone as there is always a caregiver, it was assumed that the caregiver's dreams may further illuminate and add meanings to the childreamatrix. The teachers' dreams were also included as part of the matrix.

Altogether the matrix included thirty-nine dreams, thirty-two offered by the children during our matrix sessions and seven offered by the schoolteachers during the teachers' matrix. In addition, two dreams were offered informally and spontaneously by teachers in between sessions in the course of discussing the children's matrixes.

The children were enthusiastic participants in the matrix. The classroom teachers commented on how differently the children seemed to respond during the dream matrix compared to a regular meeting. According to one of the teachers, those children who usually participated the least were very active and spoke about their dreams with great authority. The usual leaders in the group, and those who regularly take most "airtime", were much less prominent.

It seemed that the dreamatrix had a levelling effect of sorts such that most children felt equally authorized and adept in sharing their dreams. The usual patterns of participation, determined often by popularity and "expertise", were not as prominent.

Methodology

Social dreaming as a methodology developed by Gordon Lawrence (1998c) is a relatively recent contribution. Although its roots go back thousands of years, in its current incarnation it has not yet been extended to children. The child dream matrix as described here is similar in some ways to an adult dreaming matrix, yet significantly transformed to accommodate the young participants.

Setting

The childreamatrix was conducted in an independent preschool in which the author has been consulting for the past ten years. This is a progressive school in which the children's interests and questions drive the curriculum. The dreamatrix was integrated as part of the children's study of the self. Part of the study included the study of bodies and the differences between people in terms of gender, skin colour, height, weight, and so forth. The study of dreams was presented as another aspect of the study of how they were similar yet different from each other. This idea was introduced by pointing out to the children that we all have dreams every night, yet no two people here have the exact same dream. My presence in the classroom did not evoke much reaction. The children were used to the classroom visitors, and most of the children had met me previously during my consultations with the teachers.

Groups

There were two groups. The first group included the 5-year-old children and their three classroom teachers. The second group consisted of all teachers, without the children; the teachers were invited to listen to the children's dreams, to associate to them, and to offer their own dreams. While not a formal social dreaming matrix, it was designed to allow the teachers to have a dialogue with the children's dreams.

Structure of sessions

There were a number of modifications from the adult social dreaming matrix to accommodate the difference in age and in attention span. The sessions were kept to forty-five minutes and were conducted in the children's regular setting—namely, their class meeting. This created a familiar and safe environment for the participants in which the host and the topic of discussion were the only unknowns. The children sat in a circle on the rug and basically spoke when they had a dream or an association to share. The three classroom teachers were present and were quite enthusiastic about the process. At various times they were helpful in supporting children who appeared anxious in response to their own or other children's dreams.

Getting started

Anticipating that the children may feel uncomfortable and possibly inhibited in telling their dreams, I was prepared to offer a dream of my own to start us off. I shared a dream from the night before the first matrix, which felt like an encapsulated image of the childreamatrix and how I saw my initial role as a host.

Here is the dream with which I opened the matrix:

> *I am in an aeroplane, an old fashioned aeroplane, which has only one aisle in the middle rather than the usual two. The pilot announces that there is some interesting view on the left that can be viewed through the left side windows. Everyone is rushing to the left side windows to take a look. I am nervously aware that I should not leave my seat on the right side of the plane lest the plane lose its balance. I have to counterbalance and keep the plane flying horizontally.*

I think that this dream is very much a literal representation of my feelings on taking the first childreamatrix. Will it be able to take off? Will we be able to balance the fascination with the left window of external landscapes (left-brain language and symbols) and allow for a look inwards, into the more obscure dream life?

I felt that sharing this dream at the beginning could be tricky. On the one hand, it may bias the content and the process of the group. On the other hand, it set the tone for sharing dreams as a non-authoritarian, open-ended, and democratic process. In addition this modification was supported by developmental considerations. Young children are better observers of others' subjective states of mind than of their own. By offering them my dream to discuss first, this permitted them to get into a mode of thinking about their own thinking and dreams (Baron-Cohen, 1999). It will be interesting to discover how future childreamatrixes that start without the host offering a dream vary from this one.

The development of this childreamatrix can be seen from a dream I shared in the final session:

> *I stroll in what appears like a botanical garden looking at the beautiful flowers. Suddenly I feel a bumble-bee buzzing by and suddenly getting into my right ear. It feels fuzzy and soft, tight and quite pleasant. At the same time I am frozen with fear. I am immobilized by fear that the bee might sting me.*

My dream on the night before the last matrix seemed directly in dialogue with the tenth dream of the matrix offered by K., a girl, during the first session:

> K. *"I was walking alone near a couple of flowers, until I saw a bee, I did not know what to do, I ran away, and the bee kept on following, and following and following, until I got into my home and then a bee got into my home too. And then I ran under my bed, and the bee was following me too, and then it followed me and followed me, followed me, until I was on the roof of my building, of the high rise, and then I was so scared I had to jump off the building."*

These two dreams may illustrate the distance we travelled from initially feeling haunted and persecuted by the dreams to possibly holding them and allowing ourselves to enjoy their softness. My dream, of the bumble-bee in my right ear resonated with the need to keep the childreamatrix/aeroplane from rolling to the verbal left. The right ear, now with only muffled access to incoming sounds, is inward directed. Our redirecting the attention inwards carries its own risks and satisfactions. One of the boys in the group offered this observation, speaking directly to the host: "Once there was a bee on my shoulder. I did not know if it will sting me but it did not. Bees are attracted to people, they like people. If one gets in your ear, just cry help!"

The use of art

While young children are in the process of developing their verbal expressive capacities, they are much more capable of *showing* what they have in mind rather than telling it in words. Therefore, it seemed appropriate to offer to the children an opportunity to use non-verbal means of representing their dreams. Following the sessions, the children were offered a choice of art materials such as paint, markers, collage materials, and so on. The children continued to discuss their dreams while engaged in their artwork, and for many of them the use of art material allowed for a fuller and more accurate depiction of the dreams. Soon after the second matrix the children became interested in "dream catchers", and they designed and made very elaborate ones, as described in the next section.

Children's dialogue about dreams

In parallel to the sharing of dreams, the children engaged in a kind of meta-discussion about the origin of dreams. This led to a dialogue about how to deal with bad dreams.

One of the children mentioned that he had a dream catcher (which his mother had brought home from her trip to the Southwest of America), a "device that protects you against bad dreams". Dream catchers became very popular, and as they designed their own catchers they discussed why they had constructed them in a certain way. They made them out of pipe cleaners, beads, paper, fishing lines, and feathers (see Figure 8.1).

Here are some excerpts from the discussion, starting with one of the scariest dreams in the third matrix:

> K. (girl): *I was walking on the street with my mom and dad, and this crazy cab ran into the sidewalk . . . and knocked me and mom and daddy over and dad was dead and mom said "no way! We are not taking this cab!"*

Another boy pulled up his dream catcher and demonstrated how he would use it if he had a similar dream:

> M. (boy): "Bad dreams catch on it, stick on it, and never come off. I think I need it around my brother's bed—he always has bad dreams."
>
> E. (girl): "It will catch the bad dreams."
>
> M.: "I hanged all three dream catchers in the same place so that if they come from different directions it would catch them all. . . . It did not work, the dreams came in through the holes."
>
> J. (teacher): "So did you have some bad dreams while the dream catchers were hanging?"
>
> M: "Yeah . . . *there was a monster who wanted to eat me, green, mean, and slimy. He was always in ponds. He ate fish and frogs. He was always wet. He was eating me as I was swimming in my hot tub 'cause I can't see anything when I swim in my hot tub.*"
>
> Host: "Is there anything you can do to make the dream catcher work better?"
>
> M: "yeah, you can fish him [the monster] with a fishing rod."

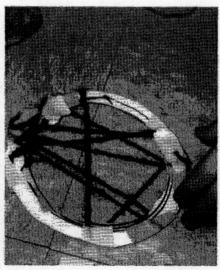

Figure 8.1.   Dream catchers

E. (teacher) (associating to a dream story she had heard of the Chippewa people): "*A grandmother watches over her grandchild's crib while the baby is sleeping. A spider weaves its web by the baby's crib. Someone finds the spider and is about to kill it but grandma saves the spider, and the spider in return promises to keep the bad dreams away in his web.*"

A. (girl): "I had a dream on Saturday. It was a day-dream. It was a dream about my tooth. *I touched my tooth and then it was bleeding . . . and I called my mummy and the tooth came out.* A dream during the day, with my eyes open."

Host: "I could sit here with my eyes open and still have a day-dream. I could dream about my day at the beach."

E. (girl) (referring to the host's dream about the bumble-bee from earlier this session): "Bumble-bees are kind of fuzzy, but they are not bad, they just help flowers, but when they are in the flower they don't want to be annoyed."

Host: "So what would be something to put on my dream to catch a bumble-bee dream?"

E. (girl): "Maybe a web."

A. (boy) : "Maybe make a small hole in the net so only flies can come in."

(Quite a few children suggested putting honey on it as bait.)

Teacher: "Anything a monster would like to find on a dream catcher?"

M. (boy): "Witches! Spiders!"

(Much excitement, with children making many suggestions.)

W. (girl): "A spider web will stop a bad dream"

Host: "Can they become good?"

Someone: "They can become yummy for a spider."

K. (girl): "I'll put a . . . I'll draw on paper something like a gold coin and put some real money so the bad dreams will take it and will turn better. . . . I will cook . . . a good dream-catcher concoction.?"

On losing and being lost: anxiety dreams of children

Nineteen of the dreams in the matrix depicted scenarios in which some danger was imminent or some frightening event was about to happen or was taking place. The danger present was most often either a loss of a caregiver or danger to one's person.

The situations described in the dreams below are those in which the children felt threatened by the loss of the attachment figure—that is, the caregiver. Attachment theory as developed by John Bowlby, Tom Main, and others has become the dominant frame of reference in assessing children's developing capacities to optimally regulate the tension between dependency and security needs and the pull for exploration and autonomy.

The sequence of anxiety dreams in the matrix offers a unique window into how the children narrate their attachment stories. That is, how accessible and effective are the caregivers in re-establishing safety. However, what is unique in the childreamatrix is that it goes beyond the assessment of an individual's security of attachment. As a group the dreams may tell us about the typical dream experience of 5-year-olds in our culture.

The following are some of these dreams in sequence (the numbers preceding each dream indicate the place that dream had in the sequence in which the dreams were offered):

2. A. (girl): "Two weeks ago I had this dream, kind of funny, like a nightmare. *Me and my mummy and dad were in the third bedroom in our apartment going around the house. . . . Two little mean old guys . . . mummy said do not get stung by that stinger and I held this thing back but there were two of them.* (What were you holding?): Well there were these two meannie guys in the house and mummy told me not to get stung by it, so I had to hold the stinger back. One had a stinger that looks like a toothpick. The other dream guy was short."

3. E. (boy): "Some people know this dream . . . it really is a spooky one. *I had a dream that me and my mom and dad were just coming home from a picnic outside . . . it was really a bad dream. . . .* Actually it was the wrong dream. I think some people know this dream. . . . *I had a dream that me and my mom and dad were in the third bedroom in my house trying to find a movie to watch 'cause all of us wanted to choose together, then an alien came in, and said I will take your mummy away and turn her into a squid, and I was really scared. And then a really bad. . . . A really bad. . . . It was this green thing, and it took people into space. Five aliens appeared. The aliens took my mummy away, they tried to take my daddy away but he was too strong to take my mummy away, instead they took my daddy away. That was actually the dream, five aliens appeared and there was a little alien dog . . . a bulldog, had really sharp teeth, really alien dog and had really bad powers. And he could turn anyone into a squid, and he took my mummy away. And turned her into a squid. And said tonight at midnight we will steal her and turn them both into squids.* Then I woke up and yelled 'Ahhh!' And then I called my mom."

11. K. (girl): *I was walking with my mom on the road where it says walk, and this big 79 bus goes down the road, and I was so scared I had to go on the top of a tunnel and to the top and then I was on the top of the tunnel and back on the road, and the bus came and almost ran me over, and I had to go on the sidewalk again, I put on these shoes that I could walk on tunnels, and they stepped on the tunnel and they would not come off, but they were not double-knotted, and I fell off and the*

shoes landed on another 79 bus, and I was riding on a 79 bus on the top of it. (Cheers.)

22. E. (girl): *"Me and mom and dad and sister were walking to the old house. I asked mom did you hear something? No. It was a wolf. A werewolf. The werewolf jumps through a little hole. He could go in, that hole went into our house. I went through the door . . . the werewolf jumped on me and licked me. It tasted me and then ate me. It was half man, half wolf."*

26. M. (boy): *"There was a spider web and I was afraid that the spider is gonna eat me. But I asked my mommy if she could save me and she did and she smacked it, Boom! Boom! Boom!"* (Laughter—what size was it?): The size of your big toe."

27. M. (same boy): *"My mummy was in a spider web it is a little like the first one and the spider wanted to eat my mummy but I was catching it. And the spider almost died but suddenly it turned back to life automatically and it ate my mummy . . .* that is a nightmare. And I when I woke up a caterpillar was on my neck." (Nervous laughter.)

A. (girl): "Was the caterpillar for real when you woke up?"

M.: "Yeah. . . . Yes . . . and it had three little babies on me."

31. K. (girl): *"I was walking on the street with my mom and dad and this crazy cab ran into the sidewalk . . . and knocked me and mom and daddy over and dad was dead and mom said "no way! We are not taking this cab!"*

Host: "So when you woke up did you check on mom and dad?"

K: "I ran all the way and snuggled up in the office chair and then I got my mummy and she snuggled with me and then I checked on my daddy and he was there."

A sense of fear and foreboding permeates these dreams. The parents, when represented in the dream, appear ineffectual, dismissive, and preoccupied. Is it possible to take the dreams at their face value, the "manifest" one? What can they tell us? Is it possible that the children's depiction of their parents as dismissive, preoccupied, as offering superficial reassurances, has a kernel of truth to it?

This, of course, is not an actual description of a particular parent. It is likely to be a composite of a parent as it appears to a 5-year-old who is about to enter school and leave his or her primary caregivers behind. It seems that the child experiences a growing disjunction between his perception of the world as possibly mysterious and uncharted and the parents' anachronistic way of seeing it which belongs to an earlier time in their relationships. The parent in the dream has no clue as to the nature of the dangers and the struggles that the child is about to encounter.

Consistent with the idea that the parents in these dreams have lost their capacity to evoke feelings of safety, the teachers seem to emerge as the new "rescuers", potentially the more effectual and protective figure:

> 5. J. (girl): "*I was going into a world that was made out of candy. And only bad guys were dentists.* (Laughter.) *There were weird guys with rotten teeth* (Why?): *Everybody tried licking the candy world. Then all the things turned back into vegetables, but nobody wanted vegetables because they never tried it . . . and they did try and then they threw up . . . and then the world turned again into candies, and the dentists came back. and then they came to school but the teacher* (points at classroom teacher) *poured sprinkles all over the floor so that the dentist won't come in. Then he slipped all over the floor and he crashed his head in a wall.*"

> 6. E.S. (girl): "I had a dream about the whole class, There were monkeys in my dream. It was last week. I will really get scared. . . . *There was a man who was really big and he could drive, who drove us in his car. He drove us really fast and then the monkey put his hands around our feet.* (Our feet?) Yes, the monkey would grab your feet. Yes everyone here was there in the dream. *He grabbed someone's feet but he got away. E.* [the classroom teacher] *said to him 'do not grab my feet because my feet are strong!' so he got away.*"

Beyond the unsafe situations of immediate external danger that are depicted in these dreams, I believe that the children are wondering about the safety of coming so close to their own dreams. Thus, it may not be surprising that the two children whose dreams depicted the teacher as a rescuer from the bad dentist and from the grabby monkey singled out their lead teacher as the rescuer. They probably recognized her authority and interest in the dream world that we were investigating.

Losing a child: teachers' dreams

There was an uncanny resonance between the children's dreams of being lost, kidnapped, and hurt and the dreams of two of the teachers.

A.: *"I lost my child, my son, and I was mortified and terribly ashamed. He was going to school here in John's classroom. I cannot ask John if he saw him, so I casually ask him how my son was doing that day in school. John reports that he is just great and doing well at drawing, playing etc. etc. From his response I gather that my son is not lost and I feel relieved. I have to keep my relief hidden as well."*

C: *"I am sitting with parents at a parent–teacher conference discussing their child. I haven't got the faintest idea who their child is. Of course, I cannot ask them who he is, so I tell the parents that he is doing just great, he had improved a lot since last year. He likes such and thus arts and stories etc. Inside I am wondering who he is, without giving away that I do not know who he is. I am nervous about how long I can keep it up and what to do if they ask me specific questions about him."*

The theme of losing children and the humiliation and guilt that is evoked is prevalent in both dreams. As the first teacher said after telling the dream: "As a teacher I should be the last one to lose my own child. I could not tell John how concerned I was about losing my son, much less to show relief when I realized he was safe."

Juxtaposing the teacher's dreams offers a counterpoint that emphasizes the futility in covering up this absence. The parent who conceals her "losing her child" in the first dream is falsely reassured by a teacher who has no idea who her child really is. It seems that the matrix contains both sides of the hidden troubling secret that parents (teachers) and children have lost each other. They act as if they had not, and try to cover the alienation that they feel, but the proof is irrefutably there in the matrix.

Double split: adult/child–dream/reality

In the context of a social dreaming matrix, taken together these dreams offer a glimpse into the disquieting disjunction between children and adults. It parallels the wedge that is driven into the child psyche as the child enters school age between an innate, more fluid mode of experiencing and a binary, logical and dualistic right/wrong mode. The dreams about a loss, a loss of a child, a loss of a parent—could they be an allusion to a loss of the direct way of living one's own experience? Do the children in the dreams stand in for the lost dreams of our childhood? Perhaps these dreams, arising from each side of the gulf between the adult and child mind convey what Ernest Schachtel (1959) so eloquently described. He asks us all why we adults are so severed from our first years of life? How and where have we lost the capacity for direct experiencing?

> No Columbus, no Marco Polo has ever seen stranger and more fascinating and thoroughly absorbing sights than the child that learns to perceive, to taste, to smell, to touch, to hear and see and to use his body, his senses, and his mind. No wonder that the child shows an insatiable curiosity. [Schachtel, 1959, p. 292]

Schachtel suspects that the child's entry into school is implicated in this loss:

> It is chiefly during the period of early childhood that the quality of the world around him changes for the growing child from a place where everything is new and to be explored—to be tasted smelled, touched and handled, wondered about and marvelled at—to a place where everything either has received a name and a label or is potentially capable of being "explained" by such label, a process which will be pursued systematically in school. [p. 293]

How has the child's insatiable curiosity vanished is the question that Adam Phillips (1998) asks:

> The child's profundity, in Freud's view, was in the quality of its curiosity. When he refers to children who have been told the facts of life but go on believing their own sexual theories, who "go on worshipping their own idols in secret," he is paying tribute to the child as someone unseduced by reality, unimpressed by other people's truths. [1998, p. 11]

The child's curiosity is his passion:

> They weren't options—the child was not casting around for a hobby, or in some supermarket, spoiled for choice—they were urgencies. And what the child's curiosity highlighted was the child's need to know and the impossibility of his being satisfied. [p. 11]

Phillips seems to agree with Schachtel's observations regarding the effect of school : "Education, Freud implies, teaches the child either to lose interest in what matters most to her or to compromise that interest. Interest has to have something added to it, called education, to make it acceptable" (Phillips, 1998, p. 21). Thus, the function of culture is to kill curiosity, most often through subtle diversion, distraction, or dispatching.

Teacher's dream matrix: what is "real"?

An echo of these longings for a direct way of experiencing was evident in the teachers' dreams that they offered in a group after listening to the children's dreams. They seem to recall with nostalgia a time when, as children, they were undistracted by what others thought was "reality".

33. N. (female teacher): "I had a dream that I thought was a real thing as a child, that happened but my mother said that it never happened. So I wonder was that a dream. *I remember that it was this place I was going into, in this way, going to that room.* I remember the details of this room, but my mom and sister said we have never been to that room, that was never a place we went to, and I said it was real to me, so I think for a minute it was a dream I had."

34. Ni. (female teacher): "I actually do not know if I was sleepwalking or whether I was dreaming that *I was just in this other place. I walked from my bedroom to the living room. And I totally . . . I . . . just remember walking to different areas in the apartment and then not being able to find my bed again. And really wanting water really, really, really badly. . . . And seeing certain things along the way . . . visually. . . . Visual characters, like dinosaurs and things.* But I wondered whether I did actually leave my bed and go into all of these places or if I was sleeping."

35. R. (Host): "I had a recurring dream *that I was not my parents biological child but instead adopted.* My mother, when she found out, tried her best to reassure me that she really was my biological mother. She took out pictures of herself when she was preg-

nant and told me how happy she was when she carried me. I recall the immense relief and gratitude I felt after that for at least a short while. Not much later I was shattered by the thought that I still did not have any positive proof that it was *me* whom she carried in that photograph—it must have been a different child."

36. N. (female teacher): "I just thought about a dream I had in childhood, in my grandmother's house. *My brother and I shared a room in there, and there was a hallway in that house, in that old house, that went into grandma's bedroom. I remember that closet from which sometime a clown figure came out when I stood over the bed.* I was so scared that I told my brother and he said he had the same dream and that made it even more real for me, so (laughter) . . . so to this day . . . I should go back to my brother and ask him if it was really the same dream or he was just teasing me. I remember that there was a very serious talk about this clown coming out of the closet."

37. J. (female teacher): "I had a dream two weeks ago, which I am still wondering about. *A woman called me on the phone and said she was the secretary of Mr Heinz who I am still wondering if I ever knew, and that he just tested positive for HIV and they thought I should know so I could get tested, and I am still wondering if I ever knew who is that man.*"

39. C. (female teacher): I had such a vivid dream that seemed so real to me for years that only after speaking to my mother who told me that it never happened did I realize it was a dream. My big brother told me it was a dream. *I was in my old house, my brother called me on Christmas Eve in the middle of the night to the window and pointed out and said, Look! Look! You see Santa Claus with his sled, and I looked and said no I cannot see it and he said, Look ! Look! See the red sled and the reindeer! And I was, like, I cannot see anything, so he said, well you are not getting any presents for Christmas.* (Laughter.) I still say to my brother that he was so mean, although he says it never happened.

On listening to the children's dreams, we were all touched by their conviction that their dreams were substantial and deserved close listening. They attempted to reach some consensus as to what was "real" and what was a "dream". One example was the discussion of M.'s spider dream, which was described earlier. The fact that M. found baby caterpillars on his neck on waking up was of great significance. It was the end of the session, but they had to resolve the question of whether the caterpillars were real or "only" in his head. The discussion was resolved when M. mentioned casually that earlier that day his silkworms escaped from their insect box. Most of the children appeared relieved by finally being able to firmly locate the spider of the dream in M.'s "head" and the silkworms in the "real" insect box from which they apparently escaped. Unexpectedly, a few children seemed quite disappointed. The possibility that the spider of the dream could have been transported to the "real" world, just like a fuzzy bumble-bee in the ear, seemed magical, frightening, and possibly even comforting. It is difficult to trade-in magic for the unbendable laws of physics in one clean swoop.

There is a familiar dismissive adult refrain accompanying the adults' and the children's dreams, it goes something like, "It is only a dream" or "It is only in your head." It is a great source of comfort for children to find out that their scariest fantasies are not imminent. It also drives dreams away from children's attention and interest. It is quite remarkable how rapidly do young children absorb this Westernized attitude towards their own dream life.[2] Our culture seems to be preoccupied with binaries such as real–dream, inside–outside, adult–child to the exclusion of many other possible organizing categories. Contrast this attitude to dreams with the attitude of the Senoi tribe in the Malay Peninsula (quoted by Lawrence, 1998c):

> As children recount their dreams to an elder, they are transformed in their meaning. The child's common anxiety-dream of falling, for instance, is responded to by the adult saying that it is a wonderful dream and asking what was discovered on falling. If the child says that he or she awoke before falling, it is pointed out that every dream has a purpose and that the child should relax in the dream because it is the quickest way to get in touch with the powers of the spirit world. In time, this falling dream is changed for the child from an anxiety-making one into the excitement of the joy of flying. [Lawrence, 1998c, p. 38]

In the Senoi culture, it seems, referring to an experience as a "dream" does not necessarily bracket it as a less significant form of psychic life.

The future of the childreamatrix

This study bears some kinship to Richard Lewis's 1982 study of creativity and imagination with school-aged children. He met with children aged between 7 and 12 years over a period of a few months to discussed dreams:

> Perhaps, part of my desire to explore "dreaming" with children came out of my reaction to the kind of rigid thought processes impressed upon children through most of their schooling life. Factual ideas, the classification of concepts as right or wrong, sterility of feeling and perception were what children, for the most part, experienced in school. It seemed to me a fascinating challenge to make "dreaming" then, in the broadest sense of the process, a legitimate way for children to move through learning and into the equally important realm of imaginative expression. [Lewis, 1982, p. 47]

I can only agree with Lewis's hopes for the children who became wonderfully free and creative in the process of sharing their dreams with him. Lewis's experiment is, however, embedded in the psychology of the individual. His hope was for the children to use the dreams as "raw materials for the shaping of their own imaginative and artistic visions" (p. 50). Lewis is careful to stay away from interpretation and analysis, and the dreams are allowed to speak for themselves, giving them the respect that they deserve without offering a translation. Like the childreamatrix, he is not interested in the group.

The focus of this chapter has been to explore the potential of the social dreaming matrix in groups of children to develop as an instrument of more integrated knowledge. I believe that the childreamatrix can transcend the individual and will find its place among other emerging applications of the social dreaming matrix. As a culture and as a society we ought to listen to our children's dreams. They may tell us something about our culture and our society that can only be discovered in a listening and associating matrix.

NOTES

1. The neologism "childreamatrix" was coined by Dr E. Martin Walker.
2. A fuller discussion of the Native-American tradition about dream catchers is beyond the scope of this paper. However, in my study of dream catchers there

seems to emerge two different ways in which Native Americans conceive of their function. According to the Lakota tradition "When Iktomi finished speaking, he gave the elder the web and said: 'The web (dream catcher) is a perfect circle with a hole in the center. Use the web to help your people reach their goals, making good use of their ideas, dreams and visions. If you believe in the great spirit, the web will catch your good ideas and the bad ones will go through the hole'" <http://web.onramp.ca/rivernen/legend_2.htm>.

On the other hand the Ojibwe have the opposite ideas about the dream catcher: "The dream catcher will filter out all the bad bawedjigewin [dreams] and allow only the good thoughts to enter into our minds when we are just abinooji [asleep]. You will see a small hole in the center of each dream catcher where those good bawadjige may come through. With the first rays of sunlight, the bad dreams would perish" <http://web.onramp.ca/rivernen/legend_2.htm>. It seems to me dubious that authentic Native American culture, with it enormous interest and importance placed on dreaming will choose to differentiate and express such a strong preference for "good" over "bad" dreams. It appears that in the translation of the myths and the concept of dream catchers a Westernized good–bad binary began to dominate the authentic myth. The children in the matrix were arriving at strikingly similar notions as in the now "Westernized" myths about how the dream catchers may function.

3. According to Klein's *Comprehensive Etymological Dictionary of the English Language* (2000), "dream" is related to the Teutonic *"drauma"*, which literally means "deception, illusion, phantom", and on to "phantom, ghost", "to deceive", "to lie". The etymology captures our Westernized suspicious attitude towards dreams.

CHAPTER NINE

Deep calls unto deep: can we experience the transcendent infinite?

Thomas A. Michael

Deep calls to deep in the roar of your cataracts, and all your waves, all your breakers sweep over me.

Revised English Bible, Psalms, 42:6

And the earth was without form and void, and darkness was upon the face of the deep.

Revised Standard Version, Genesis, 1:2

This chapter is based on a social dreaming matrix I conduct in a main-line Protestant church with which I am associated. It is a congregation of fewer than 150 members, located in an upper-middle-class suburban neighbourhood. The social dreaming matrix was scheduled for three weekly sessions as a part of an adult education forum series.

The purpose of the matrix was to seek for new insight into the direction the congregation should follow. There has been a long-term decline in membership, and there is concern for its future. It is a lively fellowship with excellent programs, but attempts to reach out for new members have not been encouraging. It seemed clear that we needed to find new approaches to mission. Accordingly, I proposed that we institute social dreaming as a possible way to discover some new directions. This was inspired by Gordon Lawrence's idea that there is emerging a politics of revelation to replace a politics of salvation (Lawrence, 2000a, pp. 165ff.).

Lawrence suggests that a politics of salvation is characterized by the belief that for all difficulties there is a solution that transcends the skill or experience of those needing help, and this can be supplied by a higher power in the case of religious issues or, in other cases, by expert—therapists, physicians, consultants—who possess knowledge that can help them "cure" or solve the problem presented by the client. The complications of modern life and the rapid rate of change render such a model obsolete. Everyone, not just the sufferer or client, is in need of new knowledge. This requires a politics of revelation in which expert and supplicant must collaborate to discern new paths of action.

Such an approach could present difficulties in a Christian community, since it is their belief that the revelation from God has been completed in the Bible and in the life, death, and resurrection of Christ. The fact that the Christian message has been greatly changed over time is usually attributed to new understanding of the revelation rather than to new truths being revealed. The members of our congregation are mostly theologically liberal, so this issue was never raised.

The matrix

Fifteen people attended the first session. A short introduction to social dreaming was given, in which it was said that a social dream is one that a person is willing to report, even though it may be a dream that could be used privately as well. The only requirement for attendance is that the participant be available for thinking. Anyone should feel free to make associations to the dreams of others, to report his or her own dream as a response to a dream, or to make an interpretation. My role was to listen and to try to discern themes, and the members were encouraged to do the same. We would spend time after the matrix discussing what we had discovered.

The members presented dreams in which the dreamers were engaged in activities for which they were unprepared or which called upon them to do tasks that required them to do things in the correct sequence. In one, the dreamer *was under attack by aliens and she was responsible to save herself, her family, and neighbours by making a series of decisions in the correct sequence lest someone die.* Another dreamed of *driving to church in a "rickety" car, going into the church in shabby clothing, and being in a dilemma since she was to be in a committee meeting at the same time as the worship service.* Others reported dreams where they were not dressed or prepared or where they had forgotten to invite important people and prepare key things. One dream involved *a family whose son was an Eagle Scout and their daughter and he could not figure out what they or the parents were doing.*

There were two dreams in which a deceased parent or grandparent appeared: in one case, *the mother assures the dreamer that she is all right,* while in another dream *a grandfather, who was not remembered as a nice person, cries out, "Help me! Help me,"* and then her father told the dreamer something that she could not quite hear. One participant reported a recurring dream in which *he was in a wooded area with a fast moving stream. He rode on a dolphin in the stream and woke up feeling good.*

The themes that were identified were that we were not able to do things in the correct sequence, did not know how to get the right people here, and were not sure we were being open to others, without hidden motivation. One participant suggested that maybe "we accept people for who they are and that is enough". One member summed up the meeting by saying: "This is my view of this church—we do not know what the Father is saying to us and as a group we cannot answer that question."

In my experience social dreaming matrices often begin this way. There are usually several who start by relating recurring dreams from their past. Then the theme arises of being unsure of what or who should be present and which dreams should be related. These questions appear to be about the matrix itself. The participants seem to be establishing the norms. What was true of the church is also true of the matrix. The matrix is being tested to determine how much of the dreaming experience of its participants can be contained and what the subject of the matrix should be.

That was important in this particular case. Our matrix was unique in that all of the participants had known one another for a long time (some as life-long members of the congregation). They had worshipped and worked together on committees, engaged in Bible study, sung in the choir, taught one another's children in Sunday school, and interacted socially. What they had never done was to tell one another their dreams.

A second meeting began with an extended dream:

The dream began in a neighbour's home with nine bedrooms, but then they walked through walls and were in the back of a huge church with nothing down in front. He decided to go down front and sat by a woman with a bag; he bumped her and she was angry, then down the aisle there were trucks coming towards the front . . . he walked in front of the trucks and out into the street. He discovered that his wallet was lost, and when he went back into the church he was arrested and found himself in prison, clad in blue prison overalls. He was ordered to clean the fingernails of a black prisoner who was due to be executed. He found his wallet and there was a cigarette in it that he used to bribe a guard and gain release. He encountered his wife on a big horse. She stopped and he said, "You are back into the swing of things." She wanted to get a Mustang automobile at a Ford agency, but they were in the basement. She took the keys but the stairs disappeared so she went up a freight elevator. The dreamer attempted to follow but had to clamber over boards to another level where he found his wife cleaning chickens telling him that they had put her to work, so he started cleaning chickens, too. In the laughter that followed, the pastor remarked: "That sounds like a description of the life of the church."

More dreams followed:

—A dreamer was leaving a meeting where there were people on the way home. A young man wanted to go with her. He was carrying a bag, but it was not clear whether it contained a bottle of wine or a baguette. He was a nice young man but it was inappropriate, and when they got to a certain place the police were stopping cars, and though she was sure they would stop her they did not and she wondered about the young man. She wondered whether the bag contained communion elements.

—A dreamer finished reading a mystery novel and was then in a social situation with the villain and was surprised to find that he was a pleasant person.

Others dreamed of being on ladders trying to jump from one to another, with a hand on one and a foot on the other.

These dreams appeared to be a continuation of questions about the matrix itself. We were aware that we were being called upon to serve or help others—prisoners, minorities, strange young men—and to prepare food. It appeared that the dreams began to be about the future of the congregation.

The third session had dreams with more distressing experiences.

—*There were rats in the church nursery, baptism in the sanctuary with a pillar of fire and the preacher was yelling at the dreamer about original sin.*

—*Canoeing in a culvert in a treacherous ice storm.*

—*A dreamer getting bugs in her hair in the church basement but her hairdresser would not comb them out.*

—*Moving on a street where there were tarantulas on pop-up webs eating, and dead people laid out on the ground.*

—*Travelling back to Chicago, where the dreamer had once lived, but it was bombed out* [this was in the July before September 11]. *When she asked, the police explained, "Oh, those fraternity parties."*

There were also some more pleasant dreams:

—*Finding a room with friends who begin to climb a mountain. When the dreamer complains they carry her on a litter and they were cheerful.*

—*The church is an arena, there is an art museum there, and there are stained-glass doors to the exhibit hall. The walls had expanded, and there were people milling about looking at pottery and paintings, and the focus was on people wanting to do their own thing. As they left, two elders were accepting evaluation sheets.* The dreamer awoke thinking, "What a pleasant experience."

This was the end of the planned series of social dreaming meetings. However, there was such enthusiasm, with new participants attending, that they requested a continuation. Two more sessions were scheduled for the summer.

The first of these sessions involved dreamers being confused by travelling:

—*One was carrying a baby as she rode on a commuter train that expanded into an amphitheatre. She told people she had no idea where she was going, got confused and left the train, then got back on and had to breastfeed the baby.*

—Another had a vague memory of being in lots of places she knew, but every time she arrived there was a kangaroo there that became her "buddy".

—Another was with his wife in the San Francisco Bay area, went to a doctor's office in a mall to have a growth removed from his neck, and was afraid that his wife was not there.

—Another was in a seedy part of a big city with her husband, who went to look for an apartment to rent, but she insisted that they were not moving there until after Christmas.

Other dreams were about the frustrations of getting an answer and then losing it:

—Hearing the name Siddartha and wanting to go back to sleep but the name got louder so the dreamer asked her husband to remember the name since Siddartha was the Buddha.

—Another recalled from that a dream in which he was reading Joseph Campbell and in the dream he "got it from Buddha" and then woke up and lost it.

—Another mentioned that he often dreams about a problem at work that frustrates him, and in the dream he solves the problem only to wake up and go to work and the problem is still there.

—Another was driving up a hill and it felt like an uphill battle that would result in her missing her young son doing something. Then she dreams that I [T.M.] was running alongside her, saying "write it down!"

A third theme included frightening circumstances of finding rats in the house; an intruder in the house that caused her to panic; a scary dream in which she was dreaming that she was dreaming; and a difficult situation where there were evil elves.

The final session of the summer (and, as it happens, before the events of September 11) included dreams about animals, travelling or moving, and houses or walls being changed. The dreams about moving included the following:

—A dreamer was at a well-known white-water-rafting site with a friend and his teenaged son. They had no paddles, went very fast, missed the

river, and were in the clouds. They stopped and climbed down a radio tower, with his little son between them. They went to a hotel, finding themselves in the basement like an enormous mall, and there was a blast in the mall.

—There was a voice from a cylindrical vehicle, like a space ship, which said, "We are landing", then it was a subway car looking back at the space ship. He got angry at the prune-faced captain and bumped into him. He was not fazed by it, then he was at the shore at a party and he offered to push the captain and curse him out, then he was on a motorcycle speeding down the highway.

—A daughter put the dreamer and her husband on a plane at the Baltimore-Washington Airport, but when the daughter picked them up only the dreamer was there.

—A dreamer found herself in her former workplace, a school for handicapped children, where her former supervisor was changing the preschool into an aquatic centre and told her to go see the dolphins. She went into a weird, dark, slimy basement and realized she had a medical problem, a balloon on her leg. When she went to the nurse she remarked that it was unusual and then a lump came out on the floor.

—A dreamer was in a twin home he wanted to sell. It was a beautiful place but the shower wall was soggy and spongy and there were windows between the houses, and the back garden was quite large.

—A dreamer was in a bungalow with a woman sitting in an overstuffed chair who said, "I'm with walls", and then she was gone. He went outside to see that people in a car were stuck in his driveway. He got into an old Chevy, drove fast down the highway, then asked himself why he was doing that and turned around.

The kangaroo from an earlier dream appeared again at the home of a friend of the dreamer; other animals also appeared:

—The kangaroo kept hopping about, and it relieved itself in the friend's bedroom, but the dreamer had difficulty sitting on the toilet since it kept moving around.

—The dreamer was riding on a whale with an intricate rope bridle. She could breathe under water and had much fun as the whale swam very fast.

Another dreamer had a pleasant dream about her deceased father:

—They were both healthy. Her father was in a good mood but irritated and said, "It's okay, everything is find, I don't know why everyone's worried."

The session ended with a participant recounting that during the worship service that day he was looking at the Tiffany window above the dossal and cross at the front of the sanctuary. In the centre of the window is a red heart with a flame arising out of it. A voice said to him: "Do the right thing."

By this time the matrix was beginning to trust its dreams. The animals that appeared were benign creatures, such as kangaroos, meercats, and friendly whales. At the same time, harrowing experiences were becoming more acceptable.

Some members had entered the matrix even though they said they could not dream, or at least could not recall their dreams. However, after experiencing social dreaming, they began to be able to recall dreams. The first dreams were very frightening, and they usually ended when the dreamer woke up with heart pounding or with cries or screaming. A difference was that the matrix had established that the dreams were social and that the burden of fear could be shared. When a harrowing dream was presented, someone would remark, "You had that dream for all of us."

An interesting fact became apparent. The most frightening dreams were reported by participants who had endured particularly frightening experiences in their lives. One, a Vietnam veteran, had been the only American on a gunboat on the Mecong River and more recently had nearly died of a stroke. Another had been a SAC bomber pilot during the cold war, and flew many hours with nuclear weapons in his bomb bay. He had also lost his first wife and a son in automobile accidents. A woman had been sexually abused as a child. Typical of their reports were:

—I was hoarse when I woke up and had been screaming in my dream.

—I was going downhill on a kiddie-car, and I go in a house to say hello. All the people in there are slumped over dead, and I screamed and woke up.

—I was in a social dreaming session in a downstairs room when a gorilla of a man came in to stab me in the stomach and I woke up.

As the matrix became more cohesive, others were able to make associations to these dreams and to give voice to the idea that the dreams were for the whole community. Other participants who had reported mainly pleasant dreams began to report more frightening dreams. On the other hand, a woman who had been abused as a child reported that she had had the first pleasant dream she could ever recall, involving people from her past whom she hadn't seen for a long time.

A dream that illustrated this openness was presented by the former bomber pilot:

He had a dead person in the trunk of his car. He drove to a cemetery but could not bury the body since he did not know how the person had died. Then someone gave the dreamer maraschino cherries for him to cleanse his hands and then he would be absolved.

This leads me to a hypothesis that a social dreaming matrix that accepts individual dreams as being constitutive of the community can enable those whose life experiences are so frightening that they cannot remember their dreams to endure the terror of their dreams. It would be interesting to test this by including those who suffer from posttraumatic stress disorder to become part of a social dreaming matrix in the broader community. Perhaps then their hands could be cleansed.

Enthusiasm for social dreaming was, if anything, increased. Therefore, we agreed that we should meet monthly, but we were unable to schedule the next meeting until November, after the destructive attacks on the World Trade Center and the Pentagon on 11 September 2001. The effects of those events served to place the question of the survival of the parish in a world context.

We next met five weeks after September 11. A participant began the session by reporting a dream about his sister in Minnesota:

At her church there, located on Martin Luther Place, the women all have clothes but the men are naked and she was concerned that the men might suffer when they sit on cold pews.

Dreams about the consequences of the bombings predominated:

—A dreamer was driving home and there were more and more airlines in the air. She realized that we were being attacked and she wanted to get

home. She also reported that her seven year-old son dreamed of dead goldfish.

—A dreamer was on a walk when he encountered an RIP sign: there was one man dead, another strangled, and a woman shopping.

—A dreamer dreamed he went to New York with his wife, child, and mother-in-law. They looked at five skyscrapers and thought that there was something good, then Osama bin Laden said, "You haven't seen anything yet." The buildings collapsed, he ran with his son into a Wal-Mart store, they were engulfed in a cloud, but his wife and mother were not there.

Others reported daydreams of planes that could crash, that they died and wonder what will happen to their children, that if the World Trade Center can go, then anything can happen. Quite a different note was struck by a dream of *working in a factory when the telephone rang and the boss asked if Nancy was in. The dreamer said that she was, but the boss asked, "Is that your pricey car?" and the dreamer replied indignantly, "I own a beige Nova."*

In the discussion it was suggested that these dreams reveal that we are vulnerable and under the control of others. However, an older woman remarked that she did not feel particularly vulnerable and other women echoed her statement. It was then noted that what was different was that men now felt vulnerable and under the control of others—they were naked in church, the woman could speak back indignantly to her boss, two men were dead and the woman was shopping; we are not in control, we are vulnerable, we are becoming as weak as women and minorities. Several of the women said to the men: "Now you know how it is for us."

I was reminded of a matrix I had conducted in 1995. The participants were employees of the case management department in a social service agency. Their jobs were to do intake and manage cases until they could be referred to a therapist or other social worker and to assist in the institutionalization of mostly poor clients unable to care for themselves. Their perception of their work is that others in the organization do not view them as fully professional. Over a period of weeks they produced dreams that involved the dreamer in situations in which they were losing control of events. As this theme became more pronounced, they began to say that they could not dream because their own lives were so stressful. One described his family

problems and then said: "If I didn't work, I'd be a client of this place."
Others agreed, one saying, "There is a thin line between us and them,
and it scares me." They, too, expressed feelings of vulnerability and
lack of control. Before the next meeting, the bombing at the federal
building in Oklahoma City occurred. One participant said that while
the images on TV are so vivid, she was bothered that they have no
compassion and no time to dream. Another described her life as a
waking dream, living in Camden, New Jersey, then the "murder
capital of America". A boy had taken a gun to her daughter's school.
They had gunshot drills in the schools. What dreams she may have
had ended in gunshots from the streets outside her home. The department decided to end the social dreaming meetings.

The parallels between the two matrixes are striking, including the
external events that intervened. The difference is that the church
group was able to form a more inclusive matrix. Its participants had
worked through the issues about membership, goals, and leadership.
It had moved from a group to a matrix in which it was possible for
any one person to present a dream that could become available for all
to own. It was also possible for this matrix to use what the other
matrix had experienced: deep had called unto deep.

This was shown by a dream in the church matrix that appeared to
be related to the attacks on September 11.

*The dreamer was running with a crowd of people. A man came by
driving an ATV. The dreamer got on, then got off in town, but realized
that he should not have done that and began to run again. With that his
feet lifted up behind him, he flew through a tunnel and ended up in front
of the running mass.*

The theme of being attacked, and the dream of flying through a
tunnel, led to the suggestion that "We are dreaming for the Afghans!"
That statement was greeted by a profound silence.

We framed the hypothesis that the social dreaming matrix was
opening our eyes to the universality of the human experience. The
statement by the Apostle Paul that "there is neither Jew nor Greek,
male nor female, slave nor free" was being enacted in our experience.
The matrix had from the beginning included participants of all ages,
from people in their thirties to several past eighty. The men had come
to understand the vulnerability that women live with daily. Recently

several dreams have been presented in which there was an emphasis upon "black and white", and the colour brown has been featured. We had reached into the inner city of our own nation and realized that we could help the Afghans by dreaming what we suspect they were too traumatized to dream. We were dreaming for Afghans whose lives were so dreadful that they needed someone to have their dreams. We had transcended the usual sources of misunderstanding and overcame barriers of space and time.

In a subsequent session several dreams involved two old women in black; two automobiles; the second floor of a town house; two retired clergy moving in time to the music and distracting worshippers so much that a woman got up and scolded them.

A member reported her 7-year-old son's dream of *being challenged by a friend to climb a high slide. God told him he could do it, and he did and felt great.* The boy's friend is a congregant of a "new life" Presbyterian church, an evangelical splinter group. It appeared that we were being challenged and that there were two views of Presbyterian doctrine. Except for this dream, most of the dreams in the matrix were of difficulties encountered by the dreamers. These dreams usually involved climbing high on unsteady ladders and stairs.

A dreamer presented a fragment in which *she was in the church, but the cross was not there in the front. Instead, the red heart in the Tiffany window was much lower and larger, taking up the space where the cross usually stands. Beside the heart were two faces, looking generally towards the centre. They were beneficent, smiling, and it gave the dreamer a good feeling.*

Participants have insisted on continuing the social dreaming matrix. They talk about the sessions with other members of the congregation. They are eager to have more sessions despite scheduling difficulties and are considering inviting teenagers into the matrix.

Discussion

Social dreaming is having an impact on the life of the parish. Participants agree with Lawrence that "social dreaming would never give them a direct answer to the issues that they were facing, but that the experience of searching for meanings would have direct consequences on the way that they thought about problems" (1998c, p. 140). A specific result, however, has been produced. The pastor and leaders are characterizing it as "A church with a heart" and are emphasizing the warmth and caring of members for one another.

Has the matrix realized, or is it in the process of realizing, the originally stated purpose of generating new revelation? This depends partly upon what is meant by revelation. Is it meaning or understanding or explanation?

Initially the participants wanted to know what their dreams meant. They kept asking me, the "dream expert", what a particular dream was about. They had been used to the typical format of adult education in which a teacher sat facing them and expounded facts and theories. My position in the congregation strengthened this tendency, since I am a Parish Associate (what the Church of England calls a "non-stipendiary clergy"), and I occasionally preach and lead worship. Members approached me after worship to relate a dream and ask its meaning. I declined as much as possible to make interpretations and instead encouraged associations, including dreams as associations. However, we find it nearly impossible not to interpret dreams. Since we have been taught by Freud that condensation, displacement, and dramatization are important elements of dreaming, the task of understanding is to try to determine what is being condensed, what is displaced, and how the dramatization represents it. Whether this amounts to revelation is difficult to say. Interpretation appears to me to be a rearrangement of information already available. It is certainly a desirable result, but is there anything there that has not already been known, the unthought known, to use Bollas's apt description? How can we know the difference between the finite experience mediated through culture and the infinite, which could supply new revelation?

I proposed elsewhere (Michael, 1998) that dreams function the same way as parables. I used the work of John Dominic Crossan, a New Testament scholar. He contrasted the narrative of myth, which attempts to construct meaning from contradictory experience, with the narrative of parable, which attacks and critiques meaning:

> Myth has a double function: the reconciliation of an individual contradiction and, more important, the creation of a belief in the permanent possibility of reconciliation. Parable also has a double

function, which opposes the double function of myth. The surface function of parable is to create contradiction within a given situation of complacent security but, even more unnervingly, to challenge the fundamental principle of reconciliation by making us aware of the fact that we made up to the reconciliation. [Crossan, 1988, p. 40]

Dreams not only challenge our usual ways of thinking about our experience, they may also be characterized by condensation, displacement, and dramatization. Their purpose is to critique our assumptions about the nature of reality, whether they be through faulty personal decisions in the case of those who seek relief through therapy or faulty cultural assumptions for all of us.

I have come to change my view of myth as a result of an encounter with the work of Rene Girard. In a large corpus of work that stretches across four decades, he has established to my mind that myth, together with ritual and sacrifice, are strategies used by cultures to disguise and hide the fact that all culture is founded upon violence and that this violence is perpetrated by the majority against an innocent scapegoat. The perpetrators of the violence always believe that the victim is guilty and deserves punishment. A myth is nearly always a retelling of that original violence in a way that transforms the victim into a god. It is a "thing hidden since the foundation of the world", to use the title of one of his most important books (Girard, 1978).

Dreams, which so often are suffused with violence, may be thought to be a means by which the infinite transcends culture to give us a glimpse of the truth of our violence. Many of the dreams in the matrix were about people in struggles, in precarious positions on unsteady ladders, in rooms with collapsing walls and in risky activities. It is as if our culture is unable to sustain us. However, our myth requires that we hide this truth beneath distortion, displacement, and dramatization. Lawrence has proposed the hypothesis that

We are living in a time when our experiencing minds are eroding the limits between what we have known as the finite and what we construe to be the infinite, not only in terms of public knowledge but also in terms of personal insight and thinking. And this process will continue if we make ourselves available for the necessary transformations invoked. [1997, p. 2]

We have known the deepest parts of our humanity calling across the ordinary barriers to one another. We are challenged to see how the infinite deeps calls to the depth of ourselves despite the sweep of waves and breakers and the roar of cataracts.

I believe that our matrix is about more important things than the survival of our church.

CHAPTER TEN

Sliding houses in the Promised Land: unstable reality worked through dreams

Mira Erlich-Ginor

> "All life is but a dream, and every man, I see, dreams all his
> deeds and nature. The king dreams he is king, and deeply sunk
> in such a dream, commands and rules and governs, and all to
> him are subject. And yet his fortune to dust is turned by, which,
> also as a dream, forever threatens him. Of their wealth the rich
> dreams, and death yet they have no peace. To the contrary, the
> poor on earth dream of his bondage and distress. He dreams who
> starts to rise, who is afraid and runs, who loves and is afire with
> hate. Thus in this wide world what all are, that they dream,
> although not one discerns this, indeed, all life is but a dream, and
> even dreams are just a dream."
>
> Pedro Calderón de la Barca, 1636

The following is the first multifaceted dream contributed to a social dreaming matrix that took place in the shadow of the first year of the *"El-akza Intifada"*.

I am on my way between a hospital [in Hebrew literally: "house of the sick"] *and a hotel* ["house of sleep"]. *A neighbour is constantly renovating. Her husband, the lawyer, is proud of her. They lost $10,000, can't find where they put it. But never mind—they have plenty more.*

The *Intifada* (Palestinian uprising) started in October 2000, dealing a death blow to the peace negotiations. The first meeting of the matrix took place three weeks later, and its last meeting was held in June 2001. At the time of writing, the *Intifada* is being transformed into a war, becoming more bloody and hopeless.

In this chapter I want to build on Gordon Lawrence's working hypotheses concerning social dreaming, and especially that:

* it is possible to have dreams that have social contents and significance;

* the matrix is a container in which the dreams of participants are the "currency";

* as a container, the matrix alters the nature of the dreams;

* in a matrix there is a "multi-verse of meaning" (Lawrence, 1998c, pp. 136–137).

In this chapter, I first illustrate the *unconscious themes* of a society in distress as these surface in the social dreaming matrix; to do this, I present an extensive version of the programme as it unfolded. I then tackle the question of the foreshadowing power of the social dreaming matrix.

The matrix in context

The "continuous social dreaming matrix" discussed in this chapter was part of a programme of eight monthly meetings. The programme, sponsored by the Israel Association for the Study of Group and Organizational Processes (OFEK), was offered to participants who had previously participated in a group relations conference. The matrix consisted of fifteen members plus myself as a "matrix taker". The group met in Jerusalem at the Sigmund Freud Center of the Hebrew University. Each meeting consisted of three 75-minute segments.

1. social dreaming matrix;
2. lecture;
3. role analysis session.

Starting from the third meeting, I introduced a short meditation at the beginning of each session. This, of course, is a whole subject that is beyond the scope of this chapter. Suffice it is to say that it provided a transitional space that helped to cross the boundary and reconnect after each monthly interval. This space was the experience of the blurred boundary where the "I" meets the "other", which in my view *is* the social dreaming space. Looking at the practice with hindsight, I see it as the equivalent of the contribution of my dream to the matrix. Some participants were easily attuned to the meditation, others had to overcome resistances. The inward gaze during the meditation helped to recollect some of the dreams.

Following each meeting I sent all the participants the notes taken during the session. From the fourth session on, I dropped all the names in the notes. Consciously, this was because of confidentiality reasons. Unconsciously, it was understood and reacted to as an assertion of the dreamer as a representative, an "unconscious citizen": "Each dreamer is potentially a 'seer' of his or her 'people' and of the relationship to that other. This has been described as 'social dreaming'. In my own terms, I consider this an aspect of *unconscious citizenship*" (Fromm, 2000, p. 289).

The participants, men and women in their forties and fifties, came from different geographical locations and from varied professional backgrounds. They were a select sample of Israeli society: educated professionals, mainly of Western origin. Many other parts of the society were not represented: there were no Arabs, no ultra-religious, no new immigrants, to name but a few of the "others" in the society. A major prevailing tension at the time was between the political "Left" and "Right." This division had to do with attitudes to the "Palestinian problem"—the different solutions to the fact that there are two populations in the "Promised Land".

"The settlers" mentioned in this chapter are Jewish people who live in the "liberated/occupied" territories that were Jordanian until the 1967 War and are a bone of contention vis-à-vis a future Palestinian state.

In order to attend the meetings, some people came from the relatively (i.e., subjectively) secure Tel-Aviv area, others came from settlements on the West Bank, crossing a dangerous shooting zone on their way to the meetings and back. The Jerusalemites came shattered by ever-growing incidences of suicide terrorist attacks and frequent Palestinian shooting at Gilo, the neighbourhood of one of the participants. The (Israeli) artillery fire was often heard on Mount Scopus where we met, providing a terrifying and unsettling soundtrack as background to the matrix.

The here-and-now of the Israeli scene during October 2000–June 2001 was a prolonged "day-mare" from which there was as yet no awakening. Parallel to the deteriorating political situation the economic situation also deteriorated, and a general sense increased during this period that "everything is falling apart", including the "Zionist Dream".

Coming to this programme was an act of hope and need in a time of distress. Participants came with an intense mixture of hopes and fears: the better judgement would have been to stay home and move out as little as possible. Yet there was a need not to give in to the depressed mood and to try to make sense of the nonsense, to assert the right to make links at a time of attacks on linking.

The "dream currency" (Lawrence, 1991, 1998c) was rich: In the eight meetings there were twenty-eight reported dreams, ranging from sessions with a single dream, to sessions with up to six dreams. It was clearly stated that participants dreamt much more then they reported, selecting from the dreams they remembered those "that made sense for the matrix". This raises the question of the influence of the group dynamics on the dreams reported and hence on the themes that were created: what was the selection criteria of participants? Did they have a preconception of what will "fit in" better? There is a partial answer to this in the sequence.

The work of "associating to dreams available to the matrix, so as to make connections and develop meanings" was presented as the primary task and was fully engaged with, creating a language, an ever-thickening web of common associations, in which meanings were always to be negotiated and renegotiated in light of the idea of a "multi-verse of meanings": "In a social dreaming matrix there is never one meaning, or interpretation, of a dream. Whereas in a group the search tends to be for universal meaning, in a matrix the 'multi-verse' of meanings to dreams is celebrated" (Lawrence, 2001b, p. 88).

This work of further negotiating meaning went on between the meetings and even after the meetings were over—as I am doing in this chapter. Whenever there were attacks on linking in the matrix, they were understood as representing a larger social dynamic.

In a social dreaming matrix, as in individual work on dreams, associations are as important to the matrix as the dreams themselves, being the means to negotiate the unconscious meanings of the matrix. Otherwise we are in the area of the narrative of the manifest dream and have to restrict ourselves to the symbolic or poetic meanings of the dreams. This issue is the focus of contemporary contributions dealing with Freud's revelations a century ago in *The Interpretation of Dreams*.

The following sequence tells the story of people who wanted to know their dreams, use them as a language, and look at them together with courage and curiosity. Participants who never remembered their dreams before "dreamt for the matrix", and a dream untold for eleven years found its way to the matrix. This is in agreement with Grotstein's assertion: "For experience generally and traumatic experience specifically are not safe until they are dreamed" (Grotstein, 1981, p. 415).

A white tall house on a bus, an island,
. . . and other escapes

Session 1

As with everything experiential, the bottom line is a far cry from the experience itself. Amos Oz, the prominent Israeli writer, in a recent interview in the newspaper *Haaretz* (1 March 2002) formulated the "bottom line" of the matrix in a few sentences: "Maybe the story of this entire period [of the Zionist movement and the state of Israel], and the whole story of this period is a story of *survivors on an island*. Maybe this is as accurate as one can get: the story of survivors on a small island. The story of a survivor." So too did the poet Yona Wallach (1997) catch the essence of the matrix in the dream-language of a poem: "How could we let ourselves become passers-by / When what we want is to be the ones returning."

Yet the discovery of these themes in the session-to-session work of the matrix was dramatic in an understated way: temporary houses, death, the Holocaust, and victimization inhabited the matrix from the beginning in dreams and in associating to them. Though it might seem trivial in retrospect, one could not have predicted the creative ways in which these deep feelings were expressed. I shall try to demonstrate this creativity through a shortened version of the unfolding of the matrix.

The first dream was offered after a short silence:

I am on my way between a hospital and a hotel. A neighbour is constantly renovating. Her husband, the lawyer, is proud of her. They lost $10,000, can't find where they put it. But never mind—they have plenty more.

This was followed by a statement that echoed throughout the matrix: "I have nightmares from which I keep waking up. My dreams are worse than reality." No dream followed this statement, which was made by a woman from a settlement in the West Bank. She postponed narrating her nightmares "for later", never coming back to them. With this she created a black hole, the hole of the "non-told dream": a dream that is mentioned, yet is shared through its absence; a dream that is too much to be told and has to remain word-less. (Was she dreaming the deterioration that was to take place, that was an untold-known?)

Following the untold dream came a told non-dream: "Shooting in Gilo—no dream." This statement was followed by the next associations:

•   "How can one dream when the guns fire? My dream-life is robbed", exclaimed the dweller of Gilo—a neighbourhood in Jerusalem that became a front line.

The next dream ending this session was, like the first one, an ambivalent mixture of hope and death: *"Broken eggs, a yellow stain of eggs mixture."* The association:

•   Eggs are the matrix of birth which life starts from.

The first session laid out a blueprint for the entire matrix: The "non-told dream" and the "no-dream"; temporary houses (a hotel, a hospital); a promise of "eggs" that you have to break but that will grow to something and "plenty more". Death on the one hand, renovation on the other.

Session 2

"I never ever dream, yet I dreamed for you": so began the second session.

I arrive for an acting class at a community centre. The director and his wife are there. There are costumes for sale. I don't buy the black one. A dance show is taking place at the community centre. Outside people are sitting on the fence. A rock star arrives: he is a dramatic, tall man. He says in German: I am late, why am I late? A "Yeke" [a German Jew] harsh with himself.

The dreamer, a manager in a large bank in Tel-Aviv, finishes telling the dream and says: "I don't understand anything, it's for you."

- Freud, the German speaking (rock) star—this is about us: since we are meeting at the Freud Center, dealing with dreams.
- Alice in Wonderland, the hurrying rabbit—a different reality, but no less real.
- We are the "acting-class"; the question is, what is the right costume in this class?
- Freud, Einstein, Marx all had moustaches: the social/psychic/metaphysical dream—the community centre, last time it came up along with hospital and hotel: public places; the common (social) place. We are trying to mix the eggs here, create connections.

A further dream follows:

A public shower. I have no booth, no soap—how will I manage? There are no proper conditions. All is difficult, very bad feeling. A nightmare.

- Shower is a private space.
- "Public shower" brings immediately to mind the Holocaust.

I offered my understanding that the two sessions are an effort to work through the difficult space of social dreaming: we are here between the public and the private. It is not easy to bring the private here; all kinds of security measures are mobilized, such as telling the dream rapidly, disowning the dream by saying, "It is yours".

- I had several dreams during the past month and debated: shall I bring my dreams here and why?
- The public shower in the Kibbutz: the Kibbutz was a social dream that turned out to be a nightmare. Social dreams when enacted can become dangerous.

This session moves from the new space of the matrix, which has to be worked through by the participants and the matrix taker to the societal meanings: it moves to the Holocaust and to the Kibbutz as a representation of the Zionist dream.

Session 3

In the third session, a woman who had hardly spoken previously presented the only dream of the session:

> *I am at a conference in England. A crowded large hall. I don't know anyone. I spot Mira there, she ignores me. Everybody is speaking in groups. I wait. Small children are playing, making annoying noise. Somebody is trying to take charge. I feel agony, alienation. There is a nice side: England, a small town, and small coffee shops. This is the compensation.*

- I looked on us as a group: representatives of our society: people that immigrated from all over the world, a gathering-in of the exiles, settlers, religious people, seculars. These are what meet the eyes, what about those things you can't see? What shall we do with this diversity? Can we build on it?
- Costumes and covers [reference to the previous session]. In the dreams we lose the covers: our grouping affiliations People in the shower look alike—but for the gender difference.
- Next session will be two days after the general elections, some of us will be happy, others will be desperate. How can we stay together?
- "The shooting on the way home" [mentioned by one of the woman-settlers] accompanies me from the first session (says a secular, anti-settler participant who lives in Tel-Aviv, the seemingly secure zone); can we have a common social dream? My social dream is so different from yours (she says in a sad tone).
- The "noise of children" is life—the present situation is that we are killing a lot of children now.
- We are killing parents of children as well.
- We bury children.
- I think of politics, another cover, another escape from myself.

- If it were not a dream (says the woman who reported the dream), I would take action; in the dream, I stayed with the chaos and anxieties.

- The political associations make the dream frightening: to run to a nice place, "eat and drink, for tomorrow you will die", a blank ballot—a blank ballot is like a non-dream: no commitment.

- (A woman-settler): I am scared to bring my dreams of the terror of the shooting. Whatever I will bring here will be tainted, will be heard as "The Settler", will be politicized [which is what I am doing as I write and refer to the "woman-settler].

- It is unfair that you don't speak your fears—we all experience fear.

I intervene by saying: All of us, regardless of political or other group-ings, have our "untold dream". Untold because I might be misunder-stood, because I as a dreamer felt alone.

- In Tel Aviv people say: "throw the settlers into the sea", says a Tel-Avivian secular woman. In Bar-Ilan (a religious university cam-pus) there are harsh words about the "leftists", says a religious woman.

- What is more difficult: to be identified or unidentified? "Call me by my true name"—the "undecided" is their name—it is a human name. People with more than one name can manage easier.

- Our task here is to give up the name of the dreamer: to contribute the dream as playdough for a common play.

This session refers to the common past: participating in a group rela-tions conference is strongly present. Since all had their group rela-tions experience in an OFEK conference in Israel, the reference is to the Leicester Conference, as a kind of "Promised Land", seems clear at the manifest level. The longings are enacted by the pull in this session to work in a "small study group" mode, as a defence against the matrix. This might be affected by the tension around the ap-proaching elections and the wish for the security that might be gained in a "group".

"We are killing a lot of children now", "We are killing parents of children", "We bury children" are all associations referring to Israeli aggression. It is notable that, though mentioned, this issue is not taken up or engaged with any further. This evidence of an attack on linking seems to represent a current trend in Israeli society: the partial blindness to the existence and suffering of the Palestinians, paralleled with the experience of "we" being The Victims.

Session 4

The fourth session took place right after the general elections, in which the right wing won by a landslide.

One of the women-settlers brings the following dream:

One of my children is going to get married. The wedding is on an island in the sea. I see the sea, can't see the island. We are all there—this group. I say: I will be able to get there, to the island, to my child's wedding, only with your help. Another scene: I am alone again, near a cave. Somebody is covering it up, like a grave. Somebody outside says: stop bullshitting, this is just nonsense."

She goes on immediately to tell another dream:

In the dream I am bringing the dream to the matrix. We start working on the dream, giving associations. I don't find myself in these associations. My truth is: "without you I can't get there". I repeat it while we are working with the dream.

- We have to get to the island—out of reality—rough sea—a wedding is a connection; in order to connect you have to depart from where you are.
- We, this matrix, became indispensable (says the man who brought the first dream, pleased).
- The unseen island: the Promised Land, I wonder what kind of a country will we have after this election? A Promised Land?. A Dream? A Nightmare?
- In several dreams I had this month, there was an "*intimate hug with a man, every time another one*".
- The couple on the island. A wish for a good partner.
- The image of the grave in the cave frightened me. Now we bury children.
- What is this wedding that only *we* can get to? What is the sea?—We

are here in a once-a-month-island. We came because we had a common experience (the group relations conference).

I wonder silently about the "couple on the island" and the "hug with a man", unconscious references to the wish for pairing with the Palestinians—those who are on this "island" with us, yet this is not taken up by participants, and as a matrix taker it seems to bring in too much of my ideas—or does it?

• A ship is a device to run away. Our parents fled on ships [as immigrants and refugees from Europe and Asia].

I offer a connection that cuts across sessions: we come up here with the transitory, temporary place. We don't have a dream here with a nice-house-with-a-garden. All is temporary or threatening: grave, cellar, fortress, community-centre, hotel, ship.

• I am coming now from a family whose son committed suicide.
• To be here is the opposite of death. to get in to this experience is to cling to life, feels secure enough, it is surprising while uncertain, and associative. Too bad the young man did not come to the matrix. [The matrix is experienced as a safe haven].

At the end of the session a dream is suddenly remembered:

I am at a gathering with lots of psychologists. A tall white house with two other houses near it. The middle house starts to slide as if it was on a rail in the direction of the sun: this is a house that is turning towards the sun, like a flower. The house I am in starts moving. The house is on top of a bus. The driver is not aware that he has a huge house on his bus. The bus is winding its way near a precipice. But it stops. A house that drives to the sun. I got up laughing.

This fantastic image of a tall house on a bus, ready to go, appears at the edge of the session. The road is dangerous, the house unstable, yet there is a sunny side to the image: the house is turning to the sun, like a flower. The dreamer wakes up laughing. Again an ambivalent dream. The "multi-verse" stance allows us to consider the sugar coating of the horrible image, as well as the bright side of the moon, like the "renovations" and "never mind the loss of $10,000—there is much more" in previous sessions.

Session 5

The dreamer had missed the previous session. She now asked for the primary task to be repeated so she could see if "a dream that was dreamt before the last session will be acceptable".

> *The dream takes place in the car-park of the university. I come to our session or perhaps to an OFEK meeting. I feel guilty, for I am where I should not be: I should have been at work. I run away. Arrive at Shuck Machne Yehuda (an open-air market hit several times by terrorists). Three men enter my car; I understand they are terrorists. They kidnap me. They leave the car. I can now run away, but I understand it will be more dangerous if they catch me. A friend appears and asks me to her car. The car is too big to move in the narrow streets, we will have to run over the tables that are there. I decide to give it a chance. It is a daring act to drive like this in this no-road road. End of dream."*

- Guilt, escape, disappearance, life, and death—did the dream prevent you from coming last time?—one feels guilty coming here, indulging oneself.
- We have three men in the matrix—they don't look frightening . . . this is a matter of interpretation.

One of the men, who had not contributed any dreams in the previous sessions, said that the fact that there were no rules about old dreams made it possible for him to bring a dream that he had had eleven years ago (!). Somehow the lack of regulations or of political correctness here made the dream feel less terrifying. He had never told this dream to anybody until some weeks ago, when he told it to his uncle. Now he wanted to bring this dream to the matrix. It was, he said, a very personal dream. He had the dream some months after his cousin's fighter-plane crashed into the Sea of Galilee. The cousin was missing for some days, then his body was found.

> *I am under the house of my parents. There is a storm, it pours, the level of the water rises. I wanted to see what happened to M. I am struggling against the current. I see that the coffin of M. is being pushed out of the cellar. My uncle goes to the entrance and with his body keeps the coffin in the cellar. I shout at him to leave the door so that the coffin can float out with the current. I am holding on to a tree. He is endangering himself, can drown. I am swept by the current.*

- Three terrorists, a coffin.
- On the one hand it seems such a personal dream, so frightening that it had to be untold, could not be spoken, but could not to be forgotten. Yet it is so much in tune with what we are dealing with here—the guilt: are you allowed to let go and move on? A storage, an attic, things are kept there unchanged but can always peep out.
- The unspoken dream of the first session; the guilt towards the dead; showers; Germany; the Holocaust.
- I just came back from a funeral at a Kibbutz. They bury there in a coffin [the usual practice in Israel is to bury without a coffin, "Earth to Earth"]. My dad's last friend, he was 90.
- We are carrying coffins—you need unusual courage to let yourself be carried by the current. It can be dangerous.

Dreams today wanted to come out, be born, get out of the closet against a danger of loss of control, of letting skeletons out, I remarked, finding it especially difficult to end this extremely moving session.

Session 6

The sixth session tool place on the memorial day for the Holocaust.

The zipper in my pants opens, I close it and it reopens, it does not work.

- Rembrandt's picture: all the internal parts are out. Here in the matrix the wishes, the fears are out.
- The wish is to put out what is in. These days are a struggle between closing and opening: spring, Passover . . . the memorial day for the Holocaust, the memorial day for Israeli soldiers.
- Yesterday, as part of the story telling of the Holocaust, a woman said that her role was to close the eyes of the dead. She would close them but she would forever see them wide open. Can you lock out what has to be open?
- When you dream you open the inner eyes; when you wake up you open your eyes and close the inner eyes.
- The zipper that opens and opens: a wish to live, but are we allowed to live, to dance, to sing?

This was followed by several moving stories about family members of participants and their experiences during the Holocaust.

- The movie, *Life Is Beautiful*—the man communicates with his wife through music. People went on to sing and dance. In a way we live like this: guilty that we live, yet we go on.

- Since the beginning of the session I felt this tension between reality and fantasy, dreams are not dreams, they are reality. For me the zipper is unzipped.

- The stories of the parents are a source of strength. I held on to this story all my life: parents that came to Israel shortly after Hitler gained power. They day-dreamed the Nazi dream—this nightmare drove them to action and they survived.

Session 7

I offer here a full version of the seventh session, for reasons that will become apparent.

- "Was too short."
- "The meditation, the programme?!"
- "The dead that stay with us. Two women died this week. I did not know them but accompanied their illness and death."
- One of the religious woman-settlers says: "My dream is related to the approaching end of the programme: *A shining marble floor. Last preparations for the Sabbath meal. Huge floors of marble. Now it reminds me of death. I am in a small room handling minced meat; I am not yet in the Shabbat, only preparing for it. There is no time. The others have already prepared everything and they are in the clean area.* My association", she continues, "is that life is measured, there are preparations to be made and if I don't make them I will arrive unprepared. What will my relatives eat? They don't get the clean house and the good food they deserve."
- The countdown: how much time remains, how much has passed.
- Shining marble, the bank headquarters [the speaker is the bank

manager], a huge lobby, grey shining marble, most of the time empty. The employees nickname the building: Funeral House, Morgue, Mausoleum."

- "There is a security guard at the door."
- "Let the next world have a gate-keeper."
- Dream: "*A new shining floor. It is not connected with ending.*" In my workplace, we moved to a new building and lots of things are chaotic. In the dream: "*A glass door opens. We are not allowed in because of the work that is being done. Olmart, the mayor of Jerusalem, is lying on the floor and laying tiles. I want to get in, to go to work. How come it is not ready yet?*" A third dream follows immediately: in my dream, too, there is an unfinished place: "*I am entering a mall with my friend. The mall is redone, a floor with a wall-to-wall thick carpet, nice, seductive.*"
- The mayor is laying tiles, maybe we are already in heaven.
- Minced meat: the caricaturist Pivan portrays Arik Sharon [the Prime Minister] with minced meat.
- I am also thinking about the minced meat: how can you eat un-cooked minced meat? Steak tartar, I like to eat it, it is bold to do so.
- Minced meat is very sensual, an opposite to the marble floor.
- "The meditation was hard for me, I longed for the previous (non-analytic) meditations."

The dreamer is a religious man:

> My father came to me dressed in a one-piece leather suit, short sleeves, and short trousers. I am busy. He asked me to clean the outfit for him. I don't have time, but I take a wet sponge so the cleaning will go faster, I did not mean to rush it though my father thought that I did. I forgot the dream coming here, the meditation brought it back to me—my father within myself.

- Like purifying the dead.

The last dreamer goes on:

> "This is very strange: My father died in Thailand at the beginning of the Sabbath. My cousin and I had to do the 'purification-of-the-

dead' rite. In the dream *he pulled down his outfit so that I can get to the private places, I felt uneasy, he was sweating.* I don't remember how it was in real life. All during the flight back to Israel I stayed with my father's body."

- Approaching the end of our meetings there are feelings of life and death, being in the middle, renovating, being in contact and out of contact.

- (The last dreamer again:) "I did not feel anything at the time that it happened: I was on 'automatic pilot.' Once back in Jerusalem they did not let me accompany the corpse, did not let me see the face."

- (Another woman:) "My father died when I was out of the country on a mission. During his illness I flew back and forth. A week before he died I came home for the last time. He died as soon as I left the country, so immediately I came back. There is this religious duty where you have to identify the body. It was clear to me that I will be the one to do it. I touched my dead father."

My understanding shared with the participants was the following. The temporary (transitory) homes switched to solid floors combined with an intense preoccupation with death. Death is the transition, the giving-up. The temporary homes were an indirect way to talk about death. When you call death by its name, you could feel some solidity, exemplified by the floors.

- I came back from Rome where I visited the Catacombs. Half a million dead people. If there were to be an earthquake here, there will be another half a million dead people. For many years I carried the experience of not parting from my mother. She died when I was 12. She was covered with a sheet, I did not see her. How could I know it was her? Why didn't I look under the sheet? Last year I re-worked through my mother's death when my therapist became terminally sick.

- If we were in South America, what would we dream of?

- I was in New York at Penn Station, a horde of people swept me along, and I thought: if there were to be a bomb, how many would be killed? Even at a remote place, these thoughts don't go away [September 11 is four months away].

- While in Rome, I heard a boom and I thought: "They are shooting in Gillo."
- You are already renovating.
- We got to the permanent houses: death, mausoleum, catacombs.
- The renovation is the cleaning of the grave stone.
- The tombstone is the most solid of places, "house of the world/of eternity" [literal translation from Hebrew for "graveyard"].
- You don't have to die physically, you can kill something within yourself and then you can be stable and secure.
- It sounds terrible what you just said.
- In the movie *Chocolat* she takes her mother's ashes in a jar, only when she spreads the ashes can she stop wondering. Until you bury, you can't go on.
- Only in Jerusalem can an 86-year-old man sit in his living-room and be a hero by getting shot in the chest [referral to recent incident that happened during Palestinian shooting in Gilo]. Survival is the same here as in South America.
- In the clinic I am working at, we had an art workshop. We were doing art and heard the shooting; later it was not clear if it was shooting or fireworks.
- We need a siren code for fireworks [reference to the Gulf War, where we had an alarm system with codes for danger and for non-danger].

Three hours after this session the marble floor of a wedding hall in Jerusalem collapsed, leaving 31 people dead. The air was filled with ambulance sirens. The mayor of Jerusalem was accused of not properly supervising the building and the permit for this hall.

Session 8

The eighth session, the final one, starts with a long silence.

- There was something mystical last time: death, marble, and the mayor of Jerusalem laying tiles. Something strange. It moved me.
- Maybe we are silent so that nothing will happen out of our dreams.
- Three times we spoke about mausoleum.

- The bank was the mausoleum, three of the casualties in the wedding hall were bank employees.
- This is uncanny: what is this about social dreaming? Did we know something?
- The dreams of Germans before the war [reference to Charlotte Beradt's 1966 book], there was nothing mystical about it. It is a question of atmosphere. How do we understand our dreams and the collapse of the floor of the wedding hall?—I read once that past and future, like here and there, are all at once. We dreamt before, but maybe the "before" is the same time?
- In social dreaming there is something potent, dangerous, scary. Maybe this is why we go more to the personal, to dilute it—but even the most personal, as we have seen, is not personal—the social and the personal are all enmeshed.
- In no other country would the collapse of a floor become the symbol of a general collapse.
- Each dream was a story by itself, but when we read the whole sequence a totally new story appears.
- Is it as dangerous in other countries? This collection of terror attacks, when does it transform to a new story, different from each attack apart?
- There is a fear to be enmeshed, people, stories dreams, opinions, what are we going to lose? What will we be left with?
- Did something develop here that was not before? Do we know what we did not know before?

Only this late in the session is there a dream, the last dream of the matrix:

I meet somebody nice. The dream ends with three points. . . . I woke up not knowing what will be. It felt nice. Like now: an end with dot, dot, dot.

- All is open.
- Was anything about to be born here? Should we have had nine sessions instead of eight?

The first reaction was that in some way we predicted the collapse of the floor, followed by a defensive retreat to a "no-dream/no-prediction" strategy, followed by a necessary move to closing, it being the last session.

The matrix apparently had to end in a *reparative mode*, a legend-like, open-ended happy end, while at the same time leaving the unknown be: "I woke up not knowing what will be."

The theme that surfaced in the most pronounced way in the social dreaming matrix was the feeling of temporariness. Where did it come from? We were at the beginning of an unusual war. Was the idea of temporariness a reaction to the current situation? The immediate threat of the *Intifada* appeared in several ways: directly through the dream with terrorists kidnapping the dreamer, indirectly through the "untold dream" and the "non-dream".

Yet it seems to me that the theme of temporariness has a much deeper meaning for Israelis. Israel is a young state, most of its citizens are first or second generation of refugees and immigrants, many of them second generation of the Holocaust. In these circumstances the theme of a fragile, uncertain existence is not unexpected. It can refer to the end of the Zionist Dream, the existential situation of the Jews throughout history, or to the "human condition".

In this social dreaming matrix, this theme surfaced in the image of temporary houses. In a previous matrix in Israel in 1997, this idea was presented as: "We, here, are spare-parts."

We find this same idea in the poetic language of Amos Oz, "The Story of Survivors on a Small Island" (2002), and in Yona Wallach's (1997) wish:

How could we let ourselves become passers-by
When what we want is to be the ones returning.

We met in the matrix temporariness and death. It is noteworthy that these were almost always coupled with an optimistic counterpoint : *"renovation"*, *"plenty more"*, *"the flower house"*, *"a wedding"*, *"a hug"*, *"meeting someone nice"*.

The dreams that were brought to the matrix became "events", in Meltzer's sense, holding the dialectics between pessimism and optimism: "When such a dream (dream as event) has visited our sleeping soul, how can we ever again doubt that dreams are 'events' in our lives? In this dream-world there is determined the great option between an optimistic and a pessimistic view, not only of our lives, but of Life" (Meltzer, 1984, p. 95).

The collapsing floor—foreshadowing the future?

"This is uncanny: what is this about social dreaming? Did we know something?" "How do we understand our dreams and the fact of the collapsing of the floor in the wedding hall?" asked participants at the session following the collapse. Did we, in the social dreaming matrix foreshadow the future? Did the matrix predict the collapse of the floor in the wedding hall?

To start from the end of my argument, I do not think that the matrix predicted the actual collapse of floor in the wedding hall. Let me make my winding way to this bottom line. Yes, there was something uncanny in the fact that we had in that session three out of four dreams that had an image of a floor in them. In "real time" the meaning I gave to this fact, along with the expressive fourth dream and the associations of death, was that we can stand on firm ground (the floors) once death is named, when it becomes possible to speak of death directly, not only symbolically.

I see the *actual* collapse of the floor as a *further association* to the matrix giving an additional meaning to the multi-verse of meanings. In the interpretation I gave, I related to the floors as solid. The collapse of the floor speaks to the contrary. Considering the associations of "mausoleum, grave, funeral, death of the father" that were given in the session, the solidity of the floor can be seen as the result of *reversal* by the "dream-work" of a sense of fragility.

Does this reading propose the predictive power of the social dreaming matrix? No, it voices the "collapsibility of the floors", not necessarily of this specific one.

What this session speaks for, using the images of floors or of "deciphered" collapsing floors, is a general sense of "collapsing" that was felt consciously and unconsciously at the time in the country, a concrete actualization in reality of what weighed heavily on some dreamers' minds: "In no other country would a floor that collapses become a symbol of a general collapse", said one of the participants. "I read once that past and future, like here and there, are all at once. We dreamt before, but maybe the 'before' is the same time?" said another participant, redefining in her own terms what the unconscious is.

The social dreaming matrix surfaced, besides the instability of houses, the theme of the danger of things falling apart. I see it not as a prediction but as a *reflection of a current state*. Lawrence (2001b) says:

"It was found that the synchronicity discovered in the dreams mirrored the larger social process in society" (p. 85). Thus, assuming that the notion of fragility was in the society, we, as part of the society, held the knowledge of the collapse—"we" in the matrix, as well as "we" as citizens. This is why the collapse of the wedding floor became, beyond a tragic event costing the life of so many, a symbol growing to such mythical proportions.

Being in a matrix, participants might have been more sensitized to their unconscious knowledge. The matrix, as a container, was influenced by the dreams as well as influencing them: "All living phenomena can be viewed as content occurring in the framework of a container which circumscribes and describes the content, and, reciprocally, the content has great influence in transforming the nature of its container" (Grotstein, 1981, p. 110).

Beyond the specific question of prediction, a general note on the status of predictive dreams is due. Dreams were treated as means to foresee the future in Eastern, Oceanic, and Western civilizations as long back as we can know. Joseph's dreams and his interpretation of the Pharaoh's dream are well-known examples. The special quality of dreams that makes the dreamer experience him/herself as an object in the dream, not necessarily its author, is easily translated to the idea that dreams come from an external source and, from there, have connection to a source of wisdom that is superhuman—hence their potential prophetic power.

Dreams are still used in this manner today in several cultures (Young, 1999). It is because of its popular use that Freud, while introducing *The Interpretation of Dreams* (1900a), had to distance himself from the predictive as well as the symbolic uses of dreams, in order to gain respectability (Sand, 1999). Yet Freud left room for predictive dreams as a means for the psyche to communicate to itself facts that are unconsciously known— for example, illness before it is diagnosed and recognized (Freud, 1900a, 1917d [1915]).

A contemporary way to understand dream-life is to see it as:

an information processing activity that deals with an effort to solve the current emotional problems of the dreamer. ... The manifest content of the dream is a representation of the problem in a figurative, imagistic language that needs to be "translated" rather than interpreted and is no more to be seen as an effort at disguise than a letter written in a foreign language is necessarily intended as a disguise. [Kramer, 1999, p. 773]

We "know" more than we are aware of since we "know" unconsciously not only what is in our personal unconscious—and that of others as well: "It is a very remarkable thing that the Unconscious of one human being can react upon that of another, without passing through the Conscious" (Freud, 1915e, p. 194). This is exponentially so in a group setting: "In my opinion there is an almost complete conformity in this respect between the individual and the group: in the group too an impression of the past is retained in unconscious memory traces" (Freud, 1939a [1937–39], p. 94).

The matrix may be conceived of as a container for the collective working-through of the citizenship emotional problems. The dreams-as-content provides the information-processing activity, and the matrix provides the container that allows for the heightened sensitivity of its participants.

In this sense, we "knew" but we did not "predict". We were shattered when it appeared as if the collapsing floor had been magically dreamed, for a pull to magical thinking is always present in groups and individuals, especially in times of social anxiety.

Yet in the poet-philosopher Calderón de la Barca's words: "Thus in this wide world what all are, that they dream, although not one discerns this, indeed, all life is but a dream, and even dreams are just a dream."

CHAPTER ELEVEN

Social dreaming
and the senior managers' programme

Peter Tatham

Twice yearly since 1998, I have led a social dreaming matrix on three days during the final week of a development programme for senior managers from the British NHS and, on occasion, from elsewhere. This five-week-long senior managers' programme (SMP), spread out over four months is organized by the King's Fund Leadership Directorate and is currently led by Valerie James, a psychotherapist and fellow of the King's Fund. SMP has been in existence, as well as evolving in nature, since 1994. It is a temporary learning community, of twenty-four members, designed to help participants make sense of the increasing complexities of their work situation while enabling them still to find creative ways forward.

A key feature and the containing bedrock of the programme's design is groupwork, which takes place in two separate forums: eighteen sessions of a large group for the whole community, as well as the same number of sessions in two small groups. These are not therapy groups for individual members but are seen as microcosms of NHS organization in which participants can discover how such emotions as envy, rivalry, and affiliation can intrude upon delivery of the primary task. They also provide participants with a space in which to reflect upon and integrate their emotional and intellectual responses

179

to the various other activities of the programme. The interventions of the current directors, which are informed by a variety of different approaches—deriving from post-Foulksian theory, as well as insights from Jung and Bion—are intended to enhance understanding of the unconscious processes of the group as they unfold.

SMP also uses a combination of cognitive psychology and conative psychology to inform its educational design. The former uses logic and intellectual discrimination to address the task in hand, whereas the latter is concerned with values, as expressed through imagery, which may be revealed through drawing, diagrams, collage, art, or body language. The educational outcome of all such activities will be enhanced by a careful choice of method according to the task in hand.

SMP also works with theories and concepts that include chaos theory, metaphor, and discourse theory, as well as psychodynamic theories of groups and organizations. By week 4, it is expected that many participants will have begun to integrate their intellectual learning with their improving emotional literacy.

Individual progress in SMP is gauged by self- and peer assessment of the quality of participation in myriad, sequentially constructed, team interactions—and by the insights gained by the individual into his or her own behaviour, as well as by its effect upon others within the group, teams, or organizations.

Social dreaming has been a part of the final week of the programme since about 1999. It has been used in a great variety of settings world-wide, for about twenty years, as a tool for exploring group experiences on an unconscious as well as conscious level, and there is now a considerable literature concerning its use (e.g. Lawrence, 1998c; Tatham, 2001; Tatham & Morgan, 1998).

The process by which dreams are shared by participants and commented upon by the convenors has been well documented (Lawrence, 1991), as have the benefits that accrue from its use in a wide variety of settings, such as at conferences and congresses, in teaching situations or seminars, as part of business and organizational consultancy—and so on.

Another feature of the management of the process is that anything said and shared or any comments that might be made while the matrix is open—even if not directly about the dreams or associations—are to be regarded as significant statements about the matrix itself. The convenors will utilize these with respect to the purpose for which the dream matrix is being held.

To give an example, I was recently a convenor, along with my colleague Helen Morgan, for a group of about 120 people at the start of each day of an international congress of Jungian analysts. We had been given a large hall in which to work, but the acoustics in the hall—with its high, domed ceiling and noisy air-conditioning—made hearing the shared dreams and the participants' responses to them very difficult indeed.

On the first morning, individuals repeatedly demanded that we find somewhere else in which to work, so that they could hear all that was being said. Some even left the hall. We were ourselves, of course, very much aware of the physical difficulties, for they affected us too; but apart from arranging that in future the air-conditioning would be turned off, we resisted the demands for a different workspace. Instead, we fed back to the matrix our suggestion that in such a large congress (about 700 people in all), it was indeed hard to make one's views heard and impossible to hear all of the talks, or discussions, that were on offer throughout its duration, because of the fullness of the five-day programme. Nor was it easy to meet speakers with whom one might wish to discuss matters further on a one-to-one basis, since we were staying at various different places across the town. All such possible frustrations would inevitably lead to the irritation or anger that was now being expressed, even before the congress proper had got properly under way. Some participants, whose continued dissatisfaction could also be seen as confirming our remarks, accepted our suggestion, rather grudgingly. Yet all those present, as it turned out, made great efforts to speak louder, even standing up to make sure of being heard. It became a matter of interest, which we later remarked upon, that over the five days of the matrix, it became much easier to hear and be heard. The anticipated anxiety about not hearing everything, or of not being individually heard, had lessened, not only through physical experience but also, we believe, because of our recognition of its origins in the social unconscious of the matrix itself.

Three congresses over nine years have confirmed these impressions that everything that is said once the matrix is "open" should always be taken as referring to the matrix itself (see Tatham & Morgan, 1998).

Used in this way, the method has been found to be an excellent tool by which to gain access to unconscious processes of the group taking part, whatever its nature, and therefore to the members' hopes, fears, angers, uncertainties, and so forth. The many published accounts of social dreaming confirm this.

There is, however, one particular aspect of the matrixes that I am writing about here that is unusual to others that I have convened elsewhere: although separated by a six-month period and made up of different people, each of the matrixes shares the same setting (Dartington Hall, Devon), the same kind of professionals (mostly NHS managers), the same reason for being together (SMP), the same programme director, and the same future (the group must now split up and individual members return to their places of work). Therefore, on each day of every year for which social dreaming has been a feature of the biannual SMP, I have found myself dealing with dreams and comments that express many of the same excitements, regrets, and fears as well as future uncertainty and anxieties.

All such emotions also surface by means of other remarks that are not dreams, yet have been made during the matrices. These findings serve to confirm what we know of social dreaming as a means of accessing the group unconscious.

The social dreaming and its themes

In what follows, I shall be extracting what I see as shared themes from the number of matrices so far held, on various occasions. Differences will, however, also be noted, and these might have to do with, among other factors, the individual make-up of the different groups—for example, the type of post and seniority, the different proportion of men to women, differing psychological profiles, the average age of participants, and their present occupation. Personal circumstances at the time will also play a part—marital difficulties, a sick child at home, a dying relative. Yet all of these differences are subsumed in the work of the matrix and their meaning within it.

It should be noted as well that these are, for the most part, people who have never taken their dreams seriously, although it has been noticeable that a number will have remembered important dreams from a much earlier time, even childhood.

The first meeting is held on the second afternoon of the week, and everyone usually attends. However, on the two days that follow, the meetings take place before breakfast and the numbers attending steadily dwindle. On the final morning, there have at times been only two or three people present, apart from myself. The final abstentions may also be due to the long final evening, spent in presenting prepared performances of their artistic activities and mutual celebration, coupled with as a wish to avoid endings.

At that first session, there is usually a good deal of bantering about dreams, some of which is teasing or derogatory. My presence is usually ignored, while jokes concerning events during other group occasions, of which I can know nothing, are re-told, and the men usually take the lead in this. Understanding these sallies as integral to the matrix itself, I recognize all of this as a method by which the group is sticking together in the face of a stranger in their midst, uncertainty concerning this unknown activity, and their unease about the impending dissolution of their commonality. It also represents a way that they use to deal with anxiety-making uncertainty by means of humour, in which they can emphasize that commonality by means of "in-jokes" while excluding the odd one out (myself), who has come in just for these sessions alone. I am the outsider, at first to be ignored or made fun of, which is a safe way of dealing with insecurity. Everybody else can laugh at him, even if he laughs *with* them too. Valerie James, on the other hand, who will also be present, is regarded as one of them.

But such actions also reflect a future that is another source of insecurity for them—namely, the impending time when they will all be returning to post in their organizations. Each individual will then be the "odd one out", suffering the same apprehension as myself, as well as being the butt of similar joking, perhaps. So it is very properly a matter for exploring within the matrix, by means of projecting that role onto the stranger in their midst. In similar fashion, they may themselves soon be seen as "outsiders" with some esoteric knowledge.

During this week, at the same time as experiencing this new and suspicious activity called social dreaming, they will also be taking part in art and media groups, music-making experiences, and, more recently, both theatre and video. None of these will have been a part of previous meetings of the programme. So these are further sources of anxiety, though ultimately pleasurable ones, in which they will take pride. These new activities are, of course, additional to the usual large groups and work groups of the programme.

In my experience over the years, and from an external point of view, I have categorized the kind of experience that participants have had, or with which they are unconsciously concerned at this time, as the following:

1. The overall experience of taking part in SMP, which has, generally speaking, been a good one and at which they have made new acquaintances, some of which relationships may have become important ones.

2. This experience is now coming to an end, so that friendships and alliances, made during the times together, may very well not be continued, as individual participants disperse across the country. Understandably, this can produce mutual sadness among them, for mourning and loss are inevitable.

3. The next phase will be the return to the workplace and the inevitable strain that this involves. What do they have to bring back with them, and what will be expected of them? Will what they have learnt on SMP really be relevant? Can they put into practice the theoretical insights that they have had and experienced personally while taking part in the programme? Or will these be forgotten? Will those colleagues who have not experienced SMP be scornful or critical? After all, what on earth does dreaming, music, painting, or video have to do with the real-life "daily grind"?

All this is to be expected and would be addressed, as well, in the formal and informal meetings of the programme. It is not surprising therefore—indeed, confirmatory—that all such themes have also been seen to be taken up, at various times and in various forms, within the dream matrices, either in associations to the dreams or in other conversations unconnected with dreaming.

At the first meeting of one matrix, several of the dreams discussed concerned flying. In one, *the dreamer was perched upon a window ledge and scared to take the plunge. When he did, then it was exhilarating to soar and dip, bank and turn. It felt unbelievable that he could do this.* Another such dream concerned *a woman, chased by a man with a large dagger. She leapt into the air and soared away, while he remained earthbound. Finally, after flight, she landed safely back on her bed.* These are both about skills that people never knew they had, as well as the ability to surmount unexpected obstacles or aggressive attacks.

The opposite can also be true, as when a man dreamed of *being back at primary school and finding that he had no trousers on without knowing how that had happened.* "This is really bad", he said to himself. The latter two dreams also suggest sexual themes, but these were, however, not addressed, although they would be relevant to the experience of mixing at close quarters and in an intimate fashion, away from home, with individuals of the opposite sex.

Another person dreamt of *an important assignment that must be completed, but the dreamer did not know what the project was.* We talked of this as an expectation, possibly for all of them, of what it would be like to go back to work and the powers that their superiors, as well as colleagues, might then expect them to deliver. There was also an uncertainty as to whether the leaders of their original organizations would be assuming that they, as students, would have learnt everything perfectly, while on the programme.

Another participant, however, remembered a childhood dream of *"the midnight ballerina", in an unknown house, who danced beautifully around the room, without bumping into any of the furniture.* On a different occasion, a dreamer told of *"a little man who goes along doing things I can't do".* So there were unconscious intimations in this particular group that in fact they had indeed taken what they had been taught on board, both to do things that had previously seemed impossible, as well as the skill to avoid obstacles to the creative path (the ballerina).

At another time, a participant asked the question, "At SMP, is the workplace a dream—or will it be vice versa?" Others broke in to say that they could never explain the programme to colleagues, because it all sounded so crazy. A person of mixed nationality asked, "Which of three languages do I dream in?" and could not answer. Another talked of their dreams as being either in colour or in black and white. Dreams were said to be like watching a film, and dreams could also be felt.

In such cases, I might reflect that they were concerned with getting the different "tongues"—the colours, the shapes, a dream-like quality, the emotionality, and sometimes the apparent "craziness" of SMP—from the point of view of the workplace. Not only that, but how might they make use of these new insights, too.

This sort of conversation is, however, more typical of the second or third matrix, when there are sometimes only three or four people present and the dreams themselves are fewer. It has sometimes seemed to me that in the first session of the matrix, the participants feel that they should tell all the dreams that they have ever remembered, as if to please "the parents" sitting among them, as well as being a means of coping with the uncertainty of having a stranger present. To be a part of this process can feel like being overwhelmed by images, while it is also hard to make any sense out of them, which is perhaps in any case what this rush of dreams is expressing. Yet, most importantly of all, the dreams have been shared and will be associated to, even if unconsciously.

Expressions of the social unconscious within later matrices often avoid dreams and may take the form of general remarks on specifics of the programme, or the uncertain future. Equally, there may at times be more personal or social conversation, and it is important to regard this as if it were a dream.

It has been important, though sometimes difficult, not to be pulled into a general discussion—about, for instance, where dreams come from, as well as the impossibilities of knowing their real meaning or, in that case, how one should actively respond to them. Remarks like these can also be interpreted as expressing understandable uncertainties about the future. Such ambivalences were nicely expressed by a dream in which the dreamer *was walking up on the carpet of a grand stone staircase, with a marble balustrade, to a half-landing where the stairway split and she could walk in either direction, to left or right*, but the dream ended there. So there was an anxious uncertainty not only about possible meanings for the dream and how to take it. In the present circumstance, it also reflected her anxiety about the "right way", or correct attitude to take, in meeting her colleagues "upstairs". Also, would they have laid out a *"red* carpet" for her, or not? From a personal point of view, I took it as a reminder to myself that I could choose to stay with the unconscious meanings, or else get sucked into general conversation.

On another occasion, someone remarked that when you did a course, you usually got a certificate at the end of it, but with what would you come out of SMP? It could seem, at times, like a lot of nothing. Someone else then responded, jokingly, by saying that you were expected to have reached Nirvana. This word can be used to mean both "perfect beatitude" as well as "extinction of personality" (*O.E.D.*). So, after SMP, have they really reached some heady enlightenment? Have they lost their old selves and become someone new or strange? Can they now cope with anything that is thrown their way in the workplace? Or are all these things the same? For, post-SMP, they will certainly have changed attitudes and be different from the persons they once were. They have clearly been somewhat enlightened as to the nature of their ways of working, been given access to new skills, and have also, maybe, been brought to a state of being in which they are more able to handle uncertainty. The humorous remark certainly reflects the feelings of ambivalence about returning to work, as well. I suggested that they would have to learn to cope with not being in some Nirvana-like state, represented by SMP. I also shared the thought that they were telling me that the work they had done in the programme had been partly about those states of uncertainty, within any workplace, that had to be lived with, suffered, and even, perhaps, transcended. The spiritual component of that last verb was entirely intentional, although not expanded upon in the matrix.

Participants generally agreed that work would be the same, but that it would be they who had changed, as well as their attitudes to the work. The roles they played, within the workplace, would be the same, but, as actors, they were different—changed people because of SMP. And, besides being beneficial, this was also somewhat scary.

On one occasion, someone remembered that in a previous post she had had a colleague who went to SMP and whom she had thought must therefore be brilliantly clever. "One day, I'll do that too", she had told herself. So now, having been here and done that, she didn't feel clever at all, but just worried that she was now the one who would be expected to be clever.

On another occasion on the last morning of one of the programmes, a man was in tears, having just heard that a close relative was dying. He had decided that he must leave directly after breakfast and not wait until the end of the programme. His sadness affected others, and several of the others were soon also in tears, those nearest holding him in their arms, as supporters. This too seemed to be an expression (without any dream) of the sadness felt by people who had well bonded together over the five weeks and whose "set" was now on the verge of going out of physical existence. Leaving early could seem to be a way of avoiding the sadness that that implied.

On a later occasion, a participant talked of watching the Twin Towers disaster on television. She desperately wanted to say "good-bye" to those figures falling from the doomed buildings. But since none of the others with whom she watched spoke out; neither could she. The silence had felt horrible to her. We agreed that for SMP, now was the time and place for such expressions of sadness and loss. The edifice that was the programme was indeed "dying", just like a building that crashed to the earth, throwing out its occupants. Would they, could they, survive the shock of a safe landing, which might very well feel like ejection? Or would they "die", just like the experience of SMP that was ending? How does an infant survive the birth experience, someone reflected? In fact, it is the "foetus" that "dies", in becoming an infant. But that infant can now grow—into eventual adulthood.

But such feelings of sadness about endings are not the only ones expressed, and neither do they last. On one occasion, a dream was shared of a familiar, comfortable house that the dreamer had previously lived in but had completely forgotten. How could he have done that? Dreaming of it anew, he felt in touch with life again. Another told of *being on a beach when the tide comes rushing in, so that she must find an escape route, at all costs. But within the dream she then remembered that she had learnt to dream under water, so that all would be well.* I suggested, as I have on various occasions before, that at SMP they may all have learnt or re-learnt skills that they didn't know they had., or which had somehow been "forgotten". Or perhaps they could now think of doing familiar things in a different, or more skilful, way. And, in addition, they had learnt or been confirmed in what it is like to live with the uncertainty of not necessarily "knowing" and yet survive it—which is also a skill.

In conclusion, these experiences with SMP have confirmed what I already knew about the value and importance of social dreaming as a highly constructive tool, capable of being used in a wide variety of formal or informal group situations. Yet what I have tried to convey in this chapter is that similar (though not identical) situations such as exist in SMP, and consisting of people doing similar kinds of jobs, will contain the same kind of unconscious concerns that will be expressed by similar, multi-versal, messages from the social unconscious of the commonality. I am also directing attention to the vital importance of treating each and every remark made within any matrix once it has been "opened"—whether dream or otherwise—as a significant statement to be taken seriously as a pointer to, as well as an aid for, furthering understanding of the underlying processes presented within the matrix.

CHAPTER TWELVE

Dream intelligence: tapping conscious and non-attended sources of intelligence in organizations

Marc Maltz and E. Martin Walker

Innovation is the product of free thinking—the creative process of generating ideas that occurs when we suspend the binds of daily life and allow our dreams to be expressed and discussed. An aspiration of most organizations, innovation is forever searched for, rarely achieved, yet ever-present. Many organizations try to enhance their creative process through activities that attempt to break the organization's members out of their normal routine in order to create new ways of working, new products, new ways of serving markets, and so forth. These processes, though, are usually unsuccessful because they do not allow the participants the opportunity to break from the social and psychological restrictions that inhibit them from contributing to such an effort.

Gordon Lawrence has written many examples over the years of how dreams have been the starting point for innovative thinking (see also chapter one herein). The authors in their own writing (Maltz & Walker, 1998) and work with dreams have witnessed the capacity of organizations to understand, to learn, and to break through traditional knowledge management in order to create new and innovative approaches to work and develop a deeper understanding of what is occurring.

We believe that the process of dreaming and the freeing of a system's use of those dreams to explore their meaning and not treat them as an individual phenomenon provides for a greater understanding, insight, and learning that further develops an organization's "intelligence".

The process of innovation

Let us look at the proto-process through which ideas are generated.[1]

- *Ideas* are the currency of innovation and are generated through intelligence.[2]
- *Intelligence* is the product of both an individual's cognitive intelligence[3] or thinking and emotional intelligence[4] or feeling.
- In organizations, intelligence is constrained by the need to protect against real and imagined loss via personal, interpersonal, and group *security* needs (also known as social defence mechanisms).
- Intelligence—the product of our emotional and cognitive abilities—can be freed from these natural security needs.
- The suspension of security needs occurs when one gains access to the uninhibited intelligence that occurs naturally in the brain's processing as represented in people's dreams.
- When properly utilized, dreams release the creative energy within an organization that is necessary for innovation and the emergence of new ideas.

Where intelligence comes from:
dreams as a part of the brain's consciousness

The study of neurological impairments via magnetic resonance imaging has enabled neurophysiologists to demonstrate that dreams are a critical part of the brain's processing of information. The areas of the brain where our experience, history, knowledge, and data-intake are processed daily coincide with those areas responsible for processing dreams. This processing power is constantly working out of awareness, except for those moments when one remembers a dream or has the feeling of *déjà vu*. In this way, the brain is continually integrating and processing thoughts and feelings in a manner that generates new learning and intelligence. Bringing this innate capacity of individuals together on behalf of an organization results in enhanced organizational intelligence.

Dreams are scientifically known to be a key component in how we process our daily emotional and cognitive world. Antonio Damasio (1999a) describes how the dreaming state of the brain is the only time during a sleeping cycle that the brain is actually "conscious", that "some 'consciousness' is on" during sleep. This consciousness is free of the contextual inhibitions that are imposed during our waking life. Put conversely, our daily ability to use our brain's power is diminished by the normal defence mechanisms that we use to exist and function. Our dream state is free to process our knowledge, unencumbered by the distractions that interfere with how we use information.[5]

In the brain, dreams are the state in which conscious processing occurs, regardless of the dreamer's awareness of such dreams.[6] Beyond the dream is the non-attended information of the brain; all that is not conscious, which may or may not seep into our consciousness. Intelligence is derived from three states of conscious processing and numerous states of non-attended processing. At a conscious level, three categories of processing occurs:

1. awake and aware;
2. awake and unaware (that part of our dynamic processing which, assuming our capacity to be present in the here-and-now, is dependent on our ability to understand our defence or security operations);
3. dreaming.

In our non-attended pre-/un-conscious, there are two broad categories of brain processing:

1. neural patterning that is stored in memory and retrieved;
2. neural patterning that is probably stored yet never retrieved or used in our conscious state.[7]

In addition to the above, there is a level of brain functioning that precedes neural patterning and is made up of all of the interactions of the brain's neurochemistry. This chemical level of neural processing is noted here to emphasize that there is a tremendous amount of data, possibly knowledge, that is never utilized in our conscious states and that remains non-attended. The link between the conscious and the non-attended *is* the dream. And the dream is a function of our consciousness and contains information and knowledge that is eclipsed by our awakening, sometimes captured in fragments, and clearly an integral part of how we think, work, and gain intelligence.

Imagery, a key to the brain's process

The preceding discussion of the brain's neural processing may help us to understand how the brain functions utilizing images. Damasio (1999a) and Llinás and Paré (1991) have written extensively about how image functioning is *the* primary means by which the brain processes. Said simply, we think in images that are derived from our "sensory modalities—visual, auditory, olfactory, gustatory and somatosensory" (Damasio, 1999a, p. 318). These images occur in both our non-attended and conscious states. Imagery in the non-attended state begins with neurochemical patterns that derive neural patterns that then give way to memory that then are used in thought.[8] There are also the images created in the course of here-and-now functioning that are critical to our creation of knowledge.

There are, then, two image sources that help us form thought. One is memory, which serves as a database of stored images; the other source is the images as they are experienced and taken-in. Dream images are a combination of the two, since some of what we are dreaming draws from what is stored in our brain's memory banks and some of what we are dreaming is the processing of the day's and the moment's experience. Our consciousness becomes informed by the dream, forever altered by its occurrence. What we recall is only a fragment of what our brain utilizes. What learning takes place, while not easily measured, is a real part of consciousness and a contribution to our intelligence. In fact, sleep studies have demonstrated that artificially presenting the brain with abstract-reasoning tasks during dream states results in higher levels of abstract-reasoning performance on those same tasks during the subsequent waking state.

Organizational intelligence: freeing creativity

A key element in the efficacy of using dream intelligence in organizations is the fact that there are striking parallels between the way in which individuals process information and the manner in which organizations manage knowledge. There are many ways of representing thinking in the dynamic life of organizations; a simple construct to demonstrate what occurs is presented in Figure 12.1, which is an adaptation of the Johari Window (Luft, 1969).

The Johari Window provides a conceptual model for representing how information known to both self and others can be considered "free" knowledge. Information consciously[9] known to the self but not known to others is "hidden". Furthermore, information not consciously known to the self yet known to others is "blind" to the self. Finally, information not consciously known to either the self or others is simply "unknown".

The key to freeing creativity in an organization begins with understanding how information is managed by a group of individuals. If

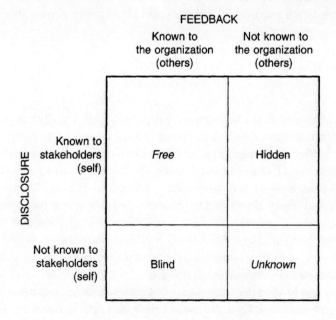

Figure 12.1.   The Johari Window (adapted from Luft, 1969)

applied to organizations, the Johari Window helps us to understand that the nature of conscious knowledge is freely available when consciously known to all, hidden when known to key stakeholders though not to the organization as a whole, and blind when known to the organization though not to key persons. Finally, the "unknown" is that which is not available to the organization or to its members in ways that would support the development of new knowledge—the development of intelligence that is essential to innovation.

By tapping into "blind", "hidden", and "unknown" realms of organizational knowledge, we access those sources of intelligence in the organization that are beyond the normal bounds of consciousness, much in the same way that the dream accesses information in the brain. This is the knowledge that is below the surface in the three conscious states (aware, unaware, dreaming) that are not available[10] or, in the deeper non-attended portions of the brain, that are preconscious. Making dreams available socially provides a mechanism to retrieve this information and make it available to free the organization from its normal operating dynamics, group processes, and security needs that disable stakeholders and the organization itself in the quest of gaining the intelligence that makes innovation possible. This is precisely the manner in which dream intelligence comes about.

Social dreaming

The technology that can release an organization's creative processes and stimulate innovation and further change is social dreaming (Lawrence, 1998c), an experiential process that frees the individual from survival needs in the present, linking the heart and mind to be available for revelation and epiphany (Lawrence, 1998d). Dreams are shared and freely associated to, collectively linking our thoughts and feelings, resulting in the deconstruction of group relations that inhibit innovation. Meaning is then freed and discovered, co-creating new experience and understanding. A dreaming matrix emerges, and a new knowledge community is formed.

The use of dreams as a means of understanding and developing organizational intelligence was originated by Lawrence nearly twenty years ago at the Tavistock Institute in London. Groups of people explored what occurred when they shared and associated to their dreams in a structured and positive way, and this resulted in astounding discoveries. Social dreaming matrices have since shown that sharing and associating to dreams allows one to tap into organizational intelligence and successfully overcome security needs. In this way, social dreaming overcomes the systems dynamics that undermine efficiency and productivity and the release of creative energy. Dreaming socially is itself not a new discovery, since dreams have always been used by numerous societies, mostly communities of indigenous populations, such as the Sioux, Senoi, Masai and Aborigines, to guide and manage the community in the collective, representing the whole community including its history, present and potential.

Contemporary organizations are plagued by complex dynamics that inhibit their ability to fully function and access the information that is contained within them. Providing a method for freeing an organization from its own dynamics (in the form of resistance) in order to free its creative energy is no simple task. These dynamics, or security needs, exist within and outside the bounds of awareness. Social dreaming has been used by Lawrence, the authors, and others as a means of helping people within organizations reach their untapped creativity and achieve innovative approaches to organizational dilemmas.

Dreams @ work

So far, this chapter has been looking at how linking an organization's cognitive, emotional, and dream intelligence can lead to increased organizational intelligence. What follows are two case examples showing how the development of a social dreaming network had a dramatic impact on the capacity of two large organizations to harness creativity, to innovate, and to change in reaction to environmental factors that threatened their existence. The first is a large entertainment-media-manufacturing firm that found itself encumbered by obsolete production methods, and the second is a financial services firm that was located in the World Trade Center when it was destroyed on 11 September 2001.

Case 1

During a complex restructuring of a multinational manufacturing company, in which manufacturing processes were being radically redesigned to improve efficiency and profitability, dreams were shared among the internal and external consultants charged with making the changes necessary for success.[11] In these dreams, the consultants became aware that workers were fearing that the change would cost them their jobs and that the system would be radically changed forever, disrupting seventeen years of full employment, caring management, and an atmosphere of family-first. The external consultants were alarmed by these dreams and the understanding associated with them. They used this data to confront management about the unspoken, unknown dilemmas that the management faced. This breakthrough allowed the management to rethink their strategy and realize that not only was the new production system unable to sustain more than 50% of the current workforce; more importantly, the new system under development would not sustain the current management structure. Six months later, only six of the twenty-one executives in the leadership team and 1,500 of the nearly 4,000 employees remained, and the son of the founder of the business retired to be replaced by the first non-family CEO. Radical change that the organization could not face or come to terms with was exposed in the dreams of those charged with planning the transition and, once shared, enabled the organization to achieve a smooth transition to a new way of life.

Case 2

The following is a discussion of four dreams from a consultation with a firm affected by the September 11 attacks on the World Trade Center in New York City. This firm lost one-third of its employees when the second tower was struck. The dreams come from two employees and one of the authors who is consulting to the firm. Of the two employees who shared their dreams, one escaped from the second tower and the other witnessed the devastation from the concourse. The dreams are shared in order of occurrence.

DREAM 1: SYNCHRONIZED HEARTBEATS—"I had a disturbing dream the morning after my recent return from two weeks away in China on business for another client in November. In the dream, *I am a passenger on one of the hijacked planes and I believe that if I could only synchronize the beating of my heart to all of the other passengers on all of the other hijacked planes, we could slow the planes down and make them veer away from their targets.* When I awoke from my panicked, anxious state in the dream, I could only think about the many folk whom I had not seen for two weeks—their faces haunted me in that early morning. I felt as though I had failed in my role as consultant, that I had abandoned them by attending to other work. Or, had they abandoned me in my unconscious? For me, this dream was very much about what doing this work meant to me as well as what our work has meant to this firm. For the firm, we are in the business of synchronizing the hearts of those who survived, in order to ensure a return to health and to ensure the caring for the many families devastated by this tragedy."[12]

The vivid imagery could be understood at many levels, including the wish on the part of the dreamer to have averted this trauma and the fantasy that he or someone had the power to stop it; the management of the dreamer's guilt for attending to others; and, as a consultation to the dreamer, to establish an understanding of what was actually occurring. In the context of this particular system, it is the job of the consultants to synchronize efforts for the families, the employees, and the system as a whole. This knowledge exists within the dreamer yet is not accessible until after the dream (or perhaps through the dream). This dream, when shared, led to changes within the consultation—for instance, the merging of employee support groups, which previously had been separated by experience, into a single support group for the entire firm.

DREAM 2: THE PLANES KEEP COMING—"I keep having the same repeating nightmare. *We have bought a home on a mountain above a dam. I am sitting on our porch and I see a jet plane flying low, flying directly towards the dam. I realize it is a hijacked plane flying into the dam to destroy it. I also realize that once the dam is hit, the mountain will collapse and I might be killed.*"

This dream is from a woman who is one of the sole survivors of her department. She observed the tragedy of the day from the concourse of the World Trade Center, including having burning debris fall on her and witnessing bodies falling from windows. In addition, she received a message on her home answering machine from one of her colleagues, saying "goodbye". For the individual, the dream can be understood as guilt at being alive, disbelief that this occurred, vulnerability, and so forth. When shared with her new team, it highlighted how vulnerable the department was and how new people coming into the firm to fill the seats of those lost were experienced as terrorists flying into the dam—the dam being she and her colleague, who were holding the water back, keeping the department alive as it was being rebuilt. This shared learning enabled the group to begin working on the dynamic rift between old and new employees to ensure that the dam remained whole— to ensure that the security needs of both the new and the old were understood, respected, and worked through in order to form a functional work-group.

DREAM 3: MY BOSS IS ALIVE AND WELL—"This morning I awoke confused thinking that my boss was still alive. I had awoken from a dream in which *he was sitting across from me in my new office, dressed casually as he would be dressed on a Friday. I was ecstatic in the dream, asking him where he was, where he had been for the past five months. He responded that he had used the opportunity to have an affair with a woman and to think through a few things. Towards the end of the dream, I started to cry in front him with the joy of his being alive.* In reality, I never really got along with my boss. He was always a bit hard on me."

The dreamer was one of the few who managed to escape from the upper floors of the second tower moments before it collapsed. He is also responsible for rebuilding a fledgling part of this firm's business. The dream at the organizational level came to represent how the dreamer had so well internalized the manager; that he had become him. Hearing the dream, the group began to discuss how they could each contribute to each other's role and enhance the whole and for the first time began to understand how to segment functions and align roles. The dream enabled the dreamer to explore further how the deceased manager had prepared him for this moment, giving him new confidence and initiating a number of key improvements in his business segment.

DREAM 4: THE DISTANT COLLEAGUE—"*I am in my office and my [dead] colleague is alive and asking me what has been happening. I feel socially awkward with him. He feels reserved, cautious, not sure that he can trust me. We have a short and uncomfortable interaction. I am confused by our lack of rapport and find myself unable to say so to him.*"

This dream is the dream of the firm. How do they integrate the memories and institutional learning from those that are now gone? How do they build on the internalized experience and knowledge of those they have lost and be whole again? These and other questions were difficult to raise and discuss. In sharing the dream, the group began the conversation of what and who was missing and how to rebuild. The integration of what was held inside of each, the knowledge and learning collected from the experience of working together with those who were now gone, could be realized, discussed, and mobilized in their rebuilding.

The imagery contained in these four dreams is not surprising, given the context. Their use in open forums as a means of bringing understanding resulted in new knowledge and new initiatives that led to departmental learning and organizational change. Without these dream images being shared and associated to, the dreams would have remained in the realm of the forgotten fragment of dream consciousness or as a consciousness image that was disturbing for the dreamer and potentially contributing to the conscious nightmare the dreamers were living. Once shared, the dreams functioned as an integral part of the development of new organizational intelligence, an intelligence that helps heal grief and portend survival for the firm.

Conclusion

The process of sharing and associating to dreams in a social setting in which dreams are offered for the whole and not the individual is a direct means of bringing the imagery offered in the brain's dream-level consciousness to the foreground in the awake and aware state.

Furthermore, doing so in an organizational setting will allow for breakthroughs in thinking that can lead to innovative approaches to organizational needs. We have presented the neurological evidence for dreams as one of three levels of consciousness (awake and aware, awake and unaware, dreaming). We have offered the link between the brain's use of imagery as its primary mode of processing and imagery as offered in its dream state. We have outlined a methodology for enabling creativity and innovation within organizations, a methodology that frees persons from the security needs that inhibit such thinking. Lastly, we have described how the ongoing work in social dreaming is the ideal methodology for unleashing creativity and innovation within groups and organizations.

Dream intelligence is an extension of cognitive and emotional intelligence and enhances our ability to perceive social dynamics and learn from experience. Although the dramatic imagery in the dreams from our second case example is understandable given the social context in which they occurred, they are not at all unusual. Again, once shared, the dreams functioned as an integral part of the development of new organizational intelligence, a means of moving from intense grief and anxiety to organizational learning that provides survival for both the individual and the firm. Social dreaming provides new-found intelligence—dream intelligence—at the social systems level.

We believe that the ability to access the forgotten fragments of dream consciousness is a vital knowledge resource that organizations are currently wasting. Dreams and the intelligence captured within are freely available to all and, as we have seen, are key elements in the information environment that organizations ignore at their own peril. Gerald Zaltman has written on the importance of taking advantage of the brain's image-processing capabilities in both management and marketing (Eakin, 2002). We need to ask ourselves why we are not using the intelligence freely available to us in our dreams in *all* aspects of organizational life.

Notes

1. This section was developed in collaboration with S. Fitzpatrick, W. G. Lawrence, and B. Patel.

2. By intelligence, we mean "the ability to learn or understand or to deal with

new or trying situations; the skilled use of reason; the ability to manipulate one's environment or to think abstractly . . ." (*Webster's New Collegiate Dictionary*).

3. Often measured as intelligence quotient (IQ).

4. Measured by any number of instruments and known as emotional quotient (EQ). There are numerous publications that expand the theory of emotional intelligence and emotional quotient.

5. There are many examples and extensive literature on how the dynamics of daily life interfere with our ability to work, think, process, and so on. A good example is Bion's "basic assumptions" that interfere with group members' ability to remain on task and attending to the work they should be achieving (Bion, 1961).

6. It should be noted that neuroscience has shown that dreams occur during each REM ("rapid eye movement") cycle of the brain, a function that repeats itself numerous times during the course of a full sleep cycle.

7. For a full discussion of the neurophysiology of the brain, see Damasio (1999a, pp. 317–335).

8. We keep noting "may" since so much of what our brains create is never accessed by us consciously.

9. In this discussion, "consciousness" only refers to the "aware" state of the brain's processing.

10. As in the dream or dream fragments quickly forgotten upon awakening, they were once available and lost once the "proto-self" is confronted by the prospect of managing in the "awake" state and once the proto-self is confronted and inhibited by the security needs stimulated by its context.

11. For a fuller discussion of these dreams and the process, see Maltz and Walker (1998).

12. From "'Finding You in Me': The Organizational Clinician", a consultation conducted by M. Maltz to an investment bank that was in the World Trade Center on 11 September 2001.

CHAPTER THIRTEEN

Paul Lippmann interview

E. Martin Walker

M ARTIN WALKER: I guess I'll just start by getting a sense of what your general impressions were from attending that event [a social dreaming matrix at the William Alanson White Institute in New York City].

PAUL LIPPMANN: I was, throughout, of two minds about the weekend. On the one hand, I was ready to join in the proceedings, to learn about this approach to dreaming in a social context, to meet with persons in the organizational program, and to have a good time with colleagues. I liked the idea of thinking about dreams in a context in which I was more a learning participant than responsible teacher. The evening prior to the beginning of the workshop, I had participated in a lovely programme at the White Institute featuring Lynn Gamwell and her slide-talk on dreams, art, and the hundredth anniversary of Freud's *Interpretation of Dreams*. So I was in a dreamy mood and happy to be at White taking part in what I understood to be an interesting dream-sharing experience. I recognized some to the participants and felt happy and ready to join in.

On the other hand, I felt particularly watchful for signs of subtle indoctrination and control, since the subject matter, after all, was *dreams*—that nightly voice of free thought and unwilled imagination. I have always been worried about efforts to control through dreams, whether the control is in the hands of interpreter psychoanalysts, lucid dreaming cultists, new-age believers, shamanic pretenders, advertising marketers, or even self-styled iconoclasts like myself. So you can see, my two-mindedness was in full swing as the social dreaming weekend got underway.

Again, on the other hand, I had just written about the social nature of dreams—the role of the social universe in the basic vocabulary of dreams—also, on the socially cohesive nature of dream interpretation in pre-industrial civilization as well as within the indoctrinating nature of various schools of psychoanalysis, the role of dreams in the foundation of religion, the social effects of dream telling and dream listening, and so forth (Lippmann, 2000). So I was eager to learn from Gordon Lawrence, who has had a long and distinguished career in working with dreams.

And then there was the way I am in group experiences. While I am increasingly a private person, nestled in my practice and in writing, and in the middle of family within a small-town culture, I have had, in earlier times, my share of "transformative" group experiences. At Naropa (the Buddhist study centre) in the 1970s, in political organizations and rallies in the 1960s, and in a number of experiences over the years, I had had the mixed pleasure of yielding my private self over to the excitement and power of the group and the mass. I hadn't had such an experience for a long while, and I was looking forward to it, sort of.

At the outset of the weekend, I went back and forth between these two hands until I began to relax my guard (on the surface) sufficient to realize that my own counter-agenda, my own counter-politics, was leading me to ignore the evident fact that here was an interesting collection of individuals gathered at White to talk about dreams. What on earth was the fuss about in my own head? Why not just "be here now?" Despite some mumbo-jumbo and my reservations about trappings of cultishness, the participants were a diverse group from within and outside our field, from within and outside the organizational programme, and I began to realize that we had a lot to learn from each other.

In my teaching at White and elsewhere, patients' dreams were the subject matter. I had been looking forward to learning what it would be like to use the participant's own dreams, as Ullman had been doing for decades. As it turned out, the experience itself—sharing dreams—was more significant than any problems I was having with the "set-up." That is, the opportunity to tell and listen to and associate to dreams, without moving to interpretation, allowed us to come to touch each other and to see into each other and into ourselves in compelling and evocative ways.

MW: That sort of fits in with one thing I wanted to ask you. Given that the primary task of the weekend was for people to gather to-gether for the purpose of sharing dreams and associations, how would you compare and contrast this with your own way of thinking about dreams?

PL: In my own thinking, working, and writing about dreams—par-ticularly in relation to psychotherapy—I am drawn more and more to a naturalist approach in which dreams are allowed to unfold on their own terms and in which the goal is not so much a "correct interpreta-tion" as an engagement in "good dream conversation." The rich net-work of meaning, feelings, surprises, and learning possible in relation to dreams has a better chance of showing itself when dreams are not crowded into some narrowed compartments of interpreted meaning. Dreams are more likely to show what they are up to when ap-proached playfully, open-heartedly, from the side, and when the par-ticipants are willing to follow the mysteries of unconscious thinking. I have become increasingly convinced that much analytic dream inter-pretation amounts to reading into patients' dreams what the analyst has on his or her mind and believes might be a helpful and therapeu-tic response, thus leaving the dream itself in the dust.

The workshop experience with dreams came close to this natural-ist, "good-conversation" approach that has been evolving in my own work. This way of talking together about dreams harkened back to what I imagined to be earlier modes of relating to dreams and to old-fashioned ways of sharing dreams. I had been reading anthropologi-cal dream studies, which emphasized various cultures' pre-scientific and pre-industrial emphasis on dreams and in which dreams were a more significant part of people's everyday lives. I began to see the way psychoanalysis had been using dreams to bolster its own shaky theories about human behaviour, sort of "strip-mining" dreams for its own purposes. I valued approaches that explored dreams without domination through interpretation. As the workshop proceeded, I began to recognize that Lawrence and the social dreaming movement had been attempting to back away from the psychoanalytic misuse of dreams to a more respectful and appreciative approach. That is, I thought Lawrence was attempting, in the midst of our modern world-market culture, to harken back to "simpler" times when people shared their dreams and enjoyed the human connectedness such sharing afforded.

MW: One of ideas surrounding social dreaming is that the focus be on the dream itself, and not the dreamer. What thoughts do you have about that, and what sort of social dynamics could a dream in that context be addressing besides the intrapsychic make-up of the person?

PL: While I understand the conceptual separation between dream and dreamer, and I understand that the greater stress is on the dream and not on the person in this approach, I think the question reflects a methodological posture rather than a substantive difference. That is, the separation can be understood as a way of allaying anxieties that the sharing of dreams will be used to "plumb" personality dynamics. That is: "don't worry, we are not after you, we are simply and innocently after your nightly musings." While in earlier cultures dreams were more often shared with gusto, in our culture people are often shy to share dreams because of the analytic bias that dreams reveal unconscious (hence potentially shameful) secrets. Thus, the social dreaming group may attempt to reduce such anxieties by speaking as though a dream is an "innocent" product separable from the conflicts, problems, and secrets of the dreamer. While the intent is a good one, in my opinion the idea is not. I think this distinction may have some meaning for a social dreaming group, but it doesn't make much sense to me. For instance, calling an event a dream "matrix" and not a group may be useful for the enterprise but not for the participants who may end up calling it that more for the sake of the leaders than for their own. The same can be said for referring to the consultants as "takers". Dream and dreamer separated echoes the idea of thoughts without a thinker, an idea of interest to the Bionists and to others in the English group more than to myself or to the Interpersonalists in general who, despite Harry Stack Sullivan's difficult language, do seem mostly to prefer plain speech and to avoid tricky metaphysics. In brief, the dream is the dreamers' night thinking. It reveals the dreamer's private musings and creations. The dream is indistinguishable, in my opinion, from the dreamer. One can playfully think of the dream as the product of a social fabric, or an era, or a group, or series of ideas—but it is, after all is said and done, the dreamer's.

MW: I'm trying to get a better idea of the dream that fits something we talk about at White a lot, which is the two-person space.

PL: Okay, but there is also the spiritual space, there's the relation between the living and the dead space, there's consciousness, there's regression, etc. There are all kinds of spaces we inhabit when we talk about dreams.

MW: When you mentioned the death space, I was thinking about the . . .

PL: There was a lot of stuff on death that weekend.

MW: Yes—what about that powerful segment about people dying and those who were already dead?

PL: The dreams of the participant concerning the recent, untimely death of her dear husband who left behind a young family was a defining experience for this group. We shared in the spirit of this terrible loss. Furthermore, as a group we experienced directly the profound relationship between dreams and death, in general via the large number of such dreams that were presented. More and more, I think that dreams are the natural home for inner reflections on death. The interweaving between the tragic element of our long foreknowledge of death and our life-long denial of the inevitability of our ending are found on the dance floor of our dreams. Perhaps thought-in-sleep is a more natural way than awake, though, to explore the mysteries of death. Our modern culture specializes in the denial and repudiation of the natural, universal processes of ageing and death. Thus it may be more difficult, in the awakened state, to consider the full range of meanings of dying (our own as well as that of loved ones) without the flooding experiences of anxiety and dread. In sleep, when the barriers are down, we can engage in all sorts of reflections and connections within the safe boundaries of sleep and may be in a better position to explore, learn about, imagine, worry about, hypothesize, and conclude about death and dying. Also, as the ancients have always known, sleep comes closer to death than does waking. Sleep was seen as something of a miniature nightly rehearsal for the enormity of death. In sleep and in dreams, the disembodied soul was seen as being free to wander, perhaps as it did in death. Dreams in which dead persons are seen again was once taken as direct sensory evidence for the existence of life after death. Whether or not sleep and dreams come close to the experience of death, the social realm of dream interpretation has historically placed dreams and death in close affinity.

At last spring's conference on the clinical use of dreams in celebration of the hundredth anniversary of Freud's *Interpretation of Dreams*, a significant majority of the dreams reported by a diverse group of psychoanalysts concerned one or another aspect of the experiences of death and dying. When interpretative comments were added, most every dream could be seen as touching on death. This was really a surprise at that meeting, since psychoanalysts do not ordinarily connect dreams with death. It may be time for us to look at dreams for what they tell us about the dreamer's thoughts about our finite existence.

Since most ancient cultures include ideas about dreams as prophecy, perhaps it need not surprise us that dreams concern themselves with our inevitable ending—the certain future of us all. Dreams, thus, may be an arena of virtual reality and thought for exploring not only the "what was" (i.e., the infantile as well as day-residue sources of dreams according to Freud), but also the "what wasn't" (paths not taken) as well as the "what is to be" (the future). The focus on Freud's wish-gratification and infantile hypotheses may turn us away from the ubiquitousness of death themes in dreams, such as the appearance of a dead person, anticipation of the death of loved ones, and anticipation of one' own death. The wish-fulfilment hypotheses may therefore represent a wish not to think about dying and may be yet another way in which modern culture—psychoanalysis in this instance—takes part in the denial of nature.

We should also remember that only a very small portion of dreams are remembered and reported. Therefore, it is possible that in our night thinking there is a vast outpouring of thinking about death in one guise or another, as one way we prepare, mostly unconsciously, for the fact of our ending. Dreaming, forgetting, dreaming, forgetting, experiencing, digesting, forgetting—over and over the mind in sleep plays with every manner of experience in a life-long exploration of the major mysteries of human experience—including death. Again, this may represent one of the ways we prepare and rehearse for death, without being flooded by anxiety.

I don't think there was anything particularly significant about the appearance of so many death themes at the workshop, because dreams about death are much more common than we suspect and will show themselves if given half a chance.

MW: Changing the subject, I wanted to ask you about the sequencing of dreams that were presented that weekend. For example, the first two dreams were presented by therapists about incidents in which it was unclear to them whether a contact with a patient was a therapy session or just an informal conversation. Also, sometimes the associations seemed to link up in a similar way. Like after the dream in a beautiful gorge, the association was made to going down a river in Alaska and then to some other profound experience of nature which could then trigger the recall of dreams about nature, etc.

PL: That is an interesting question concerning the way in which dreams affect each other, build on each other, perhaps even subtract from each other. Images from architecture and mathematics show up here. We know little—or, I should say, I know very little—about this aspect of dream connection under the surface. Leaving aside for the moment the complicating effects of associations to dreams and of the effects of telling a dream to another or to a group, dreams exist in a world in which they probably communicate with and determine one another in ways yet unknown. While telling a dream in psychotherapy, people will often spontaneously remember a whole category of earlier dreams of which this particular dream is an example, a repetition, or an extension, or a further elaboration of. In the underworld of dreams, there often seems to be a separate library of dreams, an encyclopaedia of one's own dreams, most of which are unremembered, that may cross-reference one another in an active process of dream interaction. This hypothetical process goes on beneath the active interaction between conscious day thinking and dreams. Thus, we can speculate that dreams create, interact with, and comment upon each other while at the same time interacting continually with awake thought. As a dreamer myself, and as an analyst working with individuals and mostly with one dream at a time, I only get occasional glimpses of the way dreams address one another. They often seem so discontinuous, so unique, so individual. But this uniqueness may be an illusion of the manifest if we consider the possibility that all dreams draw upon on another for influence and commentary.

Things get even more interesting and complicated when we add free-association thinking to the mix, and still more complicated when we consider the effects of group dream-telling, as in the social dreaming project. In the latter situation, we can sometimes see additional evidence of dream connections, as Person B's dream seems directly to be commenting, adding to, and taking off from the dream presented the day before by Person A. This could, of course, just be an example of day residue, but it suggests something more complex when we look carefully at the dream elements that give rise to one another.

The social dreaming project, when it works, seems to provide the freedom to interact socially, emotionally, and intellectually but also in the deeper recesses of what we usually consider the private mind. This probably is brought about in many ways, but one of the ways may have to do with the ancient property of dreams in bringing people together. Dreams often can fly beneath the radar of ordinary paranoid thinking. They have a way of disarming the armed. Their ambiguity, strangeness, playfulness, zaniness may loosen the ordinary defences of social interaction. We all have dreams; we all are capable of being frightened of and pleased by dreams; we all share in their mystery; and none of us is free from the common bond of puzzlement about them. Also, they always can change the set of the thinking and interacting going on. Within a social dreaming context, the changes in set are frequent and sharp. This has the effect of displacing the power of logical, coherent, linear thinking and allowing more room for uncertainty, unknowingness, hunches, feelings— that is, for the softer and fuzzier sides of our mental activities. When this takes place within a group of *gemütlich* participants and with coordinators who are not bullies or know-it-alls, it allows a high degree of freedom of thought. This freedom is often very pleasurable and allows a group of relative strangers to begin to care for each other in subtle ways.

Perhaps in modern life, relative strangers can learn to interact in myriad ways. One such way is through proscribed "exercises" and activities. A dance class, a yoga group, a lecture series, a bar room, a political rally, a social dreaming workshop—all provide ways of being with others and with a sense of freedom and range enhanced. Another way is the teaching that can occur between teacher and student where there is this freedom of thought that can occur between both. I don't believe that the social dreaming exercise is qualitatively different from these other modes of bringing strangers together in ways that provide an increased sense of aliveness and well-being. Although I must say that telling dreams to one another seems pleasingly anachronistic—like sitting around a fire and telling stories or like writing letters, wonderfully old-fashioned.

MW: Speaking of teaching, the weekend was greatly enriched by your perspective and historical knowledge of dreams. At the same time, you expressed some ambivalence about getting into the teaching role.

PL: On the most superficial level, it was a clash of roles between being a teacher and being a student in relation to dreams. At the institute, I've been a teacher of dreams for a long while. Yet I always feel like a student of dreams. How could it be otherwise? Dreams, as a phenomenon, just do not permit of the experience of expertise, of settledness, of finality. Quite the opposite: they always reveal that one knows nothing. With a great deal of work and luck, one may come to know a little something—for a moment. But with dreams and in dream conversation, knowledge is fleeting, constantly changing, inevitably undermined by the very next association or idea or image, subject to continuous revision. And yet, still, I may turn out to know a thing or two—not so much about dreams as about how not to talk about them with patients.

Since I was a new participant, I was very much a student in the workshop. And yet I am a teacher of dreams, so almost each time I spoke I felt my teacher role asserting itself. I couldn't divorce myself from that role, no matter how hard I tried. I became concerned that the teacher was my way of keeping distance, but it's also my way of bridging distance. After a while, I just stopped trying and became this funny mix of teacher-student, of expert-amateur. My guess is that it was trying on some people, and I apologize for being so two-headed, but that's how it is inside me as well, most of the time. In the world of dreams, I know and I know not. It's probably not so different for all of us in the realm of psychotherapy. . . . So, what are you up to with all this?

MW: I'm trying to apply dreaming to organizations, but I've learned that this requires staying away from some of the psychoanalytic language and being more focused on the creativity aspect of it. We [Gordon Lawrence, Marc Maltz, Martin Walker] are working on ways of talking about dreams that is easier for people to connect with, to relate to. Personally, these experiences also make me feel much more comfortable about dreams and dreaming, and letting my own "dreaming space" come into my analytic work with patients.

In my growth as a therapist, I am trying to work out where to allow this dreaming aspect to develop. In the analytic tradition, dreams are incredibly important, but often without one's own dream aspects. Social dreaming has allowed me to bring this more into my work. Also, I think it has something to do with my feelings about community. Looking for an underlying sense of connection and connectedness probably has a lot to do with my own experiences of growing up in many different countries. Also, this work seems congruent with Sullivan's concept that we're all more human than otherwise, in that it makes me feel that we're all more connected than otherwise. It's just that we don't experience that connectedness all the time. The anthropological sources on social dreaming certainly affirm this community aspect of dreaming.

I have often thought that in my own work with groups. Before attending my first Tavistock conference, I ran groups based on a method developed by a Swiss analyst named Ruth Cohen partly as an outgrowth of her experience of the Holocaust which led her to seek ways for people in society to interact non-destructively. I agree with you that the negative aspects of group life have to do with the possibility for manipulation versus opening things up. My fantasy is that dreaming socially can provide an antidote to that.

Lawrence has recently been referring to Bion's idea that there is an opposition between the establishment and the mystic in any social enterprise. For an organization to stay alive, to keep growing, it has to keep the mystic alive so it won't develop a manipulative aspect that ultimately leads to its own self-destruction. I think that's what I'm really after in using the dream world organizationally.

I also think that this type of dream work belongs at the institute because this is where the post-authoritarian psychoanalytic tradition has really developed, at least in the United States. By saying that the repression of awareness itself is the main problem, Clara Thompson reframed the entire focus of the psychoanalytic inquiry, just as

Sullivan did with the two-person model. So now we are struggling with how to take the psychoanalytic approach to group work beyond a Kleinian approach to groups, which, as applied in the Tavistock tradition, is all about psychotic regression and splitting, as opposed to Winnicott's, or Marion Milner's, much more creative versions of regressive experiences. Thus, in the theoretical realm, there hasn't been any incorporation of Sándor Ferenczi or any of the eclectic interpersonal tradition. I hope that changes.

I also hope that at White we can continue to differentiate ourselves from other institutions at a time that psychoanalysis is becoming homogenized around the world. The real challenge is how to connect group theory to interpersonal theory. Perhaps we can find a way to further apply psychoanalysis beyond the one-person and beyond the two-person. Perhaps we can apply this sort of radical eclecticism, or whatever you want to call it—the ability to think diversely—to organizational life itself. The institute is a great model for that, since people often talk about the feeling that this is a place where people with very different approaches can sit in the same room and still talk to each other.

PL: There is a new project that some of us are working on at the institute. With Todd Essig and Ken Eisold, we are thinking about the effects of contemporary technology—particularly the electronic revolution—on psychology. Our group is called the "Project on Mind, Culture, and Technology". Although there are a wide range of interests and concerns, my own focus in on the place of dreams and dream psychology in the new cyber-culture that is fast shaping out human environment. I believe that the dream is the original and built-in model for our contemporary fascination with virtual reality and that psychoanalytic as well as ancient and other ideas about dream life are especially relevant for an understanding of the new electronic life we are increasingly living. In the absence of body, in the absence of physical environment and nature, dream experience takes over in an absolute relativism in which "eternal truth" is less important than the inner narrative. Thus, dream-condition is fast becoming the condition of waking life for many who are affixed to the electronic universe. The disembodied world of information flow within cyber-culture is very close to the disembodied world of dreams. I think that Freud's dream psychology is entirely relevant to this new universe, as are Sullivan's ideas of the social web of human thought and interaction.

MW: One of the hypotheses that often arises in the dream matrix is that dreams can tell us something about the future of modern culture and technology.

PL: The dream *is* the model for the virtual world. The disembodied mind is what the electronic world is all about, and that's what dreams are about.

MW: I'm amazed that you have that association, because its precisely what Ed Levenson said to me about social dreaming. After wondering out loud why anyone would want to spend a weekend sharing dreams, he suggested that perhaps it was because such an exercise parallels the World Wide Web. Something about people trying to come to terms with a future that has already arrived. Interestingly, he recalled the example of the "horseless carriage" and how people had tried to take in the future at that point in history. He suggested that this was the name applied to the automobile because those were the only words they had around to which they could compare the car.

PL: Edgar Levenson always has interesting things to say, and they are profound. His ideas about dreams and about social dreaming are most welcome. What a gift to have his teaching at our place.

   One last word: I want to thank you, Martin, for this opportunity to talk with you about dreams. You are a very open-minded guy and always fun to talk with. Also, I want to thank you for the chance to edit my often rambling incoherence into a rational version of my thoughts.

   The idea of social dreaming is an idea, in my opinion, whose time has come. Along with Montague Ullman's work and others who see in dream communication a way to correct for the alienating effects of contemporary social life, Gordon Lawrence and his co-workers are making use of an ancient social custom: talking together about dreams. Psychoanalysis, while it kept a warm place for dreams on its couches throughout the twentieth century, also paradoxically increased a kind of alienation from dreams. Since dreams were "always" about repressed infantile sexuality and other unconscious matters that could cause shame were they uncovered outside the safe confines of an analyst's office, dreams simply could not be talked about between friends or neighbours. Dreams became professionalized, privatized, commercialized, if you will. But since dreams had always been the sort of stuff people talked about with each other, we would have to progress beyond the psychoanalytic realm to reclaim for dreams their deeply social nature—not just in their telling and discussion, but in their very creation. Both so deeply private and deeply social—that is the dialectic of dreams that the social dreaming project has helped us rediscover.

CHAPTER FOURTEEN

The confusion of dreams between selves and the other: non-linear continuities in the social dreaming experience

E. Martin Walker

Ferenczi's "Confusion of Tongues between Adults and the Child" (1933) reformulated prevailing Freudian ideas on symbolic material, or fantasies, in ways that remind me of Lawrence's (1998c) reformulation of dreaming as a social experience.

In this chapter, I begin by describing social dreaming in the context of contemporary interpersonal/relational psychoanalytic theory. I then elaborate on the "confusion" of dreams with a cross-cultural perspective on individual versus collectivist views of the self and apply dynamic systems theory to dreaming socially. I conclude the chapter by presenting a dream narrative from a social dreaming matrix that lends itself to the self-organizing emergence of meaning creation in a social context.

Social dreaming and contemporary psychoanalysis

In Ferenczi's "Confusion of Tongues", now an icon of relational psychoanalysis, Ferenczi challenged the idea that childhood images of abuse were fantasies and that transference was necessarily the "replay of infantile and childhood conflict" (quoted in Zaslow, 1988, p. 213). Ferenczi suggested that, in both cases, these were based on actual events in a person's lived experience of the world. In the first instance, he departed from Freud's seduction theory by proposing that memories of sexual abuse were based on real experiences, and in the second he proposed that transference included a . . ." commentary on the experienced person of the analyst." (in Zaslow, 1988, p.213) Finally, Ferenczi suggested that the analytic exploration of transference and sexual abuse revealed interpersonal links between self and others, both inside and outside the consulting-room, that are normally outside awareness.

So what is the confusion of dreams? Lawrence's (1998c) proposed social role for dreams that defines their significance beyond exclusively individual, intrapsychic, domains of interpretation opens dreaming to a vast range of possibilities. Building on his idea that dreams reflect elements of shared experiences of the world, as it actually exists, I describe how the dreams of a social aggregate reveal interconnections between individuals which we are not normally aware of. The latter, extending beyond the dyadic realms addressed in psychoanalysis, have been extensively reviewed by Lippmann (2000).

During many social dreaming matrices over the past twelve years, I have observed that an aggregation of the dreams of different people engaged in the activity of freely sharing dreams and associations to dreams functions as a window into an "interpsychic" (Poland, 2000, p. 29) space that links people with each other, reveals interconnections between our thought processes and fosters the emergence of new thinking (Lawrence, 1997, 2000b). I have also seen how this occurs in normally unattended aspects of organizational life (Maltz & Walker, 1998). Another key innovation to a social theory of dreams is Lawrence's (2000b) adoption of Bion's notion of the "infinite" to describe what would have previously been called the unconscious in groups. In so doing, he has provided a context for emergent thinking that saves participants in social dreaming matrices from the pitfall of prematurely assigning "meaning" to dreams, since no particular "theory" can encompass the infinite: "Only if we are not preoccupied with the question of the 'correct' interpretation of dreams can we begin to appreciate the[ir] extraordinary richness . . ." (Lippmann, 1998, p. 219). This "extraordinary richness", refracted through the social dreaming experience, gives rise to an appreciation of relational matrices that I describe here.

The observation that dreams of a social aggregate dreaming socially reveal interconnections between individuals parallels the contemporary psychoanalytic idea that the unconscious does not exist in a polarized relationship with the "conscious", but that it signals the way that within the analytic situation there exists the possibility of discovering how two individuals give rise to their relatedness to each other (Mitchell, 2000). "The road to the patient's unconscious (read; the real data about what is actually going on in the analytic situation) is created non-linearly by the analyst's own unconscious participation in its construction while he is consciously engaged in looking for it" (Bromberg, 2000, p. 686). With this statement, Bromberg encompasses the arrival of psychoanalysis to a Heisenbergian universe that Sullivan (1937) had hinted at with his insistence on the participant-observer stance of the analyst. Social dreaming demonstrates that the "real data" about what is actually going on in a social situation arises from the co-participation of dreams that are allowed to surface by listeners who share their dreams, and who allow themselves to associate freely to both dreams and associations. This is the equivalent of the non-linear creation of the road to the patient's unconscious by the participation of an analyst who is unconsciously co-constructing that which she or he is consciously engaged in looking for (Bromberg, 2000).

Two other perspectives on how social dreaming addresses the inherent interconnectedness between individuals are the cross-cultural literature examining individualism/collectivism and the application of dynamic systems theory to the social sciences. After a brief look at these two areas, I provide an example of how dream material gathered in September 2001, reflected a shared social experience of the terrorist attacks on September 11.

Dreaming between self and other

Lawrence (1998c) has previously noted anthropological references to dreaming socially in cultures around the world, so here I will expand this cross-cultural perspective and examine indigenous psychologies of the self (Sampson, 1988) and rabbinic views of the self that have been overshadowed by Greco-Christian traditions (Sampson, 2000). Cross-cultural views of the self define individuality in terms of boundaries, locus of control, and inclusiveness versus exclusiveness, or that which is intrinsic versus that which is extrinsic to the self (Heelas & Lock, 1981; Sampson, 1988). Cultures that emphasize firm boundaries and high personal control tend to view the self as exclusionary or "self contained." Fluid boundary, strong field-control cultures view the self as "ensembled", meaning that the self is inclusive of other individuals. While "self contained" individualism is indigenous to the United States and to the European countries from which its dominant ethnic groups draw their roots, "ensembled" individualism is far more prevalent as a percentage of all known cultures (Sampson, 2000). Ensembled individualism is also indigenous to Aboriginal, Native American, Senoi, and other cultures that are known to use dreams for social purposes.

The structural characteristic of the social dreaming matrix resembles ensembled-individualism cultures in terms of the permeability of its boundaries, locus of control, and self–other relationships. Its boundaries are purposely fluid, particularly in contrast to traditional psychoanalytic settings. The role of matrix conveners or "hosts" is limited to creating a supportive environment for sharing and associating to dreams, as well noticing links between them. Lawrence (2001b) had adopted my suggestion of renaming the role from that of "taker" or consultant to "host" in order to emphasize his notion that the authority to "understand" dreams in matrix is located in the unorchestrated aggregate of multiple participant's associations, or in the "infinite". This de-emphasis of "expert" opinions results in strong field control—versus internal control—that is characteristic of ensembled-individualism cultures. Finally, the focus on the *interpsychic* content of dreams neutralizes the exclusive-of-others nature of traditional dream interpretation and thus mimics the inclusive-self characteristic of ensembled individualism as well.

Overall, the dreams of a matrix tend to reflect elements of shared social experiences of the world as it actually exists and interconnections between the individuals present. The fact that the social dreaming matrix is, in itself, a cultural framework that differs significantly from traditional psychoanalytic settings, and from the prevailing "self contained" cultural milieu, exerts a powerful selection process on the dreams themselves. Social context has always had this effect on dreams and on the experience of telling and hearing them (Lippmann, 1998, 2000). From a "contained self" perspective, one may not initially accept the possibility that the contents of one's own dreams are social. However, when participating in a dream matrix that extends itself over several days with intervening periods of sleep and dreams, one inevitably dreams about the dreams and associations being shared, and about the social aggregate in which one has been telling and hearing them. Dreams that are experienced "within" the self, but not "of" the self, allow for an experience of ensembled individualism that is rare within the prevailing Western culture.

A less polarizing cross-cultural view of individualism–collectivism that is embodied in rabbinic traditions has been harnessed to illustrate contemporary psychoanalytic perspectives by Levenson (2001). Its roots are found in holy texts that differ significantly from the Bible in that they are composed of "fundamentally open-ended and indeterminate discussions ... where no finalized meaning or single interpretation was either possible or felt to be desirable" (Sampson, 2000, p. 1429). Modern rabbinic extensions of this tradition suggest that the self cannot exist in the absence of a lived dialogue with others and that what is most essential about the self can be found neither individually nor in the collective but in a third sphere that Buber (1965) referred to as "the between". Social dreaming invokes this "third sphere" by locating the meaning-making capacity of dreams between the unorchestrated aggregate of multiple participants' associations and the "infinite". Poland (2000) has also referenced the rabbinic tradition by noting that Emmanuel Levinas, a student of both Husserl and Heidegger, "emphasized a constant feeling of strangeness that is the sense of the universe in which any individual comes into being, [where] the self is always opening in awareness of otherness as an irreducible aspect of being" (p. 31). Otherness, as an irreducible aspect of being, taken together with ensembled individualism, describes the experience one has in social dreaming matrices of participating in an activity whose periphery is nowhere and whose centre is everywhere—and, at the same time, is uncannily familiar.

A self-organizing dynamic systems perspective
on social dreaming

A social dreaming matrix—whose periphery is nowhere and whose centre is everywhere—that gives rise to a novel self-state evokes self-organizing structures described by dynamic systems theory (Ghent, 2002). Self-organizing or "emergent" systems have been noted in fields ranging from neurology to computer-game design and urban planning (Johnson, 2001). Variously described as synergistics, non-linearity, or chaos and complexity theory, dynamic systems theory has evolved to account for the way in which an array of inputs can give rise to patterns of action, structures, or states that are not predictable from the nature of the inputs themselves (for a review, see Ghent, 2002). My own favourite example of this comes from driving down the FDR Drive in Manhattan and experiencing the frustration that mounts when I join the aggregate effect of too many cars shifting into the "fast" lane that results in the traffic there becoming slower than in the "slow" lane. Here, each individual "right" choice, when aggregated, results in a "wrong" outcome.

Applying dynamic systems theory to individual wishes, needs, and motives, Ghent suggests that the evolution of purposeful behaviour can be accounted for by motivational systems in dynamic interaction with experience, without the need for overarching genetic, structural, or drive theories. Here is how he describes Prigogine and Stengers's (1984) understanding of dynamic systems:

> Given a source of energy, all open systems can create internal organization without the need for a pattern or design . . .[that] is characterized by both stability over time and instabilities that lead to new state properties within the existing organizations. Perturbations of the system are likely to destabilize it, providing the opportunity for change. The situation most pregnant with the possibility of change is a system poised on the edge of chaos. [Ghent, 2002, p. 769]

A visual model may help. Imagine a landscape with a variety of hills in which balls are placed either on the crest of each hill or in each of the valleys. On the peaks, the balls will be set in motion by the slightest state change, with unpredictable results, whereas a relatively large state change is required to shift a ball in the valleys up and over into some other valley. The net result is that self-organizing systems—regardless of whether the elements that create such systems are people, organs, tissues, cells, molecules, or photons—will have a dynamic essence characterized by a sequence of complexity to simplicity to complexity, giving rise to the appearance of order without the need for an underlying explanatory structure (Ghent, 2002).

Applied to cognition and action, Thelen and Smith (1994) state:

> there is a multiple, parallel, and continuously dynamic interplay between perception and action, and a system that, by its . . . nature, seeks certain stable solutions. *These solutions emerge from relations, not from design* [italics added] when the elements of such complex systems cooperate; they give rise to behavior with a unitary character, and thus the *illusion* [italics in original] of structure. The order is always executory, rather than rule-driven, allowing for the enormous sensitivity and flexibility of behavior to organize. [Thelen & Smith, 1994, p. xix]

Edelman's (1992) further application of this to neuronal development in the brain is beyond the scope of this discussion, but the key concept derived from it is that the interaction between neuronal maps created by developmental selection and those developed by experiential selection accounts for both pattern recognition and the capacity for "the spontaneously emergent and relatively unpredictable patterning that is independent of experience" (quoted in Ghent, 2002, p. 780).

If we think of a social dreaming matrix as a dynamic system whose elements are dreams and associations to dreams, we would expect to see a system that moves from complexity to simplicity to complexity, driven by the relations that develop within the dream elements themselves and not by some other rule-driven structure. The experience of spontaneous emergence of coherent patterns is not predicted by the elements themselves. One of these coherent patterns I have already mentioned: the emergence of a self-state in which others are included that feels uncannily comfortable. Another is that after hearing many dreams in a matrix, participants often report losing a sense of differentiation about whether any particular dream was dreamt by them or by somebody else. Finally, there develops a vague sense that there exists a "repository" of all the dreams that can be dreamt that dreamers tap into when they go to sleep. When participants in matrices attempt to explain these uncanny experiences to others, they often resort to saying simply: "Well, you had to be there

to understand it." Further observation and research of these spontaneous emerging coherent patterns will probably identify others, as
well as elaborate on the characteristics of those mentioned here.

A social dreaming narrative

So what can this "confusion" of dreams actually look like? Let us
examine dream material from a social dreaming matrix held in
Philadelphia, Pennsylvania, at a location roughly equidistant from
the three unprecedented terrorist attacks that occurred two weeks
earlier on 11 September 2001 (PCOD, 2001). These events, which
television has etched indelibly in all of our minds, were the destruction of the World Trade Center, an attack on the Pentagon, and the
aeroplane likely brought down by its own passengers in western
Pennsylvania. Besides the obvious representations of those events in
the dreams, let us try to see what we can discern about the interconnectedness—or ensembled nature—of the individuals in the matrix and its self-organizing characteristics as a non-linear dynamic
system. What follows is the content of twenty-seven dreams reported
among twenty-two individuals during the 90 minutes that opened a
two-and-a-half-day dreaming matrix. I present the dreams here as a
single narrative because this makes the non-linear dynamic system
easiest to discern, something that I first noted in reading the children's dream matrix that Balamuth created and writes about (see
chapter eight herein).

> *I had jumped out of an airplane at forty thousand feet and the parachute*
> *opened. I was clinging on to a very dear friend from high school whom I*
> *had not seen in twenty-five years, and I suddenly realized I was clinging*
> *more to him than he to me. I saw the face of my only brother, but he was*
> *dead and I was at the funeral. I was driving with a friend down a broad*
> *open street very fast at dusk and the road became very narrow. There*
> *were all these people on it and I was honking to get them out of the way.*
> *I kept driving very fast and the road narrowed until the car started*
> *running on rails, faster and faster. The rails were made of marble and it*
> *turned out we were on a grave, ricocheting along in a city of the dead.*
> *There were tall sarcophagi-like buildings. I was racing away from head-*

stones and banging on the car, but my knuckles were hitting a coffin instead. I reversed suddenly and flew out of there. I was surrounded by the smell of clowns, rather then the smell of the flag. I was in the city among these extraordinarily tall, very dark buildings. I saw the St. Louis Arch, the enormous landmark in the American Midwest, with two horses hanging from it. The horses had been skinned and were still alive, somehow trying to stay on the arches. I started driving in a black Cadillac down a very narrow dirt road with tremendous amounts of rocks. My destination was an area with a lot of flagpoles where an acquaintance was having a dedication in his honour. My tires sank in the dirt, but I wanted to get out and say hello. Trying to re-park the car, I told my friend, who was now driving, not to spin the wheels. Then I walked towards a bridge in Philadelphia through some very high gates and arrived at a room in which there was an old man in a faded suite. There was a brass plaque in front of him like a monument. He started toddling along like he could hardly walk, and then tumbled down like a 2-year-old. He got up quickly as if to show he was all right, and I looked around to see if my acquaintance that was being honoured had left.

I invite you to go back and read this again before proceeding and to imagine yourself listening to it as a dream from a single source.

I'm in the air flying. I had taken off and though I usually go up in recurrent flying dreams, this time I decide to fly down. I flew right into a house and was ashamed and very puzzled to discover that I had become naked. I was standing holding my infant son who had had a bad fall but landed face up. His eyes were closed and I thought maybe I should take him to the hospital but I resisted, claiming that there was nothing wrong with him. I got a phone call from a woman who asked me to facilitate a workshop with Gordon Lawrence, the leader of this social dreaming matrix. I agreed to do it but couldn't find a location for it because it had to be at a place beginning with the letter "P". I found myself travelling around to organize adventure trips in the Sierra Nevada. It was raining and the programme stated specifically that one was not to study Italian grammar. Suddenly there was a huge torrent of red, bloody water. I saw an aeroplane on a golf course whose underbelly was completely transparent. It was behaving erratically, rolling violently in a manner that shifted the contents inside and then it crashed. I ran over to a large crater where a man is pulling out a survivor. All the people are naked and huddled. One particular woman is cowering, naked and ashamed. I pull her out of the hole and cover her with a sheet. When I get her to the hospital a young doctor tells me vaguely that she has been treated incorrectly and had been x-rayed too many times in the face. I thought at that moment that I was actually in some sort of Science Park where experimentation with humans was going on. I was eating from a plate of vegetables. They looked very unappealing but I realized I had to eat for what lies ahead. Looking around I saw that I was in a cafeteria where all the food was extremely peculiar.

Again, you are encouraged to reread this set and this time paying attention the themes that were introduced. Newly recurring themes of teaching, blood, injured people, and food were added to the previously recurring episodes of flying, falling, relatives, aeroplanes, and death. New events were children, medical malpractice, and a golf course, which also happened to be what surrounded the building in which this matrix took place. Earlier references to speeding automobiles, buildings and landmarks are not mentioned, but do recur in the material that follows.

It was after 9/11 and there were fences being built. I noticed that the old fences that had been built before had been turned into hedgerows for jumping over. There was a long windy road that a friend and I were taking a walk together on. We were gliding along at thirty miles an hour and came back to a large stone mansion with flames coming from a tower. The whole house was on fire, and there was a body inside. I was waiting for I.D. photos with 20 other people because we were told we had to have them. I filled out a sheet of paper, and a roll of film was casually shot to get pictures in order to attend this conference on dreams. Mine was the only picture that turned out, but it showed only two ghostly black-and-white images that looked like ectoplasm. I needed a photo I.D. card so I stopped off at the passport shop to get two clear pictures. Those photos came out nicely in colour, but they showed me sitting next to a beautiful woman. I was standing in a jungle forest in Indonesia looking at a stone carving of a religious figure that belonged to all cultures. The figures right eye was sewn shut. Later, I was standing at the ocean with a man/ shark whose eye was also sewn shut and I felt this must be the leader. I was supposed to be teaching a new class that President George W. Bush was attending as a new student, but I had to race home to get the teaching notes that I had left behind. I was in England in the living-room of friends. They are explaining that they want to live in the United States. I'm stunned and ask why they would want to do such a thing but after a while said, "Okay, come and stay in the empty rooms of my home." I went on to Oxford because I had been a student there and had been called back to discuss my orals. Strangely, I discovered I was actually in Venice and I couldn't get back to Oxford.

Rereading this segment, we see a newly recurring theme of fences and I.D. photos that meld the public-security measures that had transformed American life with participation in the dream matrix itself. This invokes the issue of locus of control by raising the question of who is in control of what, which reverberates through the image of a body burning inside the house, to a universal "leader" with one eye sewn shut, and to the president of the United States as the new kid in class.

My husband and I are arriving at a colourful, verdant farm where we are going to get some vegetables. It was very safe and pleasant. A field opened up in front of us to reveal vegetables that were suddenly all autumn coloured and larger than life. I thought: "Why not get some strawberries." I got some beautiful fruit and felt very fortunate, but I ended up in a tractor that got stuck in the mud. I was on an old truck that was driving through circuitous overpasses in Rome. I got separated from my husband. I was with a group on an island where there were demonstrators protesting. My son was in charge of the protesters, but for some reason he wasn't there. There was a gathering with a lot of people. One woman had all these registration materials filled out and there was a large card on the door to the room. Her name was Hope and she was waiting for others to come in. I was with my 10-year-old daughter, who was going to get chemotherapy. Her eyes were closed, but I saw her open them and she said: "Mom." She turned on her side and became a spiralling light that looked like a womb. I knew then that she would die from the cancer. I was left in a hall that had pews like a church with an academic friend and a War Lord from the story '"Dune." There were dark winds and the back of the church looked like an x-ray of the contents of a suitcase. Then there was another image being projected on the wall that was the colour of dawn, and then a blue/black image. I urgently told a woman to look, saying: "There's the answer!" The black spirit winds

226 EXPERIENCES IN SOCIAL DREAMING

were blowing across her face when she looked back at me and said: "You will see nothing outside the church."

Reading this narrative provides convincing evidence that all the dreams involved individuals sharing in a social reality that revealed previously unacknowledged links between them and an emerging social reality that crystallized the new world they were all suddenly living in after the events of September 11. The narrative content by itself provides the feel of an ensembled self, while the process of reading it conveys the experience of actually participating in a dreaming matrix that provides outlines of a non-linear dynamic self-organizing system in a variety of ways.

The dream narrative lays down a consistent set of patterns surrounding issues of flying, falling, danger, aeroplane and building disasters, security issues, personal loss, and learning groups that make obvious references to both the wider and the immediate social contexts in which the matrix takes place, right down to the golf course. The repeated references to Italy are not predicted by a current social context, but remind me of the fact that Lawrence was at that time about to embark on a series of lectures and matrices at several locations in Italy. This information was not "known" to those who dreamt about Italy but reflected future events in a manner similar to previous matrices within an organization that have functioned as previews to future events (Maltz & Walker, 1998; see also chapter eleven). The tractor getting stuck in the mud at the verdant farm with beautiful vegetables and fruits mirrors the car that got stuck at the beginning of the narrative in the midst of a distinctly more funereal setting. The fact that the first introduction of positive experiences to this narrative brings with it a reference to "getting stuck" creates the impression that the dream itself is rebalancing the entire narrative towards the "bad". This is strongly reinforced by the subsequent reference to the actual death of a child, evoking the earlier real death of a brother.

Although this line of reasoning may be difficult to follow at times, any participants in a matrix will find themselves able to peel back layer upon layer of meanings by drawing on their subjective experience of what ends up being a long sequence of non-linear events. The reader of this narrative, with a little effort, can do the same thing. The result is the experience of a reality co-created by the participants in a manner analogous to the contemporary psychoanalytic position that the analyst is unconsciously co-constructing—that which she or he is consciously engaged in looking for. The radical nature of Lawrence's contribution to the confusion of dreams confirms a process now familiar to interpersonal/relational psychoanalysis and provides a window onto the social creation of consensus reality that binds the present, the past, and the future for a particular group of people at a particular point in time. Ongoing exploration in this area could lead beyond Winnicott's (1966) idea of culture as a transitional phenomena and expand our theories on the social creation of culture itself.

CHAPTER FIFTEEN

Theatre of dreams:
social dreaming
as ritual/yoga/literature machine

Stephen Fitzpatrick

> Is not sleep perhaps the true home of the self, like the sea from
> which mankind first emerged at the dawn of time . . .? But if that
> is so, how can man re-enter that other life *and yet remain awake*
> *enough to know it?*
>
> Gabriel Josipovici (1979, p. 4)

> The truth of art lies in its power to break the monopoly of
> established reality . . . to define what is real.
>
> Herbert Marcuse (1977, p. 9)

What is social dreaming?

I shall try to clear a space and occupy a ground in which this
liminal object—social dreaming—can come more clearly into
view. To do so I have deliberately "bracketed off" and put aside
the putative meanings of any given set of themes made available in
any given matrix. I have made this manoeuvre—foregrounding the
structural, functional, and experiential/transformational aspects of

social dreaming while recessing the epistemological—in order to attend not to the traces left by the process of social dreaming but to the object itself. Furthermore, the eventual process that is social dreaming in fact problematizes any attempt to fix and stabilize meaning(s) generated by matrix. According to this reading of social dreaming, the medium is the message.

In pursuing the experiential matrix, I shall offer an account of social dreaming as a process generative of experiences that, in "deep matrix", are beyond semiosis and entail ontological modulations of self and world.

This account regards social dreaming not as a therapeutic technology but as a late-modern form of communitarian ritual or social-dream yoga that binds aspects of the self—essentially its personal and interpersonal modes—in order to free others; the self experienced in an impersonal and collective modality. Yet paradoxically this binding or elision of the personal is experienced by participants as a finding of the self, as a deep authentication of selfhood, that is at the same time an immersion or dissolution of the self in the collective.

Central to this analysis of experiential matrix is a discussion of the way in which social dreaming deploys language in extraordinary ways in order to reprocess the subjectivity of participants. (This, of course, assumes the centrality of language as a mediating agent of perception.) This consideration of the uses of language in social dreaming leads to a brief comparison with the uses of language tropes in modernist art practise and theory and their relevance to our understanding of the practice of social dreaming.

This chapter is divided into three distinct but related sections. The first section discusses the social dreaming matrix as a transformational object; the second offers an account of transformations in deep matrix in terms of the Buddhist concept of Sunyata or emptiness; and the third consists of a number of tentative hypotheses about the nature and significance of the social dreaming matrix.

The social dreaming matrix as transformational object

In a social dreaming matrix, participants access and realize dimensions or aspects of world that would otherwise remain merely latent, recessed, or potential.

In becoming what they only potentially were, the social dreaming matrix effects a rite-of-passage through a series or procession of life-worlds that conform to a succession of reality principles different to, and distinct from, that which is hegemonic in everyday life as it is experienced in extroverted, late-modern, urbanized, technologically enabled Western(-ized) societies.

Social dreaming brings about transformational effects. These dramatic transformations lend to the experience of participation an imaginal kinship with the religious rituals of traditional societies as described and theorized in anthropological accounts of ritual. The speed and profundity of these transformations, their social-participative nature, the states of reverie induced, their air of gravity, and their circumscription in time (one- to three-day events) are distinctive not only of social dreaming but of traditional ritual activity.

But the commonalities go deeper than this: I shall attempt to show that the transformations, the life-worlds, or the states of mind and society realized in social dreaming, generate experiential phenomena that scatter and dissolve subjectivity across a register of intensities so profound that they might properly be characterized as "religious".

I offer an account of the manner in which these integrations are realized via a procession through a series of life-worlds, which are first realized and then stabilized as states of mind *and society* by the centrifugal action of the matrix.

The numinous

Social dreaming generates experiences that can be most effectively characterized by the philosophical category of the "numinous", a term coined by Rudolf Otto (1950, p. 7) to capture the experiential, non-discursive, non-rational, and ineffable aspect of religion.

In the state of numinosity, discursive reason—the ordering principle of reality in secular Western society—may not disappear entirely, but, as Rappaport (1999, p. 219) observes, metaphoric representation, primary-process thought, and strong emotion become increasingly important as the domination of syntactic or syllogistic logic, or simple everyday rationality, recedes.

When the numinous is manifest, boundaries shift and shatter, the self overflows, and individuals are transformed, marvelling at a revelation of the hidden oneness of things. But the numinous shows itself according to many faces. This revelation of the hidden faces of the world is accompanied by powerful affects. It is not definitively cognitive.

Otto (1950, p. 36) articulates yet another face of the numinous that is of relevance here: the experience of the numinous may also generate feelings of love and beatitude, experiences that are non-rational, indescribable, and inexpressibly tranquil. Access to the numinous is facilitated in traditional societies by participation in ritual activities:

> for most people in most societies . . . the way to numinous experience is through participation in communitarian ritual, for in communitarian ritual the need for extraordinary sensitivity . . . or the special exertions to successful vision quest or mediation, regulated by the compelling characteristics of ritual itself, its tempos, its repetitiveness, its union, its strangeness, . . . drive many, or even most participants from mundane consciousness into numinous experience. [Rappaport, 1999, p. 380]

It is precisely this phenomena—*communitas*, the collective experience of the numinous—that captures the singular experiences of participants in the social dreaming matrix and that requires that we re-categorize social dreaming not as a therapeutic technology or as an heteredox psychoanalytic school, but as a late-modern form of communitarian ritual or social-dream yoga.

Psychoanalysis and language behaviour

It is an axiom of this chapter that forms of language imply and are implicated in discrete and distinctive types of relationship, forms of behaviour, and world views. In social dreaming, introverted language use is deployed in an extroverted, social context. Changes of state ensue in the wake of this extraordinary deployment of language.

There is an obvious family resemblance here with the psychoanalytic setting and the withdrawal or separation of the analysand from habitual relatedness and the dominance of extroverted (denotative-referential) language behaviour and the foregrounding of an associative-connotative language behaviour in the form of free association.

In the psychoanalytic setting, withdrawal from ordinary relatedness and the putting into interpersonal space of introverted language behaviours is one of the moves that facilitates the devolution of the ego or false self and the emergence of hitherto unrealized aspects of the self. Social dreaming brings about comparable effects in a social context, but is not defined or exhausted by therapeutic effects and objectives. Social dreaming has more in common with Eastern disciplines, in that the self is "re-ontologized" in order to permit a transition to experiences of selflessness or impersonality in *communitas*. This extraordinary re-ontologization cannot be captured by a philosophical ontology of the subject that conceives of that subject as distinct from others nor over and against a world from which it is separate and distinct.

The emergence of social dreaming constitutes a new convention— a form of communitarian ritual—establishing a break with psychoanalysis, for here the dream is not transfigured in order to reveal the hidden, but taken at face value, re-inscribed, and redeployed in a new context where it functions as part of a set of techniques (matrix) that serve to realize experience in its impersonal aspect and thereby bring into focus previously occluded and unthematized aspects of reality.

Linguistic messages transmitted in the matrix do not refer to or designate some independently existing "objective reality" that can be sought out to guarantee the truth or falsehood of statements about, or statements of, this class of statements. The messages—narrated dreams and associations—that constitute the "social dreaming liturgy" are not "denotative"—that is to say, an objective, fixed, and more or less stable referent cannot be assumed. Rather, the messages that constitute the social dreaming liturgy conform to the class of statements designated by Anglo-American analytic philosophy as "performatives" (Austin, 1962): speech acts that are first and foremost actions—they effect transformations or modulations in the real, bringing into being a new state of affairs.

Performatives bring about the state of affairs to which they refer. They are not simply mimetic but *invocational*. In a performative speech act, the utterance is itself the performance of the language act in question, and not a report of that performance. The utterance of the minister, "I pronounce you man and wife", spoken in the marriage ceremony, is performative and calls a new state of affairs into being.

Rappaport (1999) comments:

> to say that performers participate in or become part of the orders
> they are realising is to say that transmitter-receivers become

fused with the messages they are transmitting and receiving. In conforming to the orders that their performers bring into being and that come alive in their performance, performers become indistinguishable from those orders, parts of them, for the time being. [p. 119]

The linguistic messages articulated by participants in a social dreaming matrix are of this type, effecting a separation and rupture with the established reality principle in order to conform to and realize an impersonal order of experience. This impersonal mode, however, is experienced as a paradox: it is both impersonal and yet at the same time a new-found and deep sense of freedom and self-authentification. Rappaport again: "Performatives . . . are self-fulfilling and make themselves true by standing in a relationship of conformity to the states of affairs with which they are concerned" (Rappaport, 1999, p. 117).

The transformations wrought by social dreaming are an effect of the ways in which meaning is configured and conveyed by the process. The meanings produced in the matrix can be owned by no individual participant—all participate in its making. This polysemous text cannot be claimed or definitively named—it eludes semantic closure, and meaning is indefinitely deferred. The territorialing tendency of the ego-self to define, own, and defend its utterances as private property is refused.

The social dreaming "liturgy"—the messages transmitted and received by participants in the matrix—is a co-emergent phenomena, woven by the participants, who are re-inscribed in communitas by the dense allusive patterns of its whorling warp and woof.

The social dreaming liturgy:
rehearsing and realizing impersonality

Although the meanings generated in any given matrix may differ radically, the form—that is to say, dreams and associations—remain constant. In this sense the messages transmitted and received by participants function in an analogous way to the invariant liturgy of traditional ritual.

As the social dreaming set takes hold, the personal aspects of the participants are gradually refined out of the mise-en-scène. What is rehearsed is realized. The matrix as liturgy transforms and modulates the experience of participants.

Rappaport again: "To perform a liturgical order which is by definition a more or less invariant sequence of formal acts and utterances encoded by someone other than the performer is necessarily to conform to it" (Rappaport, 1999, p. 118).

The associations and dreams narrated in matrix do not, however, exhaust the sum of meaning-bearing messages and actions that bind the personal and interpersonal and realize the condition of impersonality.

The liturgy is comprised of at least seven components, which function synergetically and holistically in the matrix.

Free association

Free association in social dreaming is both deconstructive and creative. Free association deconstructs the language behaviours and states of mind and society of the reality principle in which extroverted, denotative language behaviour is dominant, dissolving the distinctions between things and manifesting hidden connections between dreams and participants.

Owning the other's dream

Participants free-associate to the dreams of others as if they were their own. This technique rehearses a condition of impersonal field awareness, which is subsequently realized according to the performative logic of ritual: the personal recedes into the background as communitas is realized.

Impersonal speech—impersonal dream

The subject identifies with an impersonal aspect of her or his experience and speaks from this "place". The focus upon the dream and not the dreamer facilitates the loosening of the personal relation to experience and cultivates an impersonal relation to one's own dreams and the dreams of others. Dreams and associations are spoken to from a point of view beyond one's immediate personal and interpersonal concerns. Often these points of view are expressive of social, cultural, political, philosophical, and aesthetic issues, riddles, dilemmas, and conundra. Dreams and associations become the common property of all participants.

Evenly suspended attention

Evenly suspended attention is the ideal orientation of analyst to analysand, democratized in the context of the social dreaming matrix as the relation of participant to participant—shorn of memory and desire, impartial, open, non-judgemental, interested, patient, fearless, impersonal. If evenly suspended attention is the "receptive pole" of intentionality in a matrix, its "active pole", so to speak, is the will-to-link. The will-to-link reinforces the receptivity of the holding environment with a "tuning function" that operates at both a verbal and pre- or non-verbal level. Impartial, evenly suspended attention oscillates with the will-to-link.

The will-to-link

The will-to-link reverses the intentional centripetality of the self with its tendency to focus solely upon its own immediate needs, concerns, and projects, redirecting intentionality outwards towards others, seeking out links, connections, and meanings. The self thus posits the other as other, not as an extension of the self and its concerns. By directing one's intentionality towards links, similarities and correspondences with others, agonistic relations are deconstructed and symbiontic relations are rehearsed and processionally realized. The other emerges not as an agonistic other but as a symbiontic co-producer of the emergent dream text, generated in the social dreaming matrix.

The mise-en-scène

Just as spatial relations in the therapeutic setting are configured in such a way as to relieve both analyst and analysand of the obligation to relate according to habitual interpersonal modes, thereby facilitating the emergence of an impersonal relation, the matrix is spatially configured to disrupt interpersonal relations—for example, with seating in the crystalline pattern of a snowflake—and to facilitate the emergence of an impersonal field.

Reorientation in the matrix

As the matrix takes hold, the participants find themselves inside a text that is operating according to an extra-ordinary language game. Distinctions and fixed reference points slip and slide, meanings multiply according to a principle of infinite mutability, as denotation-reference is rendered highly problematical. This text, in which uncertainty and ambiguity is multiplied, bears comparison with Roland Barthes' (1975) euphoric account of the ideal, modernist, text—open, "writeable", admissible to manifold and endless interpretation:

> This ideal text . . . is a galaxy of signifiers, not a structure of signifieds; it has no beginning, it is reversible. . . . Systems of meaning may take over this absolutely plural text, but their number is never closed, based as it is on the infinity of language . . . it is a question of asserting the very existence of plurality, which is not that of the true, the probable or even the possible. [pp. 5–6]

In one crucial respect, however, the social dreaming text is unlike the text described by Barthes—it is immersive and existentially binding, at least for the time being. The text is not literature, but literature becomes the defining reality-principle in the state of mind and society that is the matrix: connotative-associative language behaviour is deployed in social space. It is if the participants had fallen into Eliot's Waste Land or Kafka's Castle.

Like Alice, their world has been turned upside down and inside out. They have fallen into a literature machine and are grist to its mill. This may be experienced either as a liberation or as a fight for survival, a matter of life and death. In order to adapt and flourish in this ad-hoc social order, the participants must reorient: a high degree of negative capability towards the emerging social order is necessary to process the allusive messages woven into a web of signification cut loose from its roots in the world of denotation-reference. This may precipitate a crisis as the participants struggle to maintain their orientation to the dominant reality-principle, or, depending upon the disposition of the participants, a gentle slide into a cloud of unknowing.

Transformations in deep matrix—
Sunyata as a state of mind and society

The most common experiences generated in social dreaming matrices is that of communitas, the emergence of a web of symbiotic relationships and the "reciprocal dreaming" of identical dreams or dream motifs. However, in extraordinary circumstances, this gentle dissolution in communitas accelerates towards an existential crisis. In deep matrix, the experience of communitas opens an abyss into which identity and language may disappear.

This singular experience bears comparison to Buddhist accounts of Sunyata or emptiness. In a social dreaming matrix, however, this experience is an inherently social one, and herein lies its uniqueness.

Sunyata can be cognized as "emptiness", where emptiness is experienced not as nothingness but as the dissolution and absence of both a unique self identity and a world of distinct and isolated, unrelated entities. In communitas, Sunyata is experienced as both a deeply personal experience and a transition to a new mode of collective life or state of society.

The enhancement of negative capability and the gradual tranquilization of the ego and its habitual language behaviour in referential-denotative mode—desiring, naming, classifying, and controlling its objective world of distinctions and differences—seems to fade away. A capacity for pure negative capability, contained and sustained by the symbiotic relations that now hold sway, takes the place of any residual desire to control or definitively name or hold onto experience. Existence is re-configured, emerging according to a different aspect. Things are seen "as they are".

One's habitual and instantaneous reflex to name and control one's environment is stayed. Trungpa (1987) describes this habitual process in the following terms:

> Whenever a perception of form occurs, there is an immediate reaction of fascination and uncertainty on the part of an implied perceiver of the form. This reaction is almost instantaneous. It takes only a fraction of a fraction of a second. And as soon as we have established recognition of what a thing is, our next response is to give it a name. With the name comes a concept. We tend to conceptualise the object, which means at this point we are no longer able to perceive things as they actually are. We have created a kind of padding, a filter or veil between ourselves and the

object. . . . This veil removes us from panoramic awareness . . .
because again and again we are unable to see things as they are.
We feel compelled to name, to translate, to think discursively and
this activity takes us away from direct and accurate perception.
[p. 196]

The function of the social dreaming liturgy may be compared to the
action of the koan upon the student in Zen Buddhism, where the
attempt to decode enigmatic messages are designed to frustrate the
analytical-rational faculty, liberating the linguistically bound mind of
the student so as to bring about a re-orientation in perception towards
an unmediated seeing of things as they are. In Zen, the meaning of the
enigmatic koan "What is the meaning of Wu?" (Suzuki, 1956, p. 143)
is not to be arrived at by the action of the intellect, in analysis or
interpretation. The "meaning" of the koan is the state of mind that its
"solution" brings about.

The following schematization by D. T. Suzuki (1956) maps the
progress of student and koan:

1. The koan is given to the student first of all to bring about a
highly wrought-up state of consciousness.

2. The reasoning faculty is kept in abeyance, that is to say that the
more superficial activity of the mind is set at rest so that its more
central and profounder parts which are found generally deeply
buried can be brought out and exercised to perform their native
functions.

3. The affective and conative centres which are really the foundation of one's personal character are charged to do their utmost in
the solution of the koan.

4. When the mental integration thus reaches its highest mark
there obtains a neutral state of consciousness which is errone-
ously described as "ecstasy" by the psychological student of religious consciousness. This Zen state of consciousness essentially
differs from ecstasy in this: ecstasy is the suspension of the mental powers while the mind is passively engaged in contemplation;
the Zen state of consciousness, on the other hand, is the one that
has been brought about by the most intensely active exercise of
all the fundamental faculties constituting one's personality. This
is the point where the empirical consciousness with all its contents both conscious and unconscious is about to tip over the
borderline, and get noetically related to the Unknown, the Beyond, the Unconscious.

5. A penetrating insight into is born of the inner depths of consciousness, as the source of a new life has been tapped, and with it the koan yields up its secrets. [p. 149]

It is perhaps the unique feature of social dreaming that the participants experience new states of awareness as a social breakthrough. Furthermore, any potential crisis experience is thwarted by the web of symbiotic relations that "break the fall" of participants as the familiar reality-principle waxes, wanes, and dissolves and new life-worlds emerge.

Experiences of Sunyata in the social dreaming matrix: a personal account

As this process closes down a new life-world blooms. The cultural patina of meanings that until now have been constituting "the world" are revealed to have been not "the world" but "my world". Language becomes "visible" as a medium, and the world is thrown into relief. Language, I now see, was never the mirror of nature but a strange and wonderful web of patterned subtle objects, which is tangential to the world.

Linguistic meaning seem to have become unanchored from the world; meaning floats in and around me as oil. The world accessible to verbalization has shrunk and an ineffable world of mystery bodies forth.

My rationality, however, is unimpaired. I am not swallowed up by a tidal wave of irrational forces. I am more than capable of rational analysis but, as the world unfolds before me, it seems at best irrelevant. Whereas before I inhabited a world of distinct things, I now inhabit a world in which things are mysteriously interconnected. The other participants seem to me both profoundly intimate yet infinitely distant and irremediably other. The experience is awe-ful and yet indescribably tranquil and compelling, redeemed and sustained by mystery and the supportive web of symbiotic relations.

That which can be verbalized, at this point, seems to me to be at best, trivial, at worst irrelevant. Language is falling further and further short of my immediate experience. A system of universal concepts, it seems to me at this point, cannot approximate to what I am uniquely feeling, seeing, and hearing. Perhaps this was always the case? The suspicion that this is so registers with the impact of a direct blow to the head.

The vocalizations of those around me carry an infinite pathos, like the bleating of lambs; infinitely gentle, infinitely suffering. We are fixed, immobile, bereft of consoling illusions, projects, distractions, lost, bereft, blind. But miraculously the experience is contained, its awful pathos matched by a deep sense of mystery, as the sheer uncanniness of the concrete unfolds. Like sentinels we may not act but can only attend—bearing witness to what unfolds before us.

When dreams are related or association made, the meaning of the words appear to have been unanchored from their moorings in the world. They are simultaneously meaningful and yet infinitely estranged: both meaning-bearing and pure sonic affect—this music, unutterably strange and terribly beautiful. We seem to hover at the very threshold of sense. Vocalizations pulse intermittently across the matrix.

I appear to have made a most singular gesture, returning language the favour by giving *it* the slip. I flicker across the nature–culture border. What had previously been taken for granted—the apparent separateness of things, the accessibility of others, the substantiality of the self—is a veil fallen. In its place, mystery—not a supernatural mystery, but a natural one, the mystery of things as they are.

Experience flows glacially. Awareness is intense and unconflicted, the mind smooth as mahogany. According to the Buddhist author Stephen Batchelor, it is such experiences of Sunyata that reveals to us that the origin of the conflict, frustration, and anxiety we habitually experience lie not in the nature of the world itself but in our distorted conceptions of the world. At fault is the very act of assenting to our habitual world-view and the agonistic relations it sustains *as an ultimate value* (Batchelor, 1983, p. 105):

> Through revealing that nothing at all is characterised by an independent, self sufficient identity, the desolate image of numerous isolated, unrelated entities has been dispelled. As this new vision unfolds, our basic anxiety and our sense of meaninglessness are dissolved in the growing awareness of the profound mystery of interrelatedness that permeates all phenomena. [p. 106]

In deep matrix, this new life-world is not merely glimpsed as a state of mind, as in certain meditative experiences, but stabilized as a state of mind *and society*.

The immediate

In a deep matrix the social experience of Sunyata may itself be subject to further modulations. The individual, sustained by the symbiotic relations established in matrix, may undergo an experience that threatens to shatter all categories, all boundaries, even the distinction between perceiver and perceived.

The flow of experience has stabilized, now wide and inclusive, deep and glacially slow. Adrift on this lake of negative capability, this extraordinary experience is held and contained, intense, energetic, and bright.

I am caught unawares by a sudden modulation and catch my breath—the flow of experience seems for a moment to have halted. In this stillness where experience is at a halt, the world is once more transfigured.

For an instant, it seems as if the moment and myself are one and the same. Or rather, I hover over a threshold, on one side of which there is space, time, and culture, on the other an absolute present, an identification with all that is, this moment that is neither "space" nor "time" nor "me" nor "world" but all and none of these.

The feeling is of an intense and total realization. There is nothing left out, nothing not-I, the moment is all and everything.

There is danger, however, in presenting this experience as exalted. For one has the distinct impression that this is simply how things really are, that this is the ordinary condition of experience, which is, under the sway of our everyday, conflicted and distracted lives, covered over.

Blanchot (1999) captures the nature of this mystery, of an experience that is strange by virtue of its uncommonness. This he tells us, is

> An experience that one will represent to oneself as being strange and even as the experience of strangeness. But if it is so, let us recognize that it is not this because it is too removed. On the contrary, it is so close that we are prohibited from taking any distance from it—it is foreign in its very proximity. [p. 45]

This is the experience of the immediate, but brought closer than I had imagined possible, so close that the separation between myself and my world threatens to evaporate. I anxiously resist this dissolution.

An association, a passing thought, catches and pursues me. Is this anxious flight from impossibility, from the real to the contingent, from the impossible to the possible, the engine that conjures and stirs our world into being in the first place?

Working hypotheses on the nature and significance of social dreaming

If matrix is a yoga, binding the personal in order to realize the impersonal, it is, in its current phase of development, a yoga of immanence not transcendence.

In its deployment of non-denotative language behaviours, in its unique and processional power to reframe perception, it is a liminal object that elides the boundary between ritual yoga and art-practice. The ends of social dreaming and the ends of art are perhaps one. Gabriel Josipovici's (1979) account of the ends of art could be transposed to social dreaming without addition:

> Art was not a means of piercing the sensible veil of the universe, of getting at the "unknown" for there was nothing beyond the world we see all around us. The artwork reveals to us the otherness of the world around—it shocks us out of our natural sloth and the force of habit, and makes us see for the first time, what we had looked at a hundred times but never seen. [p. 191]

Social dreaming, then, is an immanentizing method that returns us to the world by dissolving our culturally conditioned conceptual Platonism and habitual tendency to absent ourselves from our own experience: social dreaming makes it new.

Perhaps in the practice of social dreaming the insight behind Susan Sontag's (1994) claim that "the earliest experience of art must have been that it was incantatory, magical . . . an instrument of ritual" (p. 3) may be glimpsed.

Social dreaming shares with modern movements in art, literature, and philosophy a concern to recover aspects of experience that have been lost or covered over in our modern Western societies.

This attempt at recovery is described by Charles Taylor (1992) as a desire to bring about

> the retrieval of the lived experience or creative activity underlying our awareness of the world, which had been occluded or denatured by the regnant mechanistic construal. The retrieval is

felt as a liberation, because the experience can become more vivid and the activity unhampered through being recognized, and alternatives open up in our stance toward the world which were quite hidden before. [p. 460]

It shares with modern movements an extraordinary deployment of language which challenges denotative-utilitarian language use and behaviour, in favour of non-ordinary uses of language designed to break open our habitual ways of seeing and return us to the world:

In a mechanistic or utilitarian world we come to deal with things in a mechanical, conventionalised way. Our attention is turned away from things to what we are getting done through them. Ordinary prose reflects this. It deals in dead counters, which allow us to refer to things without really seeing them. . . . Poetry is meant to break through this abstraction. It always endeavours to arrest you, and to make you continuously see a physical thing, to prevent you from gliding through an abstract process. The poetic image breaks from a language of counters and gives a fresh intuitive language which restores our vision of things. [p. 460]

However, because social dreaming is more immersive and existentially binding than art, it may modulate towards an experience that is beyond or beside language.

Social dreaming facilitates a kind of *progressio harmonica*, a progressive recuperation of world to itself in which the vocabulary of subjectivity and intersubjectivity is rendered increasingly problematical and inadequate to facts of experience. Moreover, if the experiences in deep matrices mirror the progressive integrations of traditional ritual, then these integrations may be occurring at both experiential *and organic levels as the participants begin to operate as if they were one, more like a single organism than a collective* (Rappaport, 1999, p. 224).

According to Laughlin, McManus, and d'Aquili, "ritual techniques neutralize the functioning of the analytic conceptual mode, bringing to the fore developmentally earlier functioning. This mode associates aspects of experience transductively: that is, it makes lateral associations based upon class similarity, overlapping class membership, or emotional affinity" (quoted in Rappaport, 1997, p. 227).

A deep matrix may even provide participants with experiences of wholeness that are conventionally vouchsafed by only the pious or committed follower of transformational practices such as yoga or meditation. Moreover, social dreaming is uniquely suited to the Western psyche, which has become alienated from aspects of body, mind, community, and the natural world.

As Rappaport observes (Rappaport, 1999, p. 402) such experiences of oneness or participation in progressively larger systems, of which the individual mind is only a function or subsystem, may even prove to be of evolutionary value. The conventional view of the person as a self-subsistent monad that is prevalent today, the era of the individual, has been challenged by a modern intellectual and social movements as various as Marxism, deconstruction in its multiple guises, new-ageism, systems theory, and the ecology movement. Yet the "natural" tendency to experience oneself as a unique, self-subsistent individual, reinforced and underwritten by institutional conditioning, overrides the truths of reason, and the fantasy of the unique sovereign self remains inviolate. Under "ordinary" conditions, I experience myself as a separate individual and behave correspondingly:

> To ask conscious reason to lead unaided the separate individuals in which it resides to favour the long-term interests of ecosystems and societies over their immediate concerns may be too much to ask of it. Sustained compliance with the imperatives of larger systems not only may require more than ordinary reason, but may have to be maintained in defiance of a consciousness that in its nature informs humans of their separateness. [Rappaport, 1999, p. 403]

Social dreaming may provide a technology for achieving such an overcoming, challenging conventional truth inscribed in the present as ultimate, giving separate individuals experiences of the impersonal whole that are inaccessible to them under ordinary conditions:

> Although humans are metabolically separate from one another, and although consciousness is individual, humans are not self sufficient and their autonomy is relative and slight. They are parts of larger systems upon which their continued existence is contingent, But the wholeness, if not indeed the very existence of those systems, may be beyond the grasp of ordinary consciousness. Although conscious reason is incomplete, participation in rituals may enlarge the awareness of those participating in them, providing them with understandings of perfectly natural aspects of the social and physical world that may elude unaided reason. [p. 402]

The alterations of self wrought in the social dreaming experience can act

in the service of the organisation and reorganisation understand-
ings that include discursive as well as non-discursive elements
and processes. They are in the service of integration which may
be, for the novice or learner in a rite of passage, a novel synthesis,
a new and deeper understanding of the world. [p. 388]

Social dreaming is a laboratory of experimental phenomenology in
which aspects of this larger mind, in which the individual is immanent and of which the individual is merely a subsystem, may be first
verified, explored, and perhaps eventually re-inscribed in an expanded common sense.

CHAPTER SIXTEEN

Social dreaming: a paradox accepted (a psychoanalyst's condensed thoughts on social dreaming)

Judit Szekacs

"... paradox accepted can have positive value."

D. W. Winnicott

Who has a dream?

Who has a dream?—as a matter of fact we all do, but we are not used to answering such a question! Dreams are, as they often say, "silly, mysterious, embarrassing, amazing", but in the first place they are personal.

How can one ask for dreams in a public space?

The idea might sound like a surrealistic image from Bunuel's film *Discreet Charm of the Bourgeoisie*, where adding to the escalating sense of madness there comes a character announcing—out of the blue—that he wants to share his dream with the ladies and gentlemen.

Nearly a hundred years ago, Freud carved a passage through social resistance to paying serious attention to dreams by recognizing them as highly precious media carrying valid psychosocial meaning. He made dreams acceptable and available for two-person investigations in the analytic space: delegates from distinct regions of the unconscious speaking a forgotten language that we all know. Sharing dreams in the analytic process became known as "the royal road to the unconscious"—a formidable and indispensable instrument for uncovering and understanding transference and countertransference processes and possible ways of elaboration.

So . . . who has a dream?

However unusual, this is exactly the question asked at the beginning of every social dreaming matrix, which causes the matrix to become expectant, by inviting the first dream to appear and start the dream-association exchange rolling.

As I look around on Wednesday evenings, I see familiar and unfamiliar faces in the room where we meet once a month, for the third year now. I can see an ordinary set of people who gather here to spend an evening with their dreams. This is the first on-going social dreaming matrix in the United Kingdom, a unique experience for us all. (The matrix is organized by IMAGO East–West in London.)

Gordon Lawrence keeps quoting the definition: "a matrix is a place where things can grow." Regarding the *setting* the matrix can be considered in many ways an open formation: participants may come and go, but most often they come—and come. The frames are also basic in non-clinical spaces like this, as they outline the shape of the container that is being created.

Initially we have all struggled with the idea that the group of social dreamers is not to be considered a group in the traditional sense: the boundaries around it are not definite. They are penetrable in space and time and—I believe this was the most difficult concept to digest—group dynamics do not apply here.

The task—again in Lawrence's words—is "to be available for the dreams and associations related to them" and to liberate ourselves from the definition of treating each other's dreams as representations of personal inner worlds.

What makes this possible?

It has taken me nearly fifteen years to grasp the meaning of Lawrence's vision and translate it into my own language. Now, when I attempt to conceptualize phenomena that might offer some analytic insight into the dynamic processes of the social dreaming experience, I need to bring together disparate but very closely linked ideas.

John Byng-Hall, the central and most original figure of British family therapy, when recalling crucial moments in the history of family therapy describes how revolutionary it was to realize that the most fundamental transference was not to the therapists but to other members of the family. This freed the therapists from addressing individual processes and allowed them to turn their attention to the family as a unit and uncover the vast and fascinating area of family dynamics in this light. This shift has enabled the model of change to alter (Whiffen & Byng-Hall, 1982, p. 9) and created a new stance that made it possible for the participants to engage in a different *transferential* experience.

I believe that, by introducing changes in the setting and deconstructing traditional boundaries and relational techniques (basic components of the adult's self-representation, role, and identity), something similarly basic happen s in social dreaming: *the "most fundamental" transference gets established not between the individuals but between the members of the matrix and the DREAMS.*

This altered model allows the dreamers to take part in creating an associative network of images, ideas, and reflections that each participant relates to: the texture contains and is partly woven of the individuals' thoughts, affects, and memories, but they belong to the *community of dreamers* at the same time. It is all right to use the others' dream-elements, and everybody welcomes new bits that the next person adds to the construct. As the private domain is always profoundly respected, the personal opens up to be fertilized by new meanings .

There are no interpretations in the usual sense either: the meaning is being woven from dream imagery, talking pictures, tunes, rhythms, associated sensuous fragments, intellectual references, linkages to everyday events—socio-economic and human drama. A "harmonious mix-up", to borrow Balint's (1968, p. 70) expressive term, of primary and secondary processes reflected upon in this intermediary space.

Since in this atmosphere ego boundaries do not have to be guarded all the time, sharing becomes possible and the participants experience a high level of intimacy. The atmosphere sometimes gets fully charged, passionate, tense, then meditative and reflective again. The convenors are part of these processes: sometimes they will be "guides" helping the dreams stay in focus, other times participant observers, in the next moment players themselves.

As a result of these changes in this community of dreamers a new transitional container is being created

Though this all might sound like a thrilling description of discovering a never-seen land, the experience itself is utterly familiar: it takes us all back to a place long forgotten yet never unconsciously abandoned, the psychodynamic zone where playing is possible.

In *Playing and Reality* Winnicott (1971) writes:

> This intermediate area of experience, unchallenged in the respect of its belonging to inner or external (shared) reality, constitutes the greater part of the infant's experience, and throughout life is retained in the intense experiencing that belongs to the arts and to religion and to imaginative living, and to creative scientific work. [p. 14]

He postulates the existence of a transitional space where transitional phenomena take place and where transitional objects are being created.

In the social dreaming matrix, dreams acquire such a transitional nature, they became the mind-objects that make members of the matrix experience the direct continuity with the play area of the small child who is lost in play. This is exactly the magic of our Wednesday nights: being lost in social dreaming.

Looking amazed at how dreams link up, move together, follow resembling story-lines, contain similar images, colours, feelings, rhythm, the question often arises: where do our dreams come from? Are we conjuring them up from within, or do they approach us from without? Are they waiting for a dreamer to dream them? In Winnicott's (1951) words: "Of the transitional object it can be said that it is a matter of agreement between us and the baby that we will never ask the question: 'Did you conceive of this or was it presented to you from without?'"* Winnicott continues: "The important point is that no decision on this point is expected" (pp. 239–240). This advice has resonance in social dreaming too: such a question cannot be asked without the danger of invading the potential space. It might deprive the dreamer of a sense of creativity and the experience of being in touch with her or his own and others' creations.

The processes of social dreaming affect not only the dreamers: dreams, too, undergo dynamic changes

Working with "two-body" dreams in the analytic space, one's experience is that verbal elements are rather rare and always deserve special attention. In social dreaming, dreams unexpectedly start talking. Shorter and longer verbal sequences, even elaborate dialogues, alternate with more archaic, sensuous elements.

This extraordinary phenomenon seems to reflect transformations in the nature of dreams: the primary processes seem to allow secondary processes more prominence, which results in a much more balanced mix of visual and verbal.

Does this mean that the technique used in social dreaming modifies the dynamics of the dream-work?

If the emphasis is less on the private aspects of the dreams and the instinctual-affective charge does not get interpreted, do dreams become more straightforward and direct? Is there less repression and concealment necessary when the main area of exploration is our relationship and our reactions to the world in which we are living? Does the gap become narrower between the manifest and the latent content of the dreams, or is what we observe simply the result of working predominantly with the social content, hence allowing the dreams to come closer to the conscious through the formative experiences inherent in social dreaming?

The matrix presents a place where "things can grow", but also a place where the nature of dreams (dream characteristics) can be further explored as a function of external–internal changes. Observing how dreams behave during the times of social crises and traumatization—our matrix entered its second year in September 2001—we see a particularly fascinating field of inquiry being opened up.

Dreams seem to be capable of taking the matrix on a "crash course" in trauma theory and elaboration. Initially, following the trauma there was a powerful silence: the dreams refused to appear After a while, frightening dream contents swept through the shared dream-space; bizarre objects, composite creatures and plants, absurd body images, not-fitting elements, wrong colours and functions dominated—as if the trauma had blown up the dream imagery and the loose fragments had joined up in wrong combinations. Even elementary sensual features decomposed; the smell, the sight, the voice, the touch, or the pace of things went out of order. This breakdown of differentiation and representation reflected a collapse of orientation in space and time and a chaotic confusion between external and internal. The dreams bore witness to how the trauma splits the self.

Ferenczi introduces the idea of "stages" in his paper on the development of the sense of reality (Ferenczi, 1913), taking us through the steps of the decline of the feeling of omnipotence. Ferenczi, like Winnicott, believes that the "task of reality acceptance is never completed, that no human being is free from the strain of relating inner and outer reality, and the relief from this strain is provided by an intermediate area of experience (cf. Riviere, 1936) which is not challenged (arts, religion, etc.)" (Winnicott, 1971, p. 13).

The place we inhabit in social dreaming is this intermediate area, and what we explore is the capacity of the dream to function as a communicative link between external and psychic reality. Reclaiming larger territories from "the unknown" or infinite prepares us for action in a world that seems to be getting more and more out of control.

Turning to the "community of dreamers" to make sense of our dreams has proven to be, throughout these years, a complex and electrifying exercise in keeping ourselves more "fit" to understand our internal and external world. Examining changes in the environment and society through the prism of our dreams gives us access to being in touch with related conscious and unconscious impulses and wishes, thus enabling us to become more aware of changes in the psychic world.

Social dreaming opens up not only the "royal road" to the unconscious but also a very "democratic road" to a better sense of reality and a more creative relationship to our life.

CHAPTER SEVENTEEN

Associations and reflections on social dreaming

Lilia Baglioni

> What . . . will take that great mass which everyone calls "the
> dreadful horror" and break it up into these tiny, precious
> particles? art cannot replace faith: Art lacks the power for the
> task, nor does it pretend to posses this power: Nonetheless, by its
> very nature, art constantly challenges the process by which the
> individual is reduced to anonymity.
>
> Appelfeld, *Beyond Despair* (1994)

A social dreaming matrix, a participant once said, is "a social gathering where dreams are divorced from the personality of their authors and shared freely", with the common goal of freely associating thoughts and other dreams to the dream presented so as to find links and discover connections to socially relevant elements (Bion's "thoughts without a thinker", Bollas's, "the unthought known") in the environment. Thereby participants are given a glimpse of the otherwise invisible web of connectivity between nocturnal dreaming and the greater world of reality. In so doing, a transitional space (Winnicott) comes into existence, which could also be described as a mental state close to reverie.

But this concept does not totally capture it.

Connecting the idea of *reverie*, as elaborated in particular in the tradition of Bion, with the concept of *states of non-integration* described by Winnicott in the context of his conceptualizing the development of the *capacity to be alone, in the presence of another*, approximates a little more to the experience; this is how I would try to describe it outside of a dreaming matrix to a group of psychoanalysts.

To adumbrate the work of a matrix, I could also resort to the Winnicotian *squiggle play* as a way of both delicately making contact between adult and child and of developing, in a symbiotic relationship, a formal container of meaning, capable of hosting/expressing the emotional worlds of the dyad in their environment, a technique conducive to better differentiation and communication.

From the point of view of a participant, the activity in a matrix results, first of all, in a deepening of the feeling of "going on being" (Winnicott) and a strengthening of the muscle of negative capability (Keats, Bion), both of which are necessary for living creatively and responsibly.

As the work of the matrix proceeds, and the emotional-tension release patterns stabilize, surfacing in the spoken text as a harmonic admixture of dreams and associations, rhythmically expanding and contracting the breadth of possible universes of meaning, or discrete realities, this state may at times shift to one closer to a hypnagogic one, with contemporary optimal activation of primary and secondary process and partial dissolving of self boundaries.

This is the state ostensibly conducive to the kind of dreams (like Kekulé's or Coleridge's) always used in the literature as evidence of the problem-solving and creative function of dreaming—the dreams, that is, in which the thrust of the image is also "upward".

As we progress, attention freely moving and pausing, the participants become more aware of each other in the room, and of the different thinking/feeling styles present, as well as of a new, non-personal component in the room, a" presence", that for lack of better metaphor, I would describe, borrowing from Rose (1996) talking about the responsiveness to art, as a "witnessing presence", responsive itself and therefore intrinsically benevolent.

By the use of ongoing matrices or by the connection of different dreaming matrices (interfacing), the extent and the quality of the invisible network becomes ever more obvious, adding evidence to the fertility of new evolving holistic and non-reductionist paradigms.

Social dreaming has in fact pointed to the relatedness of dreams to social events, but this would not have been possible, in our Western culture, until now: a way of construing the cosmos and the mind favourable to the development of this idea had first to come into existence.

We seem to be now in the process of testing/living/creating the span of a potential symbiotic relationship between the evolving idea of social dreaming and its environment. I believe that "social dreaming" points to elements that are of crucial importance today for all of us as individuals, as creatures who are part and parcel of a collective, no matter how isolated and remote we may appear or perceive ourselves to be, related to each other by the context in which we live, reproduce/not reproduce, and die.

Lawrence proposes that this collective, which can be regarded and described in many different ways, should be looked at as a collective of dreamers, engaged in co-dreaming reality into existence, including the reality of ourselves as individuals, as groups, as species, as elements of a local ecosystem, and finally of cosmos and mind. This I regard as a promising methodological choice, a potentially fruitful basic assumption or working hypothesis strongly embedded in the matrix of scientific method as nowadays recognized by the so-called hard sciences as well as in the matrix of the so-called traditional sapiential doctrines. I see the link in the expression "learning from experience", which we paradoxically do by using the very nature of our being (mind–body) in the process of becoming, out of the pressure put on the mind–body (apparatus for thinking thoughts), by the presence or absence of a specific disturbing element called thought in the felt presence of an other and of an environment shared by both.

The world has just begun to exploit the power of connecting millions of disparate, small, privately owned computers into a colossal analytic computing procedure to find solutions to scientific riddles heretofore impossible to address for lack of large-enough computers, such as capturing and analysing for meaning the sounds from outer space, foregrounding background noise, looking for signals of presence of intelligent life in the cosmos. In this, desire and memory give, as always, the first form to the cloud of uncertainty: if something is there, will it be friend or foe? Good for mating or eating? Or . . .

What is it that is filling our scientific, enlarged sensory apparatuses with stimuli reluctant to categorization, sometimes driving them crazy, sometimes driving the "observers" to develop a better instrument?

The answer, someone maintained, is the endemic malady of the question. But what about hybrids, like sphinxes and such creatures? Do they have illnesses too? I recently read an article in a daily paper about the venerably old Sphinx, in Giza. As it seems, archaeologists and the larger circle of those concerned with the preservation of valuable cultural artefacts in the world are becoming concerned fact that restorative interventions, brought to the limits of therapeutic furor, might precipitate the beautiful although dilapidated creature into becoming a large heap of dust. An archaeologist put it this way: "The more you study it, the more you kill it."

I have a very special affection for Egypt and a familiarity with the old monument, which I go to greet almost every year on my frequent trips to Cairo, so I could not help being strongly touched by the news. A sad story, especially because this particular sphinx, the Egyptian kind, the survivor of her family, which was once much more widespread in the area, was, as it seems and as I like to believe, much more of a pacific and profound animal compared to the better-known Greek specimen so determinant in the fate of Oedipus.

The social dreaming matrix has its roots in experiences that were attained through participation in groups and psychoanalysis, as in the use of thoughts that such experiences impelled. What is social dreaming's *idée mere*? I do not know—perhaps this is something we are also exploring in the dreaming matrix. I am here using the term "idea" as Bion used it in *Memoir of the Future* (1991).

There is some agreement in recent psychoanalysis—for instance, that which moved ahead under the stimulation of the thought of Bion and of Winnicott, which also has representative thinkers in my own country, Italy—that we have to dream first what we are afterwards to call reality and play with it with another engaged in the same task (see Ferro, 1996, 1999; or, more from the group vertex, Corrao & Neri, 1981).

This builds on Bion's seminal idea of *alpha-elements* (pictograms that are a transformation of the rough sense data, *beta-elements*) and *alpha function* or *dreamwork alpha* as a continuous unconscious processing of lived experience going on, wavelike, by day and by night.

This underlying process would surface and become knowable and ready for further transformation in the form of *narrative derivatives*, including. of course dreams proper.

What do we do, then, as "dreaming souls"?

This to me amounts, at this moment, for shortage of a better metaphor, to what Bion referred to when he spoke of psychoanalysis as a probe that enlarges the field it explores, and Winnicott when he spoke of the creation of transitional space and of the created/found object. Bion was pointing to a function of the mind as yet quite primitive, embryonic in the humane individual. Bion, as I understand it, did not think of the mind of the analyst, but of the mind itself, although stating strongly that this function can be more, or less, developed in different individual minds and can be cultivated through relentless and inspired exercise. Included is the kind of exercise that people engage in during an analysis in a dyadic or multipersonal setting—that is, connecting, through an emotional experience, to the evolutionary nuclei of meaning created by the individual–individual or group–individual dyad in order to promote development and differentiation.

This, Bion thought, could better be done by putting memory and desire on the one side—a reformulation of Freudian evenly suspended attention—and by actively sustaining the state of reverie so promoted through the use of free association and imaginative conjectures.

Bion (1991) also thought that psychoanalysts and patients had some glimpses of the nature of the mind in their search, practice, and "theorizing" activity. He wondered whether, having seen the "stripes on the back of the tiger . . . we would one day meet the burning bright creature herself" (p. 12).

So we may assume, as a working hypothesis, that dream comes first, that there are "dreams in search of a dreamer", and that we have to dream reality before it can become really real for us, and maybe dream it a number of times to allow getting into contact with it effectively.

In this process we change, and reality changes too. We transform each other and our environment as we go, in a process that is at the same time finite and infinite. Evidence collected by Lawrence and other "social dreamers" around the world seems to suggest that this process of digesting, dreaming—narrating reality in common—is that which creates the web in which we are all contained or suspended and that contains and suspends us while we work at weaving its threads. It is also through this process that we come to know the unknown.

This net, generated from the inside, as in an Australian myth about the invention of the fishing-net, is a multi-verse of dreams, and dreams themselves are, in this sense, containers for meaning as well as containers of meaning (see Armstrong, 1998b). Thus, it is a cradle for evolving thoughts.

The term "matrix" comes from the Latin for *uterus*, the place from which something grows. The concept of postnatal uterus, developed by Frances Tustin (1981), comes to mind—the place in which the process of growth and development of the "child mind" continues after birth (see the work of Donald Meltzer, Meg Harris Williams, or Marion Milner, for example)—a concept not just restricted to the realm of pathology, from which it was derived.

Two other concepts might help to construe and explore a model for social dreaming matrix, borrowed this time from the psychoanalytic work with groups: protomental system (Bion, 1961) and syncretistic sociality (Bleger, 1967). The former stresses more the non-differentiation between the biological and the psychological; the latter introduces a clear image of the connecting net underlying discrete behavioural phenomena and, so to speak, "spacefies" the first concept and adds dimensions. Do dreams grow from such a terrain, and, if so, won't they be connected, made of the same elements of the soil from which they grow into the daylight of awareness?

With a quantum leap that I would not allow myself were we not in the realm of dreams and free associations (where jumping is the norm, as on the moon), I would like to put to you, as metaphor, a "scientific truth". Stars transform hydrogen into helium, and from their combination come nitrogen, oxygen, carbon, phosphorus, potassium—the elements without which amino acids would not be, nor would the proteins indispensable to life. Without the radiations coming from the stars and liberated in this cosmic process, millions of stars would freeze and die.

As living creatures we contain the same genetic code of other living creatures, including amoebas and dinosaurs (see Morrone & Mazzalli, 2000), essentially made of adenosine, cytosine, guanine, thymine—A, C, G, T—yet we are very different from each other, the forms of life being many, expanding–contracting universes themselves. So we seem also to "depend on the stars".

The social dreaming matrix is a different medium compared to a group, and we may therefore expect that different phenomena will become visible as they transit through it, adding or subtracting evidence from what we know and probably highlighting new objects. Coming back to the collective of dreamers (social dreaming matrix) and to the concept of a multi-verse of meanings created by the encounter between dreams and associations, as Lawrence puts it, I have the impression that having stated a working hypothesis (social dreaming) and having devised a technical apparatus to test it (the social dreaming matrix), we are now exposed to the effects of this new medium. This is what we set up to explore, and what we are going to discover on the way is probably that people dream socially, that individuals are continually monitoring and communicating, through dreams, about the context in which they swim, like vortexes in a pool of water, that the water seems to have a direction, that the direction changes, as for the effect of invisible undercurrents, that the feeling of disconnection usually leads to a frantic search for connection creating larger vortexes, that at the boundaries of the vortex it is virtually impossible and also useless to keep talking of vortex and pool as separate entities if we want to make some sense and keep swimming. At this point we may want to take a plunge into the current.

CHAPTER EIGHTEEN

Social dreaming:
dreams in search of a dreamer

Franca Fubini

A while ago I was called by a small firm to work on improving communication and cohesion between staff and management at a time of crisis. Reality was that the existing staff was in the process of being selected because at least a third of them had to be dismissed. Time for this project was very limited, and I decided to use in it social dreaming matrices and small discussion groups. The first matrix was scheduled for staff only, without the four managers. The room was organized with the chairs in a snowflake shape; people arrived and were told that the task for the next hour and a half was to associate one's dreams with those of the others, so as to create links and connections.

After initial ironical comments of the kind "First they give us the sack, then they send the psychoanalyst to sweeten the pill", dreams came out, mostly full of anxiety because of missed or failed examinations, invalidated degrees, shut doors, missed trains, and so on. The associations to their work situation became quite clear. They were able to talk freely about the anxiety of the moment, the uncertainty of the future.

In the next matrix they were to associate with one of the dreams and read through its images of the unrealistic expectations of secure jobs they had had towards this very young firm, caught up in the changes of market environment.

The following week a matrix was held with the participation of both staff and managers. This time the managers felt anxious, as they were new to the experience, and this was observed by the staff with some glee. However, soon they were all on common ground; dreams were flowing, and associations too; the theme of funerals became dominant, allowing everyone to talk differently about the situation they shared. Different options for collaboration emerged. When I left, the managers were discussing whether to call back two of the dismissed employees, as the roles they covered were actually needed in the firm.

In the following matrix, the last one, the feedback was that this work had acted like removing old trunks from a river so that water could flow again. In some of the dreams offered to the matrix there was the figure of an old man, loved/hated who was dying or dead. It elicited different and strong feelings from most participants, but I could not quite locate the experience in the context of what I knew. In a later meeting I had with the founding members, they spoke of another, older member who held 32% of the shares who, although not working in the firm, strongly influenced company policy through his many political contacts. He was loved by one manager but strongly resented by the other three.

Weeks later I came for the final meeting to see what had happened and whether to take the work further. The shares of "Mister 32%" had been bought by the other associates, who had realized that change was primarily related to

1. their own internal reorganization: they had only taken action in terms of reducing the staff, rather than looking at their own needs for updating management;
2. a more realistic evaluation of the changing market in such a way that they could adjust the internal environment to be more in tune with the external one.

This material illustrates how issues of change could be hidden and distorted by the innate desire to have security and adjust to a mode of precarious equilibrium. Pressure from the environment, both internal and external, was pointing to a collapse of the taken-for-granted establishment.

Dreams revealed the issues with astonishing clarity: expectations and underlying feelings emerged, connecting the participants beyond the overt hierarchical structure of the firm and the established relationships within it.

Dreams reveal and connect us to the social context in which we live. As dreams illuminate the inner life of an individual in psychoanalysis, so they do in a social context; furthermore, dreams take us to the space of knowing/not-knowing, where true creative thinking lives and a pragmatic approach to reality can betaken.

In the next pages I explore some aspects of social dreaming related to the concepts of matrix, connectedness, and "dreams in search of a dreamer".

Gordon Lawrence's paper in 1991 on social dreaming piqued my interest quite strongly, and few months later I joined a social dreaming workshop at the Institute of Group Analysis in London. At the time it was not easy for me to conceptualize the experience; intuitively, however, it was a turning point for my way of looking at groups, dreams and the context in which dreams, and the lives of the dreamers take place.

As I was already working with groups as a group analyst, social dreaming seemed to provide a missing link between the inward-looking world of therapy and the outward-looking sphere of the social.

Today I still find that to reflect and to write about social dreaming is a stimulating and very demanding task: intuitions and concepts do not always find a satisfactory meeting point. The areas revealed by the experience of being in a social dreaming matrix are vast. It is very exciting and thought-provoking to have dialogue with other participants about it, as the experiences of open space, the infinite, mobility, and connectedness that belong to social dreaming are fed by doing so, and as social meanings are discovered. The process of one dream/thought/association bouncing off of another and onto the next and to the following one, in the space of relatedness, is typical of a matrix; it becomes more of a challenge to enter the constraint/containment of definitions and finite concepts as you write on your own about it. It is challenging to sculpt the flow of a moving universe, where movement itself creates space.

And after all we don't often dream in words, or in isolation. Indeed, dreams are the mental space where known and unknown coexist, and where the unknown is our experience of the infinite, the formless, the timeless—that is, beyond and before the concepts of time and space upon which much of our mental functioning rests and is constrained.

The experience of being in a matrix is that of extreme mobility, where dreams and associations move quite freely in the space of many directions. As a therapist there is a major shift in point of observation: what Lawrence, and before him, Bion, described as the Oedipus (ego-centric) and the sphinx (socio-centric) vertexes, the reversible perspective of two complementary states of mind. In a matrix, not only can the two vertexes be seen but also, and particularly, the movement created by shifting from one perspective to another (Lawrence & Biran, 2002).

One participant in a social dreaming matrix spoke of "hearing the music"; it was not directly related to the matrix, but it clicked, and it has become a metaphor for the exploration of the matrix. In the same way as one hears a piece of music, one experiences a social dreaming matrix by hearing the whole picture created by the dreams and their associations. It is possible to focus one's hearing on a single line of music, and on individual players with their instruments, but within the context of the whole piece. The same applies for the dreams of a matrix. Indeed, we hear the composition created by the dreams, not so much the single dreamer.

"To hear the musical sound of the word, more than the meaning of the word itself" was a further association in the social dreaming matrix to "hearing the music"; by doing so, one enters an area close to mantras and sounds, which in many cultures represent the origin of creation. Rhythmic patterns are seen throughout the universe, from the very small to the very large. Quantum physics has offered the vision of energy patterns manifesting alternatively and rhythmically as waves and as particles.

Lawrence himself puts forward the hypothesis that "dream-work is a wave function and that when a dream emerges from the black hole of the psyche, it is a particle" (Lawrence, 1998c, p. 180).

Matrix

Matrix contains the root of the word *mater*, mother; it is literally a *uterus*, an original source out of which something can be created. Matrix—a fundamental concept in group analysis—is also defined by

Foulkes as the "hypothetical web of communication and relationship in a given group. It is the common shared ground which ultimately determines the meaning and significance of all events and upon which all communications and interpretations, verbal and non-verbal, rest" (Foulkes, 1964, p. 292). Foulkes addresses the group and already hints at a concept of mobility, connection, and open spaces beyond the idea of the group.

A web is by definition flexible, adjusting to the content, which the web contains; a web is made of threads and of empty spaces; it holds without the need for a fixed separation between what is inside and what is outside. Matrix in social dreaming is the open space where the shared dreams and their associations can take place, held by the flexibility of the web of connections that the matrix creates and that allows the shaping of the container each matrix needs.

A social dreaming matrix has two strong characteristics: one is that it allows the individual to come very close to the experience of dreaming itself; the other is that it allows the discovery of what a matrix is about—in other words, it is in a process of becoming, it captures the mobility of the process. There is no accent on expected phases of development to pass through, as there would be in a group context; each matrix has its own task of discovery and creation. Dreams and associations lead the way.

The process of becoming and revelation is in some ways close to the process of healthy life itself. I feel much appreciation for an approach that, without excluding other angles of vision, parallel discoveries, and spectacles of interpretation (like, for instance, the tradition of group dynamics), has as its focus that particular aspect of life that touches on the unknown, the movement of change, the coexistence of the many, the non-pathology.

Connectedness

In social dreaming, Lawrence has brought together traditional (historical, anthropological, mythological, etc.) knowledge about dreams and the discoveries of psychoanalysis, which at the beginning of the twentieth century revealed a new way of thinking about the nature and use of dreams. By doing so, Lawrence has pioneered a space for further new thinking about dreams that reflects the development of the Western culture of our present times as well as the continuation of research on the material of dream-work.

As Freud and psychoanalysis were the products of their time, creating a space for the study of the individual and of his or her psychic world, where dreams are the "royal road to the unconscious", I reckon that in the same way social dreaming is the product of a contemporary Western culture that is in the process of questioning an excessive focus on "the single lines of the music", the fragmentation of knowledge and being, rather than their polyphonic whole.

The separation between mind and body, nature and culture, observed and observer—just to mention a few—have been questioned and proven misleading, giving way to the movement towards integration and multidisciplinary views. The universe seems to be a complex web of interdependent and dynamic relationships. The results of the last decades in the field of communication and information theory (and practice) are possibly a stimulus and an end-product of such change.

Connectedness is one of the hypotheses that Lawrence has explored and which he offers as a way of reading the web of relationships revealed by the sharing of dreams and their associations in a social dreaming matrix. The hypothesis is that people in a given context are connected to each other through the context they share, be it work, cultural, political, geographical, or ultimately human.

In our culture, experiences of oneness and non-separation belong to the realm of mysticism and to the language of religion, as well as to the world of poetry and art; in psychological terms, oneness refers to the early experience of mother and baby fusion; oneness/undifferentiation occurs also in psychotic functioning. In a social dreaming matrix, one discovers that there is another possible way of accessing these experiences.

Scary it might be. I recall a matrix where, in dealing with the unexpressed question of floating in the infinite, the fear was that the matrix might be a crazy space to find oneself in and that free associations were dangerous activities. This might well be so, as they disrupt a model of thinking based on rationality and logic, so not just pulling the carpet out from under one's feet, but removing the very floor on which people often feel safer to stand.

A social dreaming matrix is usually convened by one to four convenors; the matrix convenes dreams and their associations, dreams that have been dreamt by dreamers and may reveal the dreamer and his or her particular position in the world, but which, by and large, reveal the ordinary coexistence of the many in the boundaryless space of the unconscious. In the world of dreams and free associations, there is not so much the experience of right and wrong; one shifts quite easily beyond a dualistic way of thinking and of relating in order to access the space of multi-dimensions, multi-meanings, multi-verse. What in other contexts would appear as manifestations of pathology, in a matrix can be seen and accepted as part of the many appearances of reality.

Connectedness supports, in fact, the coexistence of numberless points of view—as many as there are associations.

"Dreams in search of a dreamer"

Being in a matrix evokes images of a net created by minds tuned in to capturing echoes and signals of the presence of a continuum of dreams and thoughts, involved in the creation and working through of the environment we live in.

Where do new thoughts arise from? In my experience, first from a need, which is like an absence, even if sometimes unrecognized; then they are born from an empty (in the sense of open to the unknown) space created either by an inner tuning of body, emotions, and mind states (intrapsychic relating), or by tuning in with others in the space across individual boundaries (interpsychic relating).

This seems to come close to Bion's hypothesis that there are "thoughts in search of a thinker", where the thinker has to make him/ herself available to receive, and where thoughts are not necessarily the precious property of one individual, but make use of the individual to manifest themselves and (maybe) to carry evolution through. Traditional exploration of dreams (before Freud) belongs to humanity as a whole and dates back thousands of years; it is rich in ways of working with dreams, which in some cases, as with thoughts, have the function both of furthering evolution and of revealing what is known, yet remaining hidden as yet unthinkable thought. Lawrence has put forward the hypothesis that there are "dreams in search of a dreamer".

Human history abounds in dreams that have offered solutions to a searching mind; dreams that have predicted future events; dreams that have revealed the cause of an illness and carried the cure for that illness; dreams that have shaped the creation of a work of art; dreams of a special kind born from clarity and transcendence that have facilitated the cultural and spiritual evolution of humanity.

There are also dreams that have spoken the unthinkable. I would like to refer particularly to the working through of terrors, which may be part of the history of humanity in general, and which also seem to relate very strongly to recent world events (e.g. before and after September 11). Across different nations (the United States, Great Britain, Italy), social dreaming matrices around that time reported dreams where the running themes dealt with apocalyptic fears and ongoing terrors, fragmentation and psychotic functioning, as though at least a portion of human beings have been in the process of working through in their dreams what in daily life and alone is too scary to contemplate or, at least, often more safe to deny.

CHAPTER NINETEEN

Some thoughts on social dreaming

W. Gordon Lawrence

Milan Kundera has a short story, "The Great Return", in which he writes about Czechoslovakian émigrés living in Paris experiencing exile. Irena, the protagonist, recalls the disturbing dreams she had in the first weeks after emigrating. She talked with her husband and found that he was having the same dreams.

> Every morning they would talk about that horror of that return to their native land. Then, in the course of a conversation with a Polish friend, an émigré herself, Irene realized that all émigrés had those dreams, every one without exception; at first she was moved by the nighttime fraternity of people unknown to one another, then somewhat irritated: how could the very private experience of a dream be a collective event? What was unique about her soul, then? But that's enough of questions that have no answers! One thing was certain: on any given night, thousands of émigrés were all dreaming the same dream in numberless variants. The emigration-dream: one of the strangest phenomena of the second half of the twentieth century. [Kundera, 2002, p. 99]

Kundera points to the existence of the collective dream, which will be dreamt by many who have had similar experiences with infinite variations. These dreams echo each other. Similarly, we all dream of our lives and the telling moments of them: the death of a parent, the birth of a child, the recalled experiences of childhood, adolescence, and adulthood. In framing social dreaming and the social dreaming matrix, I wanted to capture something of these collective dreams but recognized that it would smack of omnipotence to call the venture "collective dreaming". As it is, social dreaming catches in its matrix the dreaming that relies on the pool, or reservoir, of the collective dreaming of humanity. If you will, social dreaming gives attention to a selection of dreams that arise from the well of collective dreaming.

In framing the idea of social dreaming, it was all those dreams that are never articulated, lying dormant in the collective mind, that I felt had to be captured and studied systematically. Because it had never been done before—at least in such a deliberate and studied way—there were no precedents, except for psychoanalysis. The focus of the psychoanalytic project in dreaming is to unravel what is in the mind of the analysand. It is therefore a project that has Oedipus as its guide. In psychoanalysis, through working at the transference between the professional and the analysand and the dreams, the dynamics of this relationship can be identified and worked with.

I postulated on the basis of reading anthropological texts that dreaming could also be used to gain knowledge. In this, I was following Bion's insight that one could see in a group two sets of phenomena: first, the phenomenon of Oedipus, which is that of the relations in the pair, but, second, the phenomenon of sphinx. Sphinx refers to knowledge, understanding, insight, scientific method, and how we arrive at truth as human beings (Bion, 1961, pp. 7–8).

I think that Bion's formulation can be updated, given the advances made by Maturana and Varela (1987). The interactions between a living system and its environment are cognitive interactions. Indeed, the process of living is a process of cognition. Cognition is the continual bringing forth of a world. This is an integral feature of the process of living, and cognition is the process.

Maturana and Varela were responsible for the Santiago Theory. As Capra puts it:

> Cognition, as understood in the Santiago Theory, is associated with all levels of life and is thus a much broader phenomenon than consciousness. Consciousness—that is conscious lived, experience—unfolds at certain levels of cognitive complexity that requires brain and a higher nervous system. In other words, con-

sciousness is a special kind of cognitive process that emerges when cognition reaches a certain level of complexity. [Capra, 2002, p. 33]

A matrix (which I now see as being essential to the social dreaming process), I am to postulate, embodies the idea of mental connectedness that is universal. I submit that cognition and consciousness arise from this universal mental connectedness. The act of free association enables realities to be brought into being, but it is through the complementary process of thinking that the reality comes to be substantial. One can detect the two processes interweaving in a matrix.

If free association can be likened to taking a train journey and observing the landscape and simply thinking what passes through one's mind, it is out of these random associations that thinking begins. To be sure, rationality takes over and new thoughts are thought from these novel associations. What happens in a social dreaming matrix is that after a few sessions the dreams flow as in a jazz group. This collage of dreams results in dreams speaking with dreams. From this, new knowledge emerges.

The link between dreaming and thinking has been chronicled by Becker (1968). He refers to the German chemist Kekulé, who discovered the formula for benzene. When Kekulé's research was at a standstill, a dream came to his aid:

> I turned the chair to the fireplace and sank in a half sleep. The atoms flitted before my eyes ... wriggling and turning like snakes. And see, what was that? One of the snakes seized its own tail and the image whirled scornfully before my eyes. As though from a flash of lightning I awoke. I occupied the rest of the night in working out the consequences of the hypothesis. [quoted in Becker, 1968, p. 84]

The Danish scientist Niels Bohr had a dream in 1913 that enabled him to discover the type of atom that bears his name. It is the unconscious continuity between dreams and waking that brings about these solutions. They are not always directly dreamt.

I am suggesting that cognition and consciousness arise out of thinking, which will have its basis in dreaming. A few years ago, I postulated that there were four types of thinking. I assume there are others, but I simplified thinking to four types. They are: thinking as being; thinking as becoming; thinking as dreaming; and thinking as the "unthought known", to use Bollas's concept. These four I see as being in interaction. Now, I would see the act of cognition, coming to know, and consciousness as an outcome of these four types of thinking. Through a dream, cognition is possible, as Kekulé showed. This was part of the other types of thinking. Kekulé was preoccupied with the ontological "being" of benzene and was thinking what it could "become". The link between the two was provided by a dream hypothesis, which, in a sense, was part of Kekulé's repertoire of his unthought knowns. Until they were thought, they remained unknown.

One can see something of this in a matrix. Arising from the dreaming, the free-associations expand the being of what is discussed. But this discussion can lead to transformations—that is, into a state of becoming. At the same time, the free associations will have some of their roots in the unthought known. While the dreams may be the currency of the matrix, it is the free association and the thinking that gives them value.

Matrix is the web of minds existing at any one time and which are harnessed to focus on a particular topic. A matrix continually moving, as it does, in a non-linear way lets loose thinking that could never have been predicted; serendipity and synchronicity become standard. This is perhaps because a matrix—that network of all individual mental processes—replicates the primordial breast and acts as a container, in that it receives the beta-elements—the pre-thought elements of human beings—and converts them to alpha-elements. These are duly picked up by the individual and used in the construction of his or her thoughts (Bion, 1970; Powell, 1994, p. 16).

Cognition is not the representation of an independently existing world, but is the bringing forth of a world through the process of living. As Capra (2002) is suggesting, the human mind is very active in making the world *be* alive. The Cartesian split between mind and matter is no longer sustainable. The bringing forth of a world is made possible through the quality of our mental disposition for being available for the mental connectedness that is made manifest in the matrix and, more generally, in the mental web of life that connects all humanity that is being postulated.

Being available for the thought processes is brought about by the mental disposition that can come alive in the social dreaming matrix. This mental disposition, which is recognized as a process, allows human beings to perceive that the infinite is made manifest inside our minds and is not some objective, vast space located outside of us. Centuries ago, Indian philosophers identified this, but it is only now beginning to be recognized in the West. By the same token, transcendence and the holy have to be identified inside before they can be recognized as phenomena existing outside us. Thus the mind evolves and does not grow from the outside. Mind evolves through learning, which is derived from working at the edge of knowing and not-knowing. To be in this space is to access the truth-in-the-moment. Bion urged us to "Discard your memory; discard the future tense of your desire; forget them both, both what you knew and what you want, to leave space for a new idea" (Bion, 1980, p. 11).

Leaving space for a new idea has been the hallmark of social dreaming. In a matrix, one can witness the participants reaching after the new free-association, the new idea, the new thinking, the new thought, as they dwell in the space of knowing/not-knowing. This is anxiety making, but I believe that social dreaming, with its non-judgmental posture, allows anxiety to be put into some perspective. This emotional atmosphere allows for new ideas to emerge from the free-associative matrix. To be in the space waiting for new ideas relies on negative capability. Keats identified this as being "when a man is capable of being in uncertainties, mysteries, doubts, without any reaching after fact or reason" (Keats, 1817). In this, Keats was referring to Shakespeare and identifying the latter's genius.

Social dreaming invites working with the dreaming in different ways from those of the past, from conventional ways. Social dreaming invokes a disposition for understanding that relies on not-knowing, in the first instance. This seeming paradox can have positive value.

Bollas (2002, pp. 73 ff.) writes of "mother dream and father thought". The dream is a product of sleep when the body is in a foetal posture and accessing hallucinatory thought.

Once the dream is reported, it becomes subject to father's law, which Lacan saw as "all the obligations determined by one's place in the patriarchal hierarchy" (quoted in Bollas, 2002, p. 73). This is when thinking and thought take over. Dreaming has, since the time of Freud and Jung and probably since mankind was on earth, been recognized as being the route to personal insight. I am arguing that it is also a route into creative thinking and knowledge.

The social dreaming matrix is in the process of causing an epistemological shift in the understanding of dreaming and dream work. It focuses on the gaining of knowledge and leaves the idea of personal understanding of oneself on one side. By making oneself blind to Oedipus, one can see sphinx more clearly and consider the implications imaginatively.

Something of the magic and mysterious ways of dreams was captured by Robert Jay Lifton (1987):

> We can thus view dreams as providing a perpetual dialectic between the most "primitive" psychic fragments and the most "enlightened" frontier of the formative imagination. Within this dialogue the dream flashes its powerful and yet fluid symbolization before us, ours for the using according to the mind's readiness and capacity.
>
> The dream, then, is central to our evolutionary inheritance. In it we find, most profoundly, both clue to and expression of the human capacity for good and evil—for holding visions. For prospective imagining. More than ever we must dream well if we are to confront forces threatening to annihilate us, and if we are to further the wonderful, dangerous, and always visionary human adventure. [p. 194]

REFERENCES

Abraham, R., McKenna, T., & Sheldrake, R. (1992). *Trialogues at the Edge of the West*. Santa Fe: Bear & Co.

Ambrosiano, L. (1999). Tra clinico e istituzionale: nessi possibili. *Rivista di Psicoanalisi, 45*: 475–492.

Ambrosiano, L. (2001a). Introduction. In: W. G. Lawrence (Ed.), *Social Dreaming: La funzione sociale del sogno*. Rome: Borla.

Ambrosiano, L. (2001b). Ululare con i lupi. Note su socialismo e narcisismo. *Rivista di Psicoanalisi, 47* (2): 283–302.

Appelfeld, A. (1994). *Beyond Despair*. New York: Fromm International.

Arendt, H. (1968). *Men in Dark Times*. New York: Harcourt Brace.

Arendt, H., & Heidegger, M. (1998). *Hannah Arendt and Martin Heidegger, Letters: 1925–1975*. New York: Harcourt Brace, 2002.

Armstrong, D. (1998a). Introduction. In: W. G. Lawrence (Ed.), *Social Dreaming @ Work*. London: Karnac.

Armstrong, D. (1998b). Thinking aloud: contributions to three dialogues. In: W. G. Lawrence (Ed.), *Social Dreaming @ Work*. London: Karnac.

Artemidorus Daldianus (ca. A.D. 200). *Interpretation of Dreams. Oneirocritica*. Park Ridge, NJ: Noyes Publications, 1975.

Austin, J. L. (1976). *How to Do Things with Words*. Oxford: Oxford Paperbacks.

Bain, A. (1998). Social defences against organizational learning. In: *Human*

Relations, Special Edition: Past , Present and Future. London: Tavistock Publications.

Bain, A., Long, S., & Ross, S. (1992). *Paper Houses. The Authority Vacuum in a Government School*. Melbourne: Collins Dove.

Balint, M. (1968). *The Basic Fault*. London: Tavistock/Routledge.

Barnet, S., & Burto, W. (1982). *Zen Ink Paintings*. New York: Kodansha International.

Baron-Cohen, S. (1999). *Mindblindness: An Essay on Autism and Theory of Mind*. Cambridge, MA: MIT Press.

Barthes, R. (1990). *Roland Barthes S/Z*, trans. R. Miller, ed. by R. Howard. Oxford: Blackwell.

Batchelor, S. (1983). *Alone with Others*. New York: Grove Press.

Becker, R. de (1968). *Understanding Dreams*. London: George Allen & Unwin.

Beradt, C. (1966). *The Third Reich of Dreams*. Chicago: Quadrangle, 1968.

Bernabei, M. (2001). "La funzione 'problem solving' dei sogni nei gruppi con bambini e adolescenti." Presented at the IAGP Mediterranean Conference in Zadar.

Bion, W. R. (1961). *Experiences in Groups*. London: Tavistock Publications.

Bion, W. R. (1962). *Learning From Experience*. New York: Basic Books; London: Karnac.

Bion, W. R. (1963). *Elements of Psychoanalysis*. London: Heinemann.

Bion, W. R. (1965). *Transformations*. London: Karnac.

Bion, W. R. (1967a). *Experiences in Groups*. London: Routledge.

Bion, W. R. (1967b). *Second Thoughts*. London: Heinemann Medical Books.

Bion, W. R. (1970). *Attention and Interpretation*. London: Tavistock Publications.

Bion, W. R. (1979). *The Dawn of Oblivion. A Memoir of the Future, Book 3*. London: Karnac, 1991.

Bion, W. R. (1980). *Bion in New York and Sao Paulo*, ed. by F. Bion. Strathclyde: Clunie Press.

Bion, W. R. (1987). *Clinical Seminars and Four Papers*. London: Karnac.

Bion, W. R. (1990). *Brazilian Lectures 1973*. London: Karnac.

Bion, W. R. (1991). *A Memoir of the Future*. London: Karnac.

Bion, W. R. (1992). *Cogitations*. London: Karnac.

Bion, W. R. (1997). *Taming Wild Thoughts*. London: Karnac.

Biran, H. (1997). Myths, memories and roles—how they live again in the group process. *Free Associations, 7* (Part 1, No. 4): 31–38.

Biran, H. (1998). An attempt to apply Bion's alpha and beta elements to processes in society at large. In: P. Brontalano, F. Borgogno, & S. A. Merciai (Eds.), *Bion's Legacy To Groups*. London: Karnac.

Biran, H. (1999). Relationship and relatedness between the elementary school and its violent parts. *Socio-Analysis: Journal of the Australian Institute of Socio-Analysis, 1* (1).

Blanchot, M. (1993). *The Infinite Conversation*. Minneapolis, MN: University of Minnesota Press.

Bleger, J. (1967). *Simbiosis y ambiguidad*. Buenos Aires: Paidos.

Bloom, H. (1973). *The Anxiety of Influence*. New York: Oxford University Press.

Bollas, C. (1987). *The Shadow of the Object*. New York: Columbia University Press; London: Free Association Books, 1994.

Bollas, C. (1989). *Forces of Destiny*. London: Free Association Books, 1992.

Bollas, C. (1992). *Being a Character*. London: Routledge.

Bollas, C. (1999). *The Mystery of Things*. London: Routledge.

Bollas, C. (2002). *Free Association*. Cambridge: Icon Books.

Bowlby, J. (1982). Attachment and loss. *Attachment, Vol. 1*. New York: Basic Books.

Briggs, J., & Peat, F. D. (1984). *Looking Glass Universe*. New York: Simon & Schuster.

Briggs, J., & Peat, F. D. (1989). *Turbulent Mirror*. New York: Harper & Row.

Bromberg, P. M. (2000). Bringing in the dreamer: some reflections on dreamwork, surprise, and the analytic process. *Contemporary Psychoanalysis. 36* (4): 685–705.

Buber, M. (1965). *The Knowledge of Man: Selected Essays*. Atlantic Highlands, NJ: Humanities Press International.

Calderón de la Barca, Pedro (1636). *Life Is a Dream*. Oxford: University Press, 1999.

Capra, F. (1997). *The Web of Life*. London: Flamingo.

Capra, F. (2002). *The Hidden Connections*. London: Harper Collins.

Chardin, T. de (1959). *Le phénomène humain*. Paris: Editions du Seuil.

Chopra, D. (1989). *Quantum Healing*. New York: Bantam.

Clarke, L. (1990). *The Chymical Wedding*. London: Picador.

Corbin, H. (1990). *Spiritual Body and Celestial Earth*. London & New York: I. B. Tauris.

Corrao, F. (1986). Il concetto di campo come modello teorico. In: *Orme II*. Milan: Cortina editore, 1998.

Corrao, F., & Neri, C. (1981). Introduction. *Rivista di Psicoanalisi, 27* (3–4): 363–367. (Special Issue dedicated to the work of W. R. Bion, ed. by P. Bion Talamo & C. Neri.)

Correale, A., et al. (2001). *Borderline: Lo sfondo psichico naturale*. Rome: Borla.

Crick, F., & Mitchison, G. (1983). The function of dream sleep. *Nature, 304*: 111–114.

Crossan, J. D. (1988). *The Dark Interval: Towards a Theology Story*. Sonoma, CA: Eagle Books, Polebridge Press.

Damasio, A. (1999a). *The Feeling of What Happens*. New York: Harcourt Brace & Company.

Damasio, A. (1999b). How the brain creates the mind. *Scientific American*, *281* (6): 74–79.

Davis, M., & Wallbridge, D. (1983). *Boundary and Space*. New York: Penguin.

Drury, N. (1979). *Inner Visions*. London: Routledge & Kegan Paul.

Duggan, G. H. (1968). *Teilhardism and the Faith*. Cork: Mercier Press.

Durrenmatt, F. (1976). *Das Sterben der Pythia*. Zurich: Diogenes Verlag.

Eakin, E. (2002). Penetrating the mind of metaphor. *The New York Times*, 23 February.

Edelman, G. M. (1992). *Bright Air, Brilliant Fire: On the Matter of the Mind*. New York: Basic Books.

Eisold, K. (1994). The intolerance of diversity in psychoanalytic institutes. *International Journal of Psycho-Analysis*, 75 (4): 215–233.

Ettinger, E. (1995). *Hanna Arendt–Martin Heidegger*. New Haven, CT/London: Yale University Press.

Ferenczi, S. (1913). Stages in the development of the sense of reality. In: *First Contributions to Psycho-Analysis*. London: Karnac, 1994.

Ferenczi, S. (1933). The confusion of tongues between adults and the child. *International Journal of Psycho-Analysis, 30* (1949): 22.

Ferro, A. (1996). Sexuality as a narrative genre or dialect in the consulting room. In P. Bion-Talamo, F. Borgogna, & S. A. Merciai, *Bion Between Past and Future*. London: Karnac .

Ferro, A. (1999). Narrative derivatives of alpha elements: clinical implications. *International Forum of Psychoanalysis*.

Ferro, A. (2002). Some implications of Bion's thought: waking dream and narrative derivatives. *International Journal of Psycho-Analysis, 83*.

Fosshage, J. L.(1998). "Le funzioni organizzatrici dell'attività mentale del sogno." Presented at the Instituto per lo Studio Psicoanalitico della Soggettività, Rome.

Fosshage, J. L. (2001). "Il modello del sogno come organizzatore: implicazioni teoriche e cliniche." Presented at the DPA and ISIPSÉ, Rome.

Foulkes, S. H. (1964). *Therapeutic Group Analysis*. London: Karnac, 1984.

Freud, S. (1900a). *The Interpretation of Dreams*. S.E., 4 & 5.

Freud, S. (1908c). On the sexual theories of children. S.E., 9.

Freud, S. (1908e [1907]). Creative writers and daydreaming. S.E., 19.

Freud, S. (1913i). The disposition to obsessional neurosis. S.E., 12.

Freud, S. (1915e). The unconscious. S.E., 14.

Freud, S. (1917d [1915]). A metapsychological supplement to the theory of dreams. S.E., 14.

Freud, S. (1921c). *Group Psychology and the Analysis of the Ego. S.E.,* 18.

Freud, S. (1930a). *Civilisation and Its Discontents. S.E.,* 21.

Freud, S. (1936a). A disturbance of memory on the Acropolis. *S.E.,* 22.

Freud, S. (1939a [1937–39]). *Moses and Monotheism. S.E.,* 23.

Friedman, R. (1999). Dreamtelling, as a request for containment and elaboration in group therapy. *Funzione Gamma, 1.* <www.funzionegamma. edu>.

Friedman, R. (2000). "Roman lectures" (edited by S. Stagnitta). Presented at the Psychology Faculty of Rome University "LaSapienza". <www. funzionegamma.edu/site/shome.htm>.

Friedman, R., Neri, C., & Pines, M. (Eds.) (2002). *Dreams in Group Psychotherapy.* London & Philadelphia: Jessica Kingsley.

Fromm, E. (1951,). *The Forgotten Language.* New York: Grove Press, 1957.

Fromm, E., Suzuki, D. T., & de Martino, R. (1960). *Zen Buddhism and Psychoanalysis.* London: Allen & Unwin.

Fromm, M. G. (2000). The Other in the dream. *Journal of Applied Psychoanalytic Studies.*

Gaburri, E. (1992). Emozioni, affetti, personificazione. *Rivista di Psicoanalisi, 38* (2).

Gaburri, E. (2002). Pesnioro associativo e lutto. *Rivista Psicanalisi, 2:* 345–364.

Ghent, E. (2002). Wish, need, drive: motives in the light of dynamic systems theory and Edelman's selectionist theory. *Psychoanalytic Dialogues, 12:* 763–808.

Girard, R. (1978). *Things Hidden since the Foundation of the World.* Stanford, CA: Stanford University Press, 1987.

Grotstein, J. S. (1979). Who is the dreamer who dreams the dream and who is the dreamer who understands it? *Contemporary Psychoanalysis, 15:* 110–116. Also in: J. S. Grotstein (Ed.), *Do I Dare Disturb the Universe?* London: Karnac, 1981.

Grotstein, J. S. (Ed.) (1981). *Do I Dare Disturb the Universe?* London: Karnac.

Gurdjieff, G. I. (1999). *Beelzebub's Tales to His Grandson.* New YOrk: Penguin/Arkana.

Hahn, H. (1998). Dreaming to learn: pathways to rediscovery. In: W. G. Lawrence (Ed.), *Social Dreaming @ Work.* London: Karnac.

Heelas, P., & Lock, A. (1981). *Indigenous Psychologies: The Anthropology of the Self.* London: Academic Press.

Jameson, F. (1984). Postmodernism or the cultural logic of late capitalism. *New Left Review, 146.*

Johnson, E. (2001). *Emergence: The Connected Lives of Ants, Brains, Cities, and Software.* New York: Simon & Schuster.

Josipovici, G. (1979). *The World and the Book.* London: Stanford University Press.

Kaës, R. (2002). The polyphonic texture of intersubjectivity in the dream. In: R. Friedman, C. Neri, & M. Pines (Eds.), *Dreams in Group Psychotherapy.* London & Philadelphia: Jessica Kingsley.

Keats, J. (1817). Letter to George and Tom Keats, 21 (or 27) December. In:

Letters of John Keats (p. 43), ed. R. Gittings. Oxford: Oxford University Press, 1987.

Klein, E. (2000). *A Comprehensive Etymological Dictionary of the English Language*. Amsterdam: Elsevier Science.

Knowlson, J. (1996). *Damned to Fame: The Life of Samuel Beckett*. London: Bloomsbury.

Kramer, M. (1999). Commentary on papers by Rosemarie Sand and by Ramon Greenberg and Chester A. Pearlman. *Dialogues, 9* (6): 767–778.

Kundera, M. (2002). The great return. *New Yorker*, May 20, p. 99.

Lacan, J. (1949). La stade du miroir. In: *Ecrits*. Paris: Editions du Seuil, 1966.

Lawlor, R. (1991). *Voices of the First Day*. Vermont: Inner Traditions.

Lawrence, W. G. (1991). Won from the void and formless infinite: experiences of social dreaming. *Free Associations, 2* (2): 254–294.

Lawrence, W. G. (1997). *Centring the Sphinx for the Psychoanalytic Study of Organisations*. Philadelphia, PA: International Society for the Psychoanalytic Study of Organisations.

Lawrence, W. G. (1998a). Prologue. In: W. G. Lawrence (Ed.), *Social Dreaming @ Work*. London: Karnac.

Lawrence, W. G. (1998b). Social dreaming as a tool of consultancy and action research. In: W. G. Lawrence (Ed.), *Social Dreaming @ Work*. London: Karnac.

Lawrence, W. G. (Ed.) (1998c). *Social Dreaming @ Work*. London: Karnac.

Lawrence, W. G. (1998d). Won from the void and formless infinite: experiences of social dreaming. In: W. G. Lawrence (Ed.), *Social Dreaming @ Work*. London: Karnac.

Lawrence, W. G. (2000a). The politics of salvation and revelation in the practice of consultancy. In: *Tongued with Fire: Groups in Experience*. London: Karnac.

Lawrence, W. G. (2000b). *Tongued with Fire: Groups in Experience*. London: Karnac.

Lawrence, W. G. (2001a). "Roman Lecture." Presented at the Psychology Faculty of Rome, University "La Sapienza", 14 November. <www.funzionegamma.edu/site/shome.htm>.

Lawrence, W. G. (2001b). Social dreaming illuminating social change. *Organizational and Social Dynamics, 1* (1).

Lawrence, W. G., & Biran, H. (2002). *The Complementarity of Social Dreaming and Therapeutic Dreaming*. London: Jessica Kingsley.

Levenson, E. A. (2001). Freud's dilemma: on writing Greek and thinking Jewish. *Contemporary Psychoanalysis, 37* (3): 375–390.

Lewis, R. (1982). Acting out daydreams. In: *Parabola, Myth and the Quest for Meaning, Vol. 7 (2), Dreams and Seeing*. New York: Society for the Study of Myth and Tradition.

Lifton, R. J. (1987). *The Future of Immortality*. New York: Basic Books.

Lippmann, P. (1998). On the private and social nature of dreams. *Contemporary Psychoanalysis, 34* (2): 195–222.

Lippmann, P. (2000). *Nocturnes: On Listening to Dreams*. Hillsdale, NJ: Analytic Press.

Llinás, R., & Paré, D. (1991). Of dreaming and wakefulness. *Neuroscience, 44:* 521–535.

Luft, J. (1969). *Of Human Interaction*. Palo Alto, CA: National Press Books.

Maltz, M. (2002). "'Finding You in Me': The Organizational Clinician." Consultation to an Investment Bank that was in the World Trade Center on 11 September 2001.

Maltz, M., & Walker, E. M. (1998). Simultaneity and parallel process: an online Social Dreaming Matrix. In: W. G. Lawrence (Ed.), *Social Dreaming @ Work*. London: Karnac.

Marcuse, H. (1979). *The Aesthetic Dimension*. London: Palgrave Macmillan.

Maturana, H., & Varela, F. (1987). *The Tree of Knowledge*. Boston, MA: Shambhala.

McLuhan, M. (1967). *The Medium Is the Message: An Inventory of Effects*. New York: Bantam Books.

Meltzer, D. (1984). *Dream-Life*. Strathclyde: Clunie Press.

Menzies, I. E. P. (1970). *The Functioning of Social Systems as a Defence against Anxiety*. London: Tavistock Publications.

Michael, T. (1998). Creating new cultures: the contribution of Social Dreaming. In: W. G. Lawrence (Ed.), *Social Dreaming @ Work*. London: Karnac.

Milner, M. (1957). *On the Suppressed Madness of Sane Man*. London/New York: Tavistock Publications.

Mitchell, S. (2000). *Relationality: From Attachment to Intersubjectivity*. Hillsdale, NJ: Analytic Press.

Morrone, A., & Mazzalli, M. (2000). *Le stelle e la rana*. Milan: Franco Angeli.

Murray, L. W. (1999). The Angel of Dreams: toward an ethnology of dream interpreting. *Journal of the American Academy of Psychoanalysis, 27* (3): 417–430.

Neri, C. (1990). Contentimento fusionale e relazione contenitore-contenuto. In: C. Neri et al., *Fusionalità: Scritti di psicoanalisi clinica*. Rome: Borla.

Neri, C. (1998). *Group*. London & Philadelphia: Jessica Kingsley.

Neri, C. (2001). Introducción al sueño social y relato de dos workshop que tuvieron lugar en Raissa y Clarice Town. *Clínica y Análisis Grupal, 32* (2): 41–52.

Oeser, F. (1998). After Shakespeare—the language of social dreaming. In: W. G. Lawrence (Ed.), *Social Dreaming @ Work*. London: Karnac.

Otto, R. (1950). *The Idea of the Holy*, 2nd edition. Oxford: Oxford University Press.

Oz, A. (2002). The story of survivors on a small island. *Haaretz*, 1 March.

PCOD (2001). "Social Dreaming Matrix." The Philadelphia Center for Organizational Dynamics of the A. K. Rice Institute, Upper Darby, Pennsylvania, 28–30 September.

Phillips, A. (1994). *On Flirtation*. London: Faber & Faber.

Phillips, A. (1998). *The Beast in the Nursery*. New York: Pantheon Books.

Poland, W. S. (2000). The analyst's witnessing and otherness. *Journal of the American Psychoanalytic Association, 48* (1): 17–34.

Powell, D. (1994). Towards a unifying concert of the group matrix. In: D. Brown & L. Zinkin (Eds.), *The Psyche and the Social World*. London: Routledge.

Prigogine, I., & Stengers, I. (1984). *Order out of Chaos: Man's New Dialogue with Nature*. New York: Bantam.

Rappaport, R. (1999). *Ritual and Religion in the Making of Humanity*. Cambridge: Cambridge University Press.

Riolo, F. (1982). Sogno e teoria della conoscenza in psicoanalisi. *Rivista di Psicoanalisi, 28* (3).

Riviere, J. (1936). On the genesis of psychical conflict in earliest infancy. *International Journal of Psycho-Analysis, 17.*

Rorty, R. (1989). *Contingency, Irony and Solidarity*. Cambridge/New York: Cambridge University Press.

Rose, G. J. (1996). *Necessary Illusion: Art as Witness*. Boston, MA: IUP.

Safranski, R. (1994). *Martin Heidegger: Between Good and Evil*. Cambridge, MA: Harvard University Press, 1998.

Sampson, E. (1988). Indigenous psychologies of the individual and their role in personal and societal functioning. *American Psychologist, 43* (1): 15–22.

Sampson, E. (2000). Reinterpreting individualism and collectivism: their religious roots and monologic versus dialogic person–other relationship. *American Psychologist, 55* (12): 1425–1432.

Samuels, A. (1989). *The Plural Psyche*. London: Routledge.

Sand, R. (1999). The interpretation of dreams, Freud and the Western dream tradition. *Dialogues, 9* (6): 725–747.

Schachtel, E. (1959). *Metamorphosis*. New York: Basic Books.

Selvaggi, L. (2001). Review of "Social Dreaming at Work." *Funzione Gamma*. <www.funsionegamma.edu>.

Sharpe, E. F. (1937). *Dream Analysis*. London: Hogarth Press, 1961.

Sharpe, P., & Ross, S. (1990). *Living Psychology*. Melbourne: Scribe Publications.

Sheldrake, R. (1991). *The Rebirth of Nature*. London: London Century Books, Rider.

Sontag, S. (1994). *Against Interpretation*. New York: Vintage Press.

Sullivan, H. S. (1937). A note on the implications of psychiatry, the study of interpersonal relations, for investigations in the social sciences. In: *The*

Fusion of Psychiatry and Social Science (pp. 15–29). New York: W. W. Norton, 1964.

Suzuki, D. T. (1956). *Zen Buddhism*. New York: Grove Press.

Tagliacozzo, R. (1992). *Il sogno: progetto vitale e proggetto psicoanalitico*. Unpublished paper.

Tatham, P. H. (2001). Getting to the heart of the matter: a Jungian approach to Social Dreaming. In: A. Chesner & H. Hahn (Eds.), *Creative Advances in Groupwork*. London: Jessica Kingsley.

Tatham, P. H., & Morgan, H. (1998). The Social Dreaming Matrix. In: W. G. Lawrence (Ed.), *Social Dreaming @ Work*. London: Karnac.

Tatham, P. H., & Morgan, H. (2002). Social Dreaming at Cambridge. *Proceedings of the 15th International Congress for Analytical Psychology*. Zurich: Daimon Verlag.

Taylor, C. (1992). *Sources of the Self*. Cambridge: Cambridge University Press.

Thelen, E., & Smith, L. B. (1994). *A Dynamic Systems Approach to the Development of Cognition and Action*. Cambridge, MA: MIT Press.

Trungpa, C. (1991). *Cutting through Spiritual Materialism*. Boston, MA/London: Shambhala Publications.

Tustin, F. (1981). Psychological birth and psychological catastrophe. In: J. S. Grotstein, *Do I Dare Disturb the Universe?* London: Karnac.

Ullman, M. (1975). The transformation process in dreams. *American Academy of Psychoanalysis, 19* (2): 8–10.

Ullman, M., Krippner, S., & Vaughan, A. (1973). *Dream Telepathy*. New York: Macmillan.

Unamuno, M. de (1954). *The Tragic Sense of Life*. New York: Dover.

Vallion Macció, D. (1992). Atmosfera emotiva e affetti. *Rivista di Psicoanalisi, 38* (3).

Vermorel, H., & Vermorel, M. (1993). *S. Freud et R. Rolland Correspondence 1923–1936*. Paris: Presse Universitaire de France.

Vernadskij, V. I. (1929). *La Biosphere*. Paris: F. Alcan.

Wallach, Y. (1997). *Wild Light: Selected Poems*, trans. Linda Zisquit. Riverdale on Hudson, NY: Sheep Meadow Press.

Whiffen, R., & Byng-Hall, J. (1982). *Family Therapy Supervision: Recent Developments in Practice*. London: Academic Press.

Winnicott, D. W. (1951). Transitional objects and transitional phenomena. *Through Paediatrics to Psycho-Analysis*. New York: Basic Books.

Winnicott, D. W. (1966). The location of cultural experience. *International Journal of Psycho-Analysis, 48*: 368–372.

Winnicott, D. W. (1971). *Playing and Reality*. London: Tavistock Publications.

Yehoshua, A. B. (1977). *Shoken* [*The Lover*]. New York: Doubleday & Company, 1978.

Young, S. (1999). *Dreaming in the Lotus: Buddhist Dream Narrative, Imagery, and Practice*. Boston: Wisdom Publications.

Zagier Roberts, V. (1994). The organization of work: contributions from open systems theory. In: A. Obholzer & V. Zagier Roberts, *The Unconscious at Work: Individual and Organisational Stress in the Human Services*. London: Routledge.

Zaslow, S. L. (1988). Discussions of Ferenczi's confusion of tongues. *Contemporary Psychoanalysis, 24* (2): 211–225.

Zizek, S. (2001). *Welcome to the Desert of the Real*. New York: Wooster Press.

INDEX

288   INDEX